P9-DTA-971

Architect?

Architect?

A Candid Guide to the Profession

Third Edition

Roger K. Lewis

The MIT Press
Cambridge, Massachusetts
London, England

© 2013 Massachusetts Institute of Technology
Originally published in 1985, 1998

All rights reserved. No part of this book may be reproduced in any form by any electronic or mechanical means (including photocopying, recording, or information storage and retrieval) without permission in writing from the publisher.

MIT Press books may be purchased at special quantity discounts for business or sales promotional use. For information, please email special_sales@mitpress.mit.edu or write to Special Sales Department, The MIT Press, 55 Hayward Street, Cambridge, MA 02142.

This book was set in Kievit and Minion by the MIT Press. Printed and bound in the United States of America.

Library of Congress Cataloging-in-Publication Data

Lewis, Roger K.
    Architect? : a candid guide to the profession / Roger K. Lewis. — Third Edition.
        pages   cm
    ISBN 978-0-262-51884-0 (pbk. : alk. paper)
    1. Architecture—Vocational guidance—United States. I. Title.
NA1995.L45   2013
720.23′73—dc23

2012046588

10   9   8   7   6   5   4   3   2

For architecture students, who I hope learned from me and from whom I unquestionably learned much, and for my colleagues, friends, and especially my family

Contents

Preface

When I wrote the first edition of this book about the profession of architecture, my goal was to explain the true nature of architectural education and practice. I wanted to tell beginning architecture students and prospective architects, lucidly and honestly, what to expect. At the time, such a book seemed to be missing in the literature about architecture.

In 1998, when the second edition was published, my goals for the book had not changed but the culture and practice of architecture had. The profession, as well as architecture schools and degree programs, had become more diverse. The use of computers had increased exponentially. New architectural philosophies, theories, and fields of exploration had appeared. And my own perceptions, interpretations, and judgments of architecture had evolved, along with my writing style. Consequently, in addition to updating and enhancing the text, I added more illustrations to augment the book's visually storytelling effectiveness. Once again, for the same reasons, another update is needed. Thus, similar to the previous edition, this new edition discusses changes affecting, and affected by, the profession since 1998.

Yet despite the latest revisions, *Architect?* remains faithful
to its original intent: to offer a candid account of the realities of
becoming and being an architect. A subjective work substantially
based on my own experiences, observations, and analysis, it
discloses the texture and complexity, the agonies and ecstasies, of
being an architecture student and then a practicing architect. The
book purposefully focuses on architectural practice, for which
most architects are educated and what most prospective architects
expect to do. Nevertheless, it also discusses other, related career
options that graduate architects pursue rather than practice.

Since finishing architecture school in 1967, I have taught,
practiced, and written extensively about architecture. I have
advised, instructed, or employed hundreds of neophyte architects.
But few would-be architects understood what they were getting
into, either prior to embarking on an architectural career or, in
many cases, after embarkation. Years of answering the question,
What is it really like to be an architect? so often posed by students,
clients, and others have motivated me to tell and retell the story.

This book is aimed at anyone seriously contemplating
becoming an architect: students in high school and college, those
out of school thinking about reentering, beginning architecture
students, and young architects just finishing school. Career
guidance counselors and academic advisers should read or refer
to this book before offering suggestions to their questing advisees.
Architects' clients or potential clients should read it to learn
the facts of life about the architects they hire, admire, or abuse.
Finally, architects should read this book to see the extent to which
it affirms or contradicts their own view of themselves and their
personal experiences.

Some readers seek basic information and others look for basics
plus elaboration and commentary. I have tried to respond to both

levels of interest, although readers may discover additional levels of intent and interpretation beyond these two. I hope especially that the illustrations complementing the text help illuminate and validate the book's many contentions, which nevertheless represent solely my point of view.

The contents reveal the specific topics treated but say little of the tone created by the author. For me, first writing and then rewriting this book allowed an exploration of contrasts. The inside story of architectural education and practice is one of dualities: success and failure, acceptance and rejection, tedium and elation, fulfillment and disillusionment. The experiences of becoming and being an architect can be sweet and bittersweet. Although my views about these experiences may not be shared by all, the issues raised are at least genuine and consequential. And anyone who has read this book will learn the unvarnished truth, like it or not.

Acknowledgments

I am deeply indebted to many people, too numerous to cite individually—friends, professional colleagues in practice and education, clients. The deans and faculty members at the University of Maryland School of Architecture, Planning and Preservation, where I taught for thirty-seven years, always have been especially supportive of my work beyond the design studio and classroom. And for almost three decades, the efforts of the MIT Press and its acquisitions editor, Roger Conover, have ensured this book's continued success.

Over the years, countless readers of the first two editions of *Architect?*, many of them students who are now architects, have contacted me to pose questions and offer comments, all sincerely appreciated. Much expressed in this book, including many of the revisions, comes from listening to and heeding them, although I take full responsibility for all that I say and advocate.

In 1984, when I finished writing the initial manuscript for the first edition of *Architect?*, I also began writing "Shaping the City," a weekly column on architecture and urbanism published by the *Washington Post*. This unique journalistic opportunity has enabled me to educate myself further as well as to hone my writing and cartooning skills, for which I am profoundly grateful. Many of the illustrations in this third edition first appeared in my "Shaping the City" column.

But the most important source of support has been my wife, Ellen, who always encouraged me to keep the book up-to-date. I thank her especially for pushing me and for putting up with it all.

Introduction

In 1960, during a severe sophomore year slump, I decided to switch my major from physics to architecture at the Massachusetts Institute of Technology (MIT). I was nineteen. At age seventeen I had entered MIT to become a scientist or engineer but by the fourth semester of college I faced the common dilemma of not knowing what to be or do. I knew only that I wanted to work in the tangible, three-dimensional world and that I would probably not find this in the arcane world of quantum physics.

I sought advice from family and friends and from MIT's dean of students. Because I had always loved drawing and also had reasonable technical aptitude, the very sympathetic dean suggested that I look into architecture. I had never considered architecture before and knew absolutely nothing about it. My first visit to MIT's architecture department greatly stimulated my interest when I saw drawings pinned up on walls and models scattered about. I remember thinking, "do students actually get credit for this?" In that stressful spring, architecture seemed to be just what I was looking for.

Following my decision, the little information and insight I had about architecture proved no obstacle to exciting speculation.

I could foresee a wonderfully romantic, exalted profession promising intellectual rewards, wealth, and prestige, an amalgam of art and technology fused together by social idealism and creative energy. As an architect I would someday be marshaling diverse resources and mastering many skills to create artfully designed and executed buildings, each a monument to its architect's genius. I would be a generalist and a specialist at the same time, a recognized professional, a purveyor of culture as well as a provider of services to a needy clientele.

Heroic names such as Frank Lloyd Wright, Le Corbusier, and Eero Saarinen, accompanied by visions of skyscrapers and beautiful renderings, came to mind. A heady realm of aesthetics, construction, appreciative clients, a respectful public, and the newly awakened 1960s social consciousness beckoned. Architects seemed to be in the middle of it all, orchestrating a kind of real-world opera.

In retrospect, there is nothing unusual about the way I and others have made our decisions to become architects. People choose careers for many reasons yet typically know relatively little about their choice at the outset. Many careers appear inscrutable or mysterious to the uninitiated, the nature of which is discovered only after initiation. Architecture is no exception but its real attributes differ greatly from those so often ascribed to it. Countless students, clients, and consumers of architecture possess incredibly meager and often erroneous knowledge or comprehension of how architects think and function. Indeed, most people's notions about accountants, bankers, pilots, doctors, truck drivers, attorneys, computer programmers, or plumbers better approximate reality than their notions about architects.

Few people ever hire an architect. Most do not know an architect. At best what they might know are movie and television characters portrayed as architects: the heroic Howard Roark embodied by Gary Cooper in the film version of Ayn Rand's *The Fountainhead;* urbane, blue-eyed Paul Newman reading electrical diagrams in his office boudoir in the *Towering Inferno;* or Charles Bronson in the movie *Death Wish* and its sequels, playing the vengeful, vigilante architect whose primary project activity was gunning down hoodlums in the streets and subways of New York City and Chicago. "Seinfeld" fans may recall hilariously hapless George Costanza, portrayed by Jason Alexander, who aspired and sometimes pretended to be an architect. Architects depicted in film and television can be heroes, lovers, fools, or miscreants. But there are no popular accounts about an architect being an architect in the way that doctors are shown engaged in medicine, attorneys in law practice, or police in law enforcement.

The following account is unlikely to be popularized but it will tell aspiring architects—and all who interact with architects— reasons for being or not being an architect. It relates the inside story of what studying to become an architect entails and where an architectural education can lead. It explains how architects— and those who teach architecture—think and work and what they care about as they strive to make the built environment more commodious, more beautiful, and more sustainable.

1

To Be or Not to Be . . .
an Architect?

1 Why Be an Architect?

Deciding to become an architect should be a positive decision predicated on positive motivations and aspirations. What should you expect? What leads men and women to invest five to eight years in rigorous university and professional education, three or more years in internship, and subsequent decades pursuing architectural practice, teaching, scholarship, research, and professional and public service?

Creative and Intellectual Fulfillment

Architects are driven by human intellect and rational thinking. But emotions operate as well. For architects the marriage of intellect and emotion is manifest in the impulse to be creative—to imagine, feel, do, and make. Good architects are compelled by their own passion and will to make architecture and by the intellectual and emotional gratification that being creative can provide.

The creative impulse is difficult to explain but easy to recognize. It appears early in life and is experienced to some extent by all human beings. To begin with nothing but raw materials and random thoughts, and then to transform them into something tangible, well crafted, and stimulating to the mind and senses, is the essence of creativity. For the architect, creating buildings offers countless moments of elation.

Creating something beautiful and aesthetically well composed—a work of art—is the primary goal of many architects. Their chief concern is to design artifacts, whether towns, buildings, furniture, or teapots, to use, look at, and admire as one would look at and admire paintings or sculpture. Even if others dislike a design, the architect's eye still beholds the beauty that he or she alone has bestowed on the world.

Creativity is not limited to generating works of art. The creative mind takes pleasure in making things that work, whether cities, buildings, machines, or toys. A substantial part of practicing architecture consists of creating physical structures and environments that perform successfully. In other words, in addition to being artistic expressions, buildings must effectively accommodate human functions, be buildable from many components and materials, provide shelter from the elements, resist the forces of nature, conserve energy and natural resources, and be financially feasible. Meeting performance and aesthetic objectives simultaneously is architecture's greatest creative challenge.

The Architect's Quest for Inspiration

Once that challenge is taken up, the excitement of design is matched only by the excitement of realization. Seeing a design actually constructed is elating emotionally and intellectually. And the rewards of responding to creative impulses are intensified by the struggles that accompany creativity. As we shall see, overcoming adversity absorbs much of an architect's energy because many obstacles stand in the path along which architects and their projects travel. Sometimes just getting a project built is a victory, and when architectural excellence is achieved, the victory is even sweeter.

Contributing to Culture and Civilization

Good architects see themselves as more than professionals who render services to fee-paying clients. Architecture is an expression and embodiment of culture and cultural conditions or even a critique of culture. The history of architecture and the history of civilization are inseparable. Indeed, architectural historians spend their professional lives studying architecture and urban form not only to interpret it but also to understand the political, social, and economic circumstances that produced it. By designing and building, architects know that they may be contributing directly to a culture's inventory of ideas and artifacts, no matter how insignificant. Thus the search for appropriate cultural achievement is a significant motivation for architects.

Thinking about the world's evolving cultures brings to mind countless images: pyramids in Egypt; Greek and Roman temples; Gothic cathedrals and medieval towns; Renaissance palaces, churches, and squares; English houses and gardens; Asian pavilions; and industrial-age skyscrapers. Visualize urban environments that civilization has produced, from ancient Jerusalem to Paris and London to nineteenth- and twentieth-century planned metropolises. Architecture is an indispensable component of even the most unsophisticated cultures. If asked to describe the world of Native Americans, what child would fail to sketch a teepee? Think of Neanderthals and caves come to mind.

Not all architectural work offers opportunities for cultural enrichment. But when such opportunities do arise, however modest, the architect's contribution may be unprecedented, suggesting new directions in form and style, technology, or methods of design. Or the work may reaffirm or refine already established cultural norms and iconography. Rather than inventing something new, the architect may be helping to preserve what already exists or adding to the growing collection of cultural works still in progress. Innovation and revolution require subsequent development and evolution. Architects must cover the field, respecting what's old and creating something new.

Love of Drawing—without a Computer

The discussion of creativity and intellectual fulfillment talks briefly about the rewards of graphic exploration and invention. But what about drawing in the digital age? For many architects, manual drawing is still indispensable, an extremely satisfying and stimulating use of time and energy, an activity that is its own reward. Drawing manually offers an additional reward: it teaches graphic skills and compositional judgment, which in turn enables students to compose attractive, graphically appropriate digital drawings.

You can and should love drawing. It can be therapeutic, entailing great concentration and eclipsing all other distractions or preoccupations. It is personal because no two people draw exactly alike. For generating design ideas, sketching—not mechanical drawing—is the most vital and enjoyable kind of drawing.

Through freehand sketching, architects not only record and analyze what they see but also readily explore and express new ideas or visions. Sketching, whether by hand or computer, is how architects transform design concepts into analogs of reality.

Drawing architectural and natural forms—buildings, spaces in buildings, landscapes, urban spaces, people—can become as natural for an architect as writing or reading. Some architects are happier drawing in their sketch book than doing much of the other work that architectural practice demands. In fact, because it intimately links the hand, eye, and brain, and because it can be so spontaneous, freehand drawing is fundamental to design thinking and design invention. No matter how sophisticated computer software and hardware become, they will never quite replicate nor completely replace manual drawing.

If you like drawing, and particularly freehand drawing, then you may grow to love it as an architect. If you do not like to draw, if you find it tedious or difficult, then architecture may not be the right choice. The passion for drawing and the drawing techniques architects master and employ are unique to this profession.

Service to Others

Many architects are driven by humanitarian motives. The desire to help or teach other people can be very strong, and because architecture can render public service and serve as public art, architects can easily fulfill this desire. Most architects view themselves as benefactors to society, as humanists and humanitarians. Even designing commercial projects for profit-motivated clients, architects believe that they have an additional, equally important client: the public. They feel an obligation to all who may use, occupy, or see the buildings they design, in the present and the future, an obligation not only to provide shelter and accommodate activities but also to instruct and inspire.

When buildings are constructed and put to use, it is very fulfilling for architects to know that the client, the users, and the public appreciate and benefit from their efforts. Sometimes architects create environments that measurably affect the lives of people in positive ways, perhaps by improving their living standards, behavior, sense of well-being and security, or their attitudes. Studies have shown that building occupants can feel better physically and psychologically, work more effectively, and be more productive in artfully designed environments. Well-chosen proportions, good light and color, appealing textures and details, pleasant views, comfortable furniture, desirable acoustical qualities, adequate ventilation, and thermal comfort can have great impact on body and mind. What a tremendous reward it is for architects to hear clients or users express satisfaction and gratitude for the architect's successful intervention in their lives.

Public-spirited architects contribute in ways other than designing buildings and urban communities. Being adept in matters of organization, coordination, and advocacy, as well as design, many architects devote time and effort to assisting needy individuals, communities, and nonprofit groups to undertake projects, to preserve buildings and neighborhoods, and even to change public policy affecting the built environment. Although architects in these situations may not produce designs or drawings, their service efforts and know-how may lead to better architecture, improved sustainability, or more affordable housing. And helping others enhances our sense of achievement and self-worth, which frankly makes us feel justifiably proud.

Teaching

Teaching architecture is a form of giving, and although not financially enriching, it offers architects unique opportunities for lasting educational enrichment. Professing and conveying knowledge to others is challenging but inherently stimulating and satisfying. And architects who teach can learn as much as their students.

Academic involvement and academic schedules enable teachers of architecture to keep learning through practice, writing, traveling, conducting research, providing service, as well as teaching in studios and classrooms. Thus motivated teachers are engaged in an exchange, taking in or developing new ideas and information that is in turn passed on to their students. Such interaction can be profound and enduring. Among a teacher's greatest rewards is seeing former students successfully applying what they have learned or following in their mentors' footsteps.

Nothing compares with hearing a former architecture student tell you that lessons conveyed and concepts explored with you at some earlier time are still remembered, still relevant, and still appreciated.

A Great Profession for Polymaths

Architects must deal with the complexities of design and construction, which is why many a successful architect is a polymath, someone with extensive knowledge and skills in several areas. Much of the fulfillment of architectural practice lies in applying diverse knowledge and skills to difficult problems. Polymaths enjoy solving puzzles, analyzing complicated systems, organizing data, examining options, and performing challenging tasks. Architecture provides fertile ground for such minds to plow.

Architecture entails activities of mind and body acting in concert—seeing, thinking, imagining, drawing, and crafting. The architect must know not only how to draw a line but also why, where, and when. The senses must all be engaged to observe so that the mind can analyze and synthesize. Ideas must be communicated and explained graphically and verbally. What then are the specific aptitudes or talents that contribute to mastering and enjoying the art and science of architecture?

Graphic and visual skills   The ability to observe and to represent real things graphically as well as to represent imagined things

Compositional talent   The artistic ability to compose aesthetically appealing visual forms in two and three dimensions

Technical aptitude   Proficiency in mathematics and scientific analysis, although not necessarily in a particular science

Verbal skills   The ability to read, to write clearly, and to express oneself effectively

Organizational skills   The ability to analyze and synthesize, to create order and direction out of disorder and chaos

Memory   The ability to store and recall information, images, or ideas

These are essential prerequisites for architects seeking intellectual and emotional fulfillment. They also reflect the multidisciplinary nature of the field—the need for architects to be artists, craftspersons, technologists, social scientists, managers, accountants, historians, theoreticians, philosophers, and risk takers. Mobilizing talents in an arena so rich and diverse can be tremendously exhilarating and rewarding, as stimulating as any career could be.

Money and Lifestyle

An obvious incentive for pursuing a career is to earn a living and enhance income potential. But professional incomes can vary dramatically, especially in architecture. Some architects earn only enough to ensure survival, whereas others achieve relative affluence. Each earning level enables corresponding lifestyle choices. Because architects frequently interact with people and are engaged in activities associated with costly lifestyles, the public assumes that architects are affluent, well-to-do, big-income professionals. Some are. Most are not.

It is possible to achieve substantial wealth as an architect—and no doubt some architects pursue this as a primary personal goal—but it is improbable. Instead, most architects earn comfortable or modest livings, enjoying reasonable but limited economic stability and prosperity. Average incomes in the profession of architecture are solidly middle class, comparable to what school teachers, plumbers, electricians, sales representatives, and nurses earn.

Graduate architects begin their careers as wage earners drawing hourly, monthly, or annual salaries reflecting prevailing marketplace conditions. After three years of internship and further practice, they may become associates or principal owners of firms, either in partnership with others or as sole proprietors. Larger firms typically provide larger incomes at all levels, from senior partner down to newly employed intern.

Architects who earn large incomes tend to live well. Frequently they live in interesting houses modishly decorated and furnished. They may travel to exotic places, ski, own sailboats, or escape to vacation homes in the mountains or by the sea. They may collect art, entertain extensively, make substantial political campaign contributions, or support charitable causes and institutions. All of this requires money, which most wage earners lack.

For the majority of less affluent architects, there are nevertheless ample lifestyle choices not so dependent on high incomes. Many architects find great satisfaction living modestly in cities, suburbs, small towns, or rural areas. Their lifestyles may be more basic, sometimes even approaching subsistence, but they also may enjoy flexibility and freedom of a kind not found chasing economic success, the cash flow treadmill requiring continual movement and lubrication.

Some architects discover other means, outside traditional architectural practice, to sustain themselves financially. Perhaps the ideal way to practice architecture is not to be obliged to make a living at it. Thus, architects have become real estate developers or construction contractors, sometimes making (or losing) much more money than can be earned from design practice. Architects teach in architecture schools and may earn in nine months what they could earn in twelve in an office. Still others, either by good fortune or design, enjoy a relatively stable family income thanks to their spouses' assets or earnings. Of course, the easiest route to financial well-being is to inherit money but few are so endowed. Those who are can practice architecture as an impassioned hobby.

At times, earning money can be a serious challenge for architects and, as the next chapter explains, adequate and consistent compensation is an ongoing problem for the profession. Unlike some other businesses and professions, architecture is not a field to enter to become rich by today's standards. The odds are against it. But you can earn a decent living at it most of the time, even if you are not exceptionally talented—and if you do not mind a little belt tightening from time to time.

Social Status

Social status is another reason you might choose architecture as a career. An elusive notion at best, it implies achieving and occupying an elevated place in society's hierarchy of who people are and what they do. Social status is relative, meaningful only in comparison with other professions or vocations. Society assumes that educated architects are artistically talented and technically knowledgeable. Society does not know exactly how architects operate. But it does know that they design buildings, whether modest or monumental in size, for individuals or institutions with financial resources. As a result architects may be well respected or admired by members of a social system who, unfortunately, think less of people whom they consider lacking in education, are less talented, and less acceptable in the company of people of wealth, influence, or so-called breeding.

Pursuing social status for its own sake is a dubious undertaking but most people are status conscious and high status may become a desirable and explicit goal. It is fulfilling and ego boosting to be respected, to be invited places and seen by people one admires, or to be praised by peers whose opinions one values. As professionals, architects generally associate with other professionals, people in the creative arts, or people in business or government. In many cultures architecture is among the most respected of all professions, and the United States is no exception. The American Institute of Architects (AIA) has reported that millions of Americans—especially college graduates younger than age forty-five—have expressed an interest in architecture. And any architect will tell you that frequently he or she has heard people say that they would love to have become architects.

As a corollary to social status, becoming part of the so-called establishment may motivate some architects. Read *establishment* to mean the power structure within a community, town, or city because architects rarely can become part of national political power structures. Belonging to the establishment means having close connections to business, financial, civic, and governmental interests, being seen as a force to be reckoned with among influential peers of the local or regional realm. Establishment status means having your name recognized by people you do not know, being asked to serve on boards and committees, being interviewed periodically by the media, being invited to fund-raising functions, and perhaps knowing and influencing what is going on behind the scenes. Clearly social and establishment statuses are closely linked.

Fame

Beyond achieving economic and social status is the lure of fame. Fame can come without wealth, and in architecture it often does. To become publicly recognized, if not celebrated, can be an end in itself above all others. Everyone can name at least one or two famous architects and architects can name dozens. To be famous usually requires that an individual do something exceptional and that others see, judge, and, most important, report it to a receptive and interested audience, preferably on a national or worldwide scale. Exceptional deeds may be constructive or destructive as long as they are exceptional and therefore noteworthy.

Most architects become famous in a gradual way by doing work that eventually is recognized for its originality and excellence. Often such work is seen as innovative or avant-garde in its early stages, with subsequent stages being periods of refinement and variation. Fame is usually established and measured by professional consensus, coupled with judgments made by historians, critics, journalists, and especially clients.

However, sustaining fame and professional recognition depends on publicizing and publishing what architects do, say, or write. This means not only designing and building projects but also winning awards for projects and having them featured in journals, magazines, newspapers, blogs, and online news reports. It means boosting and being boosted. In this sense architecture is a bit like show business. Lecturing and writing about one's work and philosophy, courting the media, being talked and written about by others, winning competitions: all boost fame and thrust architects into the professional and public limelight. And the Internet allows architects to generate their own limelight. They can readily feature and promote themselves using social networking and websites to display their qualifications and tout their work.

Events in the twenty-first century unfold and are publicly reported so quickly that acts of provocation and revolution promise fame more rapidly. Explicit striving for notoriety and celebrityhood can be ends in themselves. Architects, more than most other professionals, consciously or subconsciously harbor a desire for fame because much of their work is publicly visible. Being famous may have its problems but it is a form of public certification, a validation of success and a salvation from anonymity. Who has not fantasized about being on a magazine cover, not easily attainable but possible? For architects, fame yields a desirable payoff: more clients and commissions. Pursuing and nurturing fame may be good business.

Unfortunately, fame can be fleeting because of overexposure, rapidly changing fashions, and shifting tastes. For example, consider the following item published long ago in the *Wall Street Journal* (May 26, 1982, p. 33): "Fifty-eight deans and heads of accredited schools of architecture recently listed this country's top architects of non-residential structures. The overwhelming winner was I. M. Pei, who was mentioned by nearly half of the deans. . . . Rounding out the top ten were Romaldo Giurgola, Cesar Pelli, Kevin Roche, Philip Johnson, Gunnar Birkerts, Michael Graves, Charles Moore, Edward Larrabee Barnes and Richard Meier."

All these architects, well known to many older architects, are not well known to younger architects or the public. Fifteen years previously, the list would have been different. Today, few of those names would be on such a list, and fifteen years from now, today's list will have changed again.

Immortality

Fame can be not only ephemeral but also ultimately insufficient. If we contemplate basic human drives, procreation and perpetuation come to mind. What better way to transcend one's biological life than through the creation of potentially ageless and permanent structures that, even as future ruins, might tell future archeologists, historians, and cultural legatees the story of who we were and what

we did. Most people settle for their succeeding offspring and
family heirlooms to memorialize themselves but architects can
leave behind architecture as monuments to themselves.

It may seem presumptuous or self-aggrandizing, yet it
also seems natural for creative individuals to desire to make
something that could endure forever or at least for a few centuries.
I recall thinking about this explicitly when I was a student
making comparisons between architecture and other careers.
Only architecture seemed to provide the opportunity to create
something lasting and immortal. The architect, I thought, survives

and lives forever through his or her work. Even if my name were to be forgotten, I naively believed that my constructed offspring would not be.

Probably many architects share this rather romantic, immortality impulse, even if consciously denying or resisting it. Properly understood and channeled, it is a perfectly healthy impulse, not a conceit. A commendable work of architecture is in part a statement of and about its architect, the architect's progeny ultimately left behind. Of course, good architecture has many parents. Thus parenthood must be attributed not only to the architect but also to the client and those who build and to the society and culture of which architecture is a part.

Fulfilling the Dictates of Personality

In considering reasons to be an architect, don't overlook attributes of personality and their role in shaping careers. Often disregarded or underestimated by students and career counselors, such attributes are of great importance in determining career choices and outcomes. In the real world outside the classroom, personal characteristics may have a greater influence on one's professional life than technical skills, talents, and knowledge. The rewards in architecture, similar to other professions, depend as much on personal and behavioral traits as on IQ, college transcripts, graphic talent, or good intentions.

All personal attributes matter but some matter more than others.

Self-confidence, ego strength, and ambition   Strongly believing that you are capable and able to cope, compete, perform well, and succeed

Dedication and persistence   Committing and sticking to a cause or task with a willingness to work hard at it

Resilience   Coping well with setbacks, criticism, failure; being able to bounce back and overcome

Amiability   Being able to affiliate and get along, to collaborate and participate with others, even those who may not be close friends

Empathy   Recognizing, understanding, and sometimes identifying with the circumstances, limitations, and feelings of others

Charm and poise   Behaving so others see you as someone well mannered, witty, thoughtful, friendly, and comfortable to be with

Leadership   Being able to make consequential decisions, to persuade and inspire others to respect and follow you, to embrace your ideas

Courage   Being willing to take risks others avoid, to experiment, to venture into new territory, to lose as well as win

Passion   Feeling intensely about principles, ideas, activities, people, places, or things

This is not a complete list of requirements for being an architect, nor is it unique to this profession. However, these attributes characterize many successful architects. And lacking these attributes can prevent one from achieving architectural goals or even from completing architecture school. In a discipline in which criticism and negative judgments abound, lacking confidence, resilience, and persistence can be personally devastating, notwithstanding any native talents.

Ironically, an architect of mediocre design talent but blessed with great charisma—an amalgam of several attributes, especially leadership, self-confidence, and charm—may be very successful. Indeed such charisma may have more impact on an architect's career than any measurable competencies gained through education. The ability to persuade and guide other people may ultimately accomplish more for you than the ability to draw, calculate, or even think great thoughts.

Anyone contemplating becoming an architect should take stock of his or her personality. A favorable combination of personal traits, and in appropriate intensities, can make architecture an ideal profession. This is why some people seem born to be architects. They possess a mixture of intellect, talent, skills, and personal qualities—some unquestionably genetic in origin—that makes architecture their perfect cup of tea.

Freedom to Do Your Own Thing

Perhaps because architects are often viewed as artists, society accepts and sometimes even expects them to behave and think unconventionally. Some architects live up to this image, exhibiting idiosyncrasies in the ways they dress, talk, and work or in what they advocate. They strive to be individualistic and nonconformist. Frank Lloyd Wright, wearing his familiar cape and haughty expression, defied and decried all and became a prototype for iconoclastic architects.

For anyone so inclined, architecture may be more attractive as a career than, say, law, banking, accounting, engineering, or military service. There is ego satisfaction and a feeling of exceptionality that stem from being unique, from standing out, getting noticed, and being remembered.

Architects appear to have more options for doing their own thing in their own way in our culture, especially compared to other learned professions. They more freely and willfully shape their personal image as seen by their peers, their clientele, and the public. This image is reinforced by the work they do, the aesthetic values they espouse, the people with whom they associate, the causes they support, and the style in which they live. Few other careers offer this range of choice in how to behave and practice. Almost anything goes if it is done with panache. For this reason, architecture is one of the most liberal of the established professions, the most tolerant of "coloring outside the lines."

Finally, many architects know how to have a good time, to let go when necessary. Starting first as students in architecture school, architects have always found imaginative, amusing ways to have fun, to relieve the pressures and stress of architectural work. But the good times and amusing diversions are needed for another purpose. As the next chapter explains, architecture has its negative moments and having a good time can help architects cope with bad times.

2 Why Not to Be an Architect

The inside story of architecture would be incomplete and misleading if it failed to include the less-than-wonderful aspects of becoming and being an architect. Whenever we are told why we should do something, there may be unstated reasons why we should not. This is reinforced by experience, sometimes painfully. Candidly painting the entire picture of the architectural profession at least gives you the chance to make informed decisions and to know what to expect.

Reasons not to be an architect are in part a matter of perception and judgment. Therefore what follows are my own observations and interpretations of commonly encountered risks, roadblocks, and sources of frustration. Some are typical of many trades and professions and others are unique and more endemic to architecture. At one time or another, most architects have been plagued by some of these problems and have felt momentarily overwhelmed or disillusioned by them. Knowing about and anticipating them will help you prepare for them but unfortunately this knowledge makes them no less obstructive.

Odds of Becoming an Architect

Anyone contemplating a career in architecture should know that statistically there may be less than a fifty-fifty chance of ultimately becoming a licensed architect. Many undergraduate students who select architecture as their major will never complete the professional program and receive an accredited degree in architecture. Architecture students drop out along the way because of changing interests, amount and difficulty of academic work required, lack of talent, or loss of motivation.

Moreover, not all of those graduating from schools with accredited professional degrees will become licensed and practice architecture. Some will change fields for various reasons, usually related to their feelings about their prospects of becoming architects. They may be attracted to other fields for economic reasons or because they have talents more suitable to other career options. Some women with architectural degrees suspend or cut back on working to start families, finding it overly stressful to pursue their careers in architecture full-time while raising children. Regrettably, a few of those women never return to architectural practice.

Although the rate of architectural student attrition is relatively high, there is no shortage of architects in the United States, especially in metropolitan areas, where most projects are designed and built. Many architects and some educators believe that there are in fact too many architects and too many architectural firms. In addition, surveys of firms conducted by the AIA show that less than a third of architects in firms are owners or principals (proprietors, partners, or corporate officers). Thus the majority of working architects are employees, not employers.

These statistics show that someone setting out to become a practicing architect may not end up doing so and that becoming an owner or principal of a firm is even more improbable. Such statistical odds can be discouraging. Yet we know that attrition and unrealized goals are usual in any academic undertaking or career; students readily change their minds and majors. Although those who make it through and enter practice can feel good about beating the odds, they still face tough challenges.

Lack of Work

Of all the difficulties architects face, periodic lack of work is probably the most frustrating. The inability of individuals to find employment or of firms to obtain commissions is a major cause of economic and psychological suffering for architects.

Employment for firms and individuals is directly related to local and national economic conditions. When times are good and the economy grows, investment in building increases, which means architects get busier. Correspondingly, lack of economic growth, recession, inflation, high interest rates, and tight credit diminish spending and investment, especially for real estate and construction. This in turn reduces architectural commissions. Therefore the amount of work for architects is determined by volatile and unpredictable economic conditions over which architects have no control. Thus architects continually face the possibility of being under- or unemployed from one year to another.

Even when the national economy is generally strong, lack of work can result from adverse municipal, county, or state economic conditions. Architects work for clients on a project-by-project basis to which their employment fate is inexorably linked. Architects are hired by clients when projects are conceived and move forward and laid off when projects are suspended or terminated.

Projects are sponsored by property owners and developers, financed by lending institutions or government, granted permits by government agencies, constructed by contractors, and bought, leased, or used by the public. Thus the building process is complex and for many reasons projects can start and stop abruptly. Because so much time and money can be invested in the architect's work on any single project, even the loss or suspension of one or two projects can be economically disastrous for a firm. If architects rendered services to hundreds of clients at a time, this risk would be greatly reduced. Because most firms work on only a few projects over many months or years, the risk of a work slowdown is increased.

Sometimes work can fall off precipitously. For example, in the wake of the 1974–1975 Middle East oil embargo and US gasoline shortage, the economic expansion that had continued steadily for almost three decades, with only minor abbreviated recessions, abruptly ended. Architects were laid off at a rate not seen since the depression era of the 1930s. In my own office I had to let go most of my professional staff—a dozen architects—when work suddenly stopped. It was an agonizing act of retrenchment. Sizable firms became mere shadows of their former selves, shrinking by 70 or 80 percent.

During the US recession that began in 2008, the job market for architects became increasingly tight. A 2012 government survey showed that, among all new university graduates, those with architecture degrees had the hardest time finding employment in their field. Fortunately young architects can be mobile, moving from firm to firm with rising and falling workloads, as well as for personal reasons. Early in their careers, some architects can make geographic moves, relocating to other cities, states, or countries. Employment depends on and follows projects, an inescapable fact of architectural life.

Competition

The threat of having no work is made worse by another ever-present factor: intense competition. As if economic uncertainty were not enough, there is the problem of too many architects chasing too few jobs. Competition in the field of architecture is keen and unending. It begins in school, carries over into the beginning years of job seeking and employment, and continues in the marketplace of practice.

Competition is certainly not unique to architecture, being integral to any free enterprise system, but in architecture it can reach astounding proportions. For example, in the period following the 1974–1975 oil embargo and recession, it was not uncommon for more than a hundred firms, many of them very large firms, to compete for a single, small government project. When times were good, most of those firms would never have considered going after such a small project. When times are tough, architecture firms can spend months looking unsuccessfully for new jobs because the number of competitors is so great in comparison to the amount of available work. In such periods architects may be forced to survive on unemployment benefits.

The intensity of competition can be attributable not only to an oversupply of architects but also to methods by which architects compete. Architects frequently are challenged by the ability and willingness of other firms to effectively mount aggressive campaigns to woo clients and win contracts. Today competing successfully requires soft and hard selling. It requires marketing and public relations tactics that may seem distasteful and too costly for some architects who believe their reputations alone should be sufficient to attract clients.

Inadequate Compensation

It is possible but unlikely that architects can earn hefty incomes, the kinds of incomes earned by doctors, lawyers, professional athletes, movie stars, corporate executives, Internet entrepreneurs, and Wall Street bankers. Architects can earn enough most of the time to live comfortably but few will ever match income and assets of their comparably educated contemporaries. Indeed, no one should go into architecture to make a lot of money. Be an architect for many other reasons, but not to get rich.

Given the numbers of architects and the competition, financial remuneration accompanying architectural employment is not the greatest. Many architects believe that they are not fairly compensated and certainly not well compensated for what they do and the responsibilities they shoulder. When the AIA once asked licensed architects if they "feel that in comparison to other professions, architects receive adequate fees for services they provide?," 85.7 percent said no. When asked if they "feel that employers compensate their architect employees adequately?," 67 percent answered no.

For many architectural firm owners, annual income can fluctuate widely. Good years can be followed by bad years in which a principal's income could be at poverty level or even negative. Architects' dependency on economic and project circumstances differentiates their income pattern from that of other professionals whose earnings are relatively stable and consistently increase over time, and who stay busy whether times are good or bad.

For a variety of reasons, architects as a whole are unable to claim compensation appropriate to their role and commensurate with their responsibilities. The same points are always raised: so many years of education! demonstrable and unique expertise! a recognized, learned profession regulated by law! an activity entailing substantial legal and financial risks that in turn justify fair compensation and profits! Why then are so many architects apparently paid so poorly?

Architectural fees commonly fail to cover all the costs of providing services. Or fees go uncollected, flowing in unpredictable currents, just like projects. But why should fees be too low, given the architect's qualifications, risks, and efforts? Again the primary reason is competition. In the marketplace of architecture and real estate development, there is always pressure for firms to propose fees at least comparable to prevailing fees and often to cut fees below going rates just to get the job. This then lowers the going rate another notch. Many clients go shopping for architects and rarely hesitate to ask about the cost of services. If a hungry architectural firm is anxious to secure a project commission, the temptation to propose a cut-rate fee can be overwhelming, even when it means cutting corners, compromising the quality of services, spending less time than needed, and paying slave wages to employees.

Many architectural practitioners feel trapped. On the one hand, as dedicated, competent professionals, they want to invest all the time and resources necessary to thoroughly research, explore,

and present the best possible design and then to see that it is properly implemented. This implies that clients must share the architect's goals and visions and be willing to pay fully for the value of all required services. On the other hand, real-world experience teaches architects that some clients view them as just another vendor among competing vendors, clients who believe that architectural fees are excessive yet demand extra work at no cost.

To the established architect or firm, this situation is a mixed blessing. Although intense competition for projects makes it harder to obtain work, keep people employed, and ensure stable earnings, the ample supply of architects, young and old, allows firms to keep their hourly labor costs relatively low and therefore their fees relatively competitive. In fact, the economic structure of architectural practice depends on this gentle exploitation of labor to provide services that are, by their nature, extremely labor intensive. A single project can consume thousands of worker hours.

These points about architects being underpaid must be viewed in light of how others in our society are compensated. Architects still can earn more than some people ever hope to earn and typically more than many teachers, scholars, musicians, actors, and artists doing equally creative and fulfilling work. It is possible to earn more than carpenters, plumbers, electricians, and even attorneys and doctors, if that is your goal as an architect. But it is not easy.

Ego Vulnerability—Getting Lost in the Crowd

Ego involvement in architecture is high, which can lead to great frustration as well as provide the impetus for achieving. To most architects, succeeding means, among other things, gaining some measure of professional standing and reputation, if not fame. There is a natural craving for peer group recognition, beyond one's clientele, for having done well, for being exceptional in some way.

Yet in actuality many architects feel, rightly or wrongly, that they have failed to gain the status or recognition they deserve. They toil away as employees, associates, or principals in firms, carrying on the demanding, day-to-day work of producing architecture, and a handful of their colleagues receive most of the attention and credit. Some perceive themselves as anonymous cogs in a giant machine over which they have limited control. They feel unjustly treated and passed over.

Visit a large architectural office with dozens or perhaps hundreds of architects working. Many probably would characterize themselves as unfulfilled, underappreciated, underpaid, and overworked architects with plenty of talent but less luck. Some feel exploited, chained to their workstations and jobs, unable to make a breakthrough to independence and professional visibility. Most will have successfully completed professional educations, many will be licensed, and all will have useful but differing forms of talent indispensable to architectural practice. A few will feel cheated or deprived by external forces. Others will feel that various personal attributes—shyness, lack of bravado, complacency, aversion to risk—prevent them from doing or achieving more, resigning themselves to anonymity and satisfied just to keep at it. Still others will be dreaming and waiting for the right moment, the right opportunity to emerge from the crowd.

The Risks of Envy

Why should architects be envious? Envy seems more likely to be felt by aspiring actors in New York or Hollywood than by highly trained design professionals. As the first chapter explains, many architects aspire to achieve fame and to them the lack of eminence may imply that their work is perceived to be uninteresting, passé, or otherwise unworthy of notice. Whereas achieving stardom can motivate architects, not achieving it can lead to feelings of envy. Professional jealousy can arise in all lines of work but sometimes it is more keenly felt in architecture, especially by architects with big egos.

Envy and jealousy, unfortunate components of the architect's psyche, rarely surface in public and are rarely acted on. Instead, they are felt privately and coped with. These feelings can appear whenever an architect observes another architect winning and the observer is losing or is left out. They are beyond usual feelings of frustration or disappointment and can manifest themselves in subtle but gnawing, slightly malicious ways, sometimes accompanied by traces of ill will and resentment of the comparative success of others. Paradoxically, architects may have parallel feelings of respect and admiration for their envied competitors and peers.

Anything can trigger such feelings, especially at moments of vulnerability: others are busy when you are not, others are winning awards or competitions when you are not, others are being published or favorably reviewed when you are not, others are being promoted when you are not, others are making money when you are not. The negative stimuli can be unending. Losing a job or a commission you thought you should have gotten or falling out of fashion as fashions change can provoke and embitter. These sentiments are not restricted to young, immature, or unsuccessful architects. Every architect is susceptible and, indeed, the higher one's aspirations, the higher the susceptibility.

Lack of Power and Influence

Some public-spirited architects aspire to prominence not through design practice but rather through the exercise of political power and influence. They want to gain the respect and admiration of a constituency in addition to their own professional colleagues and clients. They strive to be among the movers and shakers in their community, to be consulted on matters outside the realm of architecture. Perhaps they are invited to serve on civic boards and commissions, where they often can help shape public policy. A few architects enter the political arena, running for offices and winning municipal, county, or state elections. Architects have been mayors of cities, members of city and county councils, planning commissioners, state and national legislators, and directors of public agencies.

They embark on these career paths because they understand that architecture per se is not a powerful profession. In US society, although architects gain some status as designers and technical specialists, they wield little political or civic influence. They rarely affect the course of public policy, typically determined by elected officials, attorneys, business owners, corporate and government executives, and people of great wealth.

Regrettably, architects are generally perceived as having narrow interests and expertise, limited primarily to matters of aesthetics and construction, even though many architects possess broadly based skills, knowledge, and wisdom. Architects themselves have reinforced this perception by frequently remaining aloof or uninvolved. Thus you are likely to have relatively little power and influence if your only focus is architectural practice, no matter how good your design work is. Conversely, you may become one of those rare individuals, a *citizen architect,* able to successfully combine professional practice with meaningful public engagement.

Anxiety, Disappointment, Depression

Professionally related anxiety, disappointment, and depression can be caused by rejection, failure, or the prospect of failure. Lack or loss of work, financial setbacks, unrealized design aspirations, inadequate recognition, or intense negative criticism can do the job. To be a happy, well-adjusted architect, you must be thick skinned and emotionally tough. Conversely, do not be an architect if you cope poorly with rejection and the prospect of setbacks, which are endemic to the profession of architecture.

As professional designers, architects produce work that is
continually scrutinized, criticized, compromised, and often redone.
Occasional rejection and disappointment come with the territory.
No one likes it but architects must be able to accept and deal with
it. This is not always easy, especially when setbacks are attributable
to forces beyond the architect's control. Imagine the feelings that
can well up when, after investing hundreds or thousands of hours
in a design, you are told that your work is unacceptable or cannot
be realized as you conceived it because of functional, aesthetic, or
cost problems. Imagine how it must feel not to win or receive a
prize in a design competition for which you expended great time
and effort. Rejection and disappointment are bitter medicines to
swallow but every architect has tasted them.

Rejection does not mean necessarily that extraordinary talent and effort have not been applied in creating an architectural design. Brilliant labors of love are rejected all the time along with mediocre ones. Judgment of architecture is invariably subjective, based on the values and taste of those who are judging, and architects have little choice but to endure and press on, always exerting their best efforts. Otherwise, dropping out of architecture may be the only alternative for avoiding anxiety, disappointment, and depression if compensating successes prove unattainable.

Personal Encumbrances

Architecture entails taking risks. It demands great investment of time, effort, and emotional and physical energy to achieve anything worthwhile. To be able to seize opportunities when they arise or pursue unconventional goals requires personal resources and a certain freedom from personal encumbrances.

In particular, establishing an architectural firm is often a great risk, especially financially. Yet it is the objective of many architects starting out in practice after school, an objective only some will reach. If an architect is supporting a family through his or her job, with no other substantial sources of income or assets, then giving up a regular, reliable salary to venture forth as an independent practitioner can be daunting.

Traveling and additional graduate study are other pursuits that are extremely beneficial to an architect. They too are difficult to accomplish if one is overly encumbered with dependents, debts, or doubts. Obviously those who begin with a financial support system or are personally unencumbered have a distinct advantage. Inheriting money or being married to a working, supportive spouse helps. And teaching architecture can provide time and income for young, aspiring architects to pursue practice while teaching.

An architect for whom I once worked gave me some memorable advice as I was departing my summer job to return to architecture school. After calling me into his office to say farewell, he pointed his finger toward the drafting room, then occupied by about a dozen architects bent over their drawing boards, and proposed that I should keep one thing in mind if I did not want to end up like them: don't marry or have kids too soon! He was really saying that if I wanted to travel or start a practice someday, too many premature commitments could stand in the way. Burdensome financial and personal obligations can keep an architect laboring away at a workstation in a room full of workstations.

Lack of Aptitude

Some people do not meet their professional goals because they lack the essential resources to do so. Aspiring architects should consider this possibility. If some of the key intellectual, emotional, and personal attributes noted in the preceding chapter are missing, architecture can be an uphill endeavor, even for very intelligent people. Every year teachers of architecture see bright students who nevertheless seem to be pursuing the wrong career because their aptitudes clearly lie elsewhere. Some are uncomfortable or awkward with drawing and graphics. Others lack mathematical, analytic, and technical ability. Still others have limited imaginations or visual sensitivity. These can be serious impediments for those who desire to be an architect.

Being intelligent is no guarantee of aptitude for architecture. A substantial amount of graphic and compositional talent is genetic.

Talent can be brought forth and nurtured but not taught. Similar to other personal qualities, talent can be developed in spite of, not because of, formal education. Intuition, instinct, and inventiveness are indispensable to architectural design; erudition and intelligence are necessary but not sufficient.

Lack of Passion and Dedication

Success in architecture is in part attributable to high levels of passion, dedication, and effort. Without them, the prospective or practicing architect is unlikely to do well. Because architecture is so demanding of time and energy, unwillingness to work hard and to accept often minimal rewards is a good reason not to be an architect.

Students first discover this truism in architecture school. Design is very labor intensive, requiring countless hours of mental and manual effort sketching and crafting physical and digital models. But architectural study prepares one for what is to come in practice: lots more hard work. Those fully committed to their work and impassioned about their professional ideals benefit from a quasi-religious sense of mission and purpose that inspires and helps them weather the rougher moments. All accomplished architects are motivated above all by love of design and building. For them, creating architecture is almost an obsession, an activity transcending the mere provision of services.

Legal and Financial Risks

Architects who own firms and whose designs get built are exposed to substantial legal and financial risks. The major legal risk, professional negligence, can cause clients or others to suffer monetary damages. Architects are sued by plaintiffs who believe the architect committed an error leading to injury or financial loss to the plaintiff. When such claims are made against an architect, whether groundless or not, the architect may be forced to compensate the plaintiff for some portion of the alleged damages following negotiations, arbitration, or litigation. And no matter what the outcome, substantial legal fees usually have to be paid.

Similar to others in our society who perform so-called personal services (physicians, attorneys, dentists, engineers), licensed architects are personally liable as individuals for professional negligence. This means that they cannot protect their assets against claims and judgments by incorporating but they can purchase costly liability insurance to cover most of the costs of defending and settling negligence suits.

Yet even with insurance, negotiating, litigating, and settling claims is intrusive, time-consuming, and stressful. Claims and litigation increase because of rising, often unrealistic expectations held by clients and consumers, leading them to sue architects even when there is little or no evidence of architectural wrongdoing. Thus, an architect may be slapped with a lawsuit despite his or her innocence. Furthermore the very existence of insurance invites lawsuits. If architects were impoverished and uninsured, they would rarely be sued.

Another unfortunate consequence of increased litigation risk is the practice of more defensive design and more extensive documentation—creation of a paper trail—that presumably protects the architect against the ever-present threat of lawsuits. But this can induce architects to be less innovative, to stick to the tried and true, and to devote more time to being pseudolawyers instead of designers. If you want to avoid the minefield of liability and litigation, then architectural practice is unsafe ground unless you forever remain an employee.

There is an even greater financial risk than being sued for professional negligence: the risk of not being paid for services rendered and having to take legal action to collect fees. The architect can suffer loss of income as well as time, to which may be added the stress of proving the case because, as plaintiff, the architect must assume the burden of proof. Often the only real winners financially are the attorneys.

Disillusionment

The roadblocks, risks, and uncertainties already identified produce frustration and disillusionment, perhaps the greatest overall risk in becoming an architect. When architects have met the demands of professional preparation, paid their proverbial dues, mustered their talents, and then found their aspirations and ideals compromised or their ideas rejected, disillusionment may set in. Usually there is not even the offsetting consolation of having made a lot of money. In fact architects say that they sometimes feel like prostitutes, working in a profession in which selling out one's goals and standards is commonplace. A dim view indeed.

Architects periodically feel exploited or used. They sometimes provide services for little or no pay, hoping for something in the future but ending up with nothing. Many see their career as a giant compromise, having given more than they got and accepted less than they deserved. How different, they say to themselves in retrospect, than what they imagined when they first put pencil to paper in a design studio. Some accept this condition as part of the business of architecture. They find sufficient rewards to offset the disappointments or they may even be able to disregard the problems altogether. A few abandon the profession, seeking firmer ground.

One thing is certain: for anyone contemplating or just starting a career in architecture, there is no way to predict where the choice will lead. Undoubtedly there will be rewards and frustrations, moments of delight and depression. The prospective architect can hope only that the sum of the assets will exceed the sum of the liabilities, yielding a positive net worth.

II

Becoming an Architect

3 The Structure of Architectural Education

For many architects, architectural education is among the most stimulating, challenging, and formative periods of their careers. It also can be one of the most frustrating, a period of trial and error, of discovery and doubt. To understand what becoming an architect entails, consider the structure of architectural education in the United States.

There are over 150 architecture programs in the United States accredited by the National Architectural Accrediting Board (NAAB; see http://www.naab.org/architecture_programs for a complete list of programs and schools). NAAB accrediting committees periodically visit architecture schools to ascertain whether schools are meeting NAAB criteria for conferring accredited architecture degrees. Criteria address faculty qualifications, physical facilities, budget, curricula and course content, and overall program goals. These criteria are also relevant to prospective students of architecture.

Architecture programs are typically constituent parts of universities, existing either as departments or schools within university divisions or colleges. This linkage is appropriate because the study of architecture touches on many other university-based disciplines: art, engineering, physics, mathematics, computer science, history, horticulture, geography, sociology, and even business and management. Further, introductory courses in architecture are often of interest to students in other departments on university campuses.

Most state and many private universities offer programs and degrees in architecture, with significant tuition differences between private and public or nonprofit institutions. Two-year community colleges teach prearchitecture courses for students planning to enroll eventually in accredited, university degree programs. A few wholly independent architecture schools are unaffiliated with universities. And several accredited institutions offer multisemester cooperative programs enabling employed students to attend classes at night on the way to earning a professional architecture degree.

US architecture schools offer diverse pathways to professional degrees, the source of considerable confusion for prospective architecture students.

Degree Pathways

Pathway 1   An undergraduate, four-year program leading to a BS or BA degree that is *not* an accredited professional degree. Many schools offer this program. After earning these degrees, students usually must spend at least two more years in a graduate program to earn an accredited, professional degree, in most cases a master of architecture (MArch). Also, prior to entering architecture graduate school, many students take off a year or two to work. This type of program allows students to test the waters of architecture without an excessive investment of time in the event that they change their minds. Such preprofessional programs may provide up to half of a complete architectural curriculum.

Pathway 2   An undergraduate, five-year program leading to the BArch, an accredited professional degree, or the MArch degree at a few schools. The five-year BArch was once the norm for architectural education in the United States, and many schools have retained this program despite the shift to graduate architectural education since the 1960s. Its advantages are less cost—five years of college versus six or seven, undergraduate tuition fees versus graduate tuition fees (almost always higher) — and academic continuity from freshman to fifth year. It immerses students in architecture from the outset when they are young and therefore most receptive to new ideas and experimentation. Its disadvantages are that it compresses professional and general education together into an intense five-year period, often precluding exploration through elective studies in other fields; it forces an early career choice, usually at the freshman or sophomore year levels when many eighteen- or nineteen-year-old students are still maturing and questing; and once begun, it is usually an all-or-nothing program because the BArch can be earned only on successful completion of all five years of study.

Pathway 3   A graduate-level, professional degree program leading to the MArch for students who have already earned an undergraduate, nonprofessional BA or BS degree (pathway one) with a major in architecture. These are two- to three-year programs for those without an accredited professional degree (a BArch or MArch). Students in pathway three programs enroll as graduate students and may hold undergraduate degrees from other universities.

Pathway 4   A graduate-level program leading to the first, accredited degree in architecture, usually the MArch degree for students holding undergraduate degrees in majors other than architecture. Such programs enroll students only as graduate students and usually require three to four years of concentrated studies in architecture. Students in these programs are generally assumed to have had little architectural preparation prior to entering the program. Typically these programs are populated by older students, some returning to school after working or establishing families, with degrees in the arts and humanities, engineering, science, business, or social sciences.

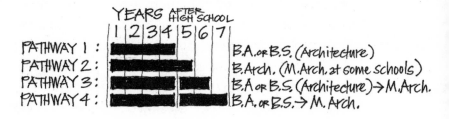

A number of architecture schools also offer specialized graduate programs leading to a postprofessional architecture degree for students already holding an accredited BArch or MArch degree. Advanced master's degree programs in architecture vary from one to two years in duration, depending on the school and area of study. In many cases, an advanced degree entails a customized study topic pursued collaboratively by a graduate student and a specific faculty member serving as the student's mentor. Some doctoral degree programs exist and entail research focusing on technology, history, theory, criticism, and urban planning rather than design.

The lack of national consistency in programs and degree names reflects the independent nature of individual architecture schools, coupled with the reluctance of the architectural establishment—those in practice and in education—to standardize architecture school programs. The NAAB's established program evaluation criteria pertain primarily to the basic subject matter all accredited degree programs must cover but it does not prescribe curricula, courses, or teaching approaches. Rather, it asks each architecture school to define its own particular goals, standards, and methods and then evaluates the school's success in meeting those goals, along with verifying that key subjects are addressed and resources are adequate. Although there are generally accepted notions of what constitutes a legitimate architectural program, schools nevertheless enjoy wide latitude in designing courses and curricula. Consequently, reading names of degrees and courses listed on websites reveals little of the quality and specifics of a school's program.

Curricular Content

Despite nominal variations in packaging of courses and curricula from one architecture school to another, there is nevertheless substantial commonality in content. Therefore what follows is not a description of specific architecture schools' curricula but rather a summary of their basic content. A course may have dozens of different names from one school to another, so it is imperative to focus on subject matter, not labels. Further, the exact chronology of subjects offered in schools varies but again these variations are less significant than the overall sequence, which is fairly uniform.

Most school curricula encompass the cumulative equivalent of eight semesters of architectural studies, which can be a mix of undergraduate and graduate work, for successful completion of a professional degree program. Some graduate schools do it in six or seven semesters (pathway four). With no previous background in architecture, you should assume that earning your professional degree will take five to eight calendar years after high school, depending on when you begin architectural course work.

Architectural programs generally focus on three main teaching areas: design, history, and technology, including digital technology. Complementing these are courses in professional practice, city planning, and perhaps historic preservation and real estate development. But studies in all these areas overlap. For example, design entails technology and history and may also involve city planning and preservation. History of architecture is the study of the history of building and city design and design theories related to cultural, philosophical, political, social, economic, and technological history. Technology courses teach students principles and techniques for exploring, engineering, and constructing architectural design concepts. Interrelation of areas of specialty and courses is the keystone of the discipline of architecture, itself an amalgam of disciplines.

Design

Studio courses in design are usually taken during every semester of an architectural program. They are the unifying pedagogical activity synthesizing the diverse contributing disciplines of architecture. Design studio courses typically account for 35 to 40 percent of the total credit hours needed for a professional architecture degree but they actually consume a disproportionately higher percentage of students' time: 50 to 60 percent.

Integral to learning design is the study of fundamental principles and techniques of architectural form making and graphic representation. These include the following:

Visual analysis and composition   Using digital and manual techniques to analyze existing forms as well as to create and manipulate invented forms in two and three dimensions; studying existing forms—buildings, urban spaces, vegetation, manufactured artifacts, painting, sculpture—to discover patterns and principles of composition applicable to creating new forms

Freehand drawing   Sketching to develop conceptual thinking and eye-brain-hand facility using different media (pencil and ink primarily but also charcoal, pastels, watercolor, or other paint); mastering techniques for making lines, tones, textures, shades, and

shadows; and learning to produce gestural sketches and scaled drawings rapidly, comfortably, and with reasonable perspectival accuracy, an invaluable graphic skill

Manually constructed drawing   Design concepts drawn using drafting tools, most notably orthogonal projections (plan, elevation, section); paraline or axonometric drawing; one-, two-, and three-point perspectives; and shadow projection. Essential drafting tools include pencils and pens; erasers and erasing shield; tracing paper; measuring scales to translate real, full-scale dimensions into proportional, scaled-down dimensions in drawings; a straightedge (T-square or parallel bar) and triangles; compass; and templates for drawing standard shapes and curved figures.

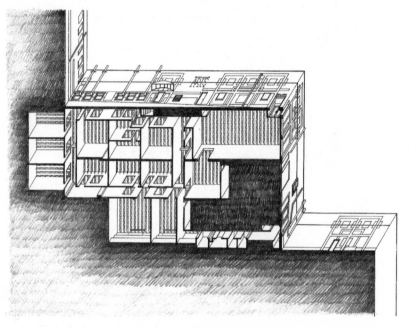

Manually drafted axonometric drawing showing a worms'-eye view

Physical models Crafting three-dimensional study models at diverse scales and levels of detail to explore design concepts; physical models can be made quickly or laboriously with simple cutting tools, almost any material—clay, polyfoam, stiff paper, cardboard, metal, wood, plastic, glass, fabric, plaster, cement—and a variety of adhesives

Digital drawing and model making Using state-of-the-art computer software and hardware to create, manipulate, and render 2-D orthographic drawings, perspectives, 3-D digital models, and video simulations; selection and control of line weights; inserting tones, textures, shading, shadows, furniture, figures, vegetation, and other objects available from digital libraries; despite sophisticated software, students must still generate design concepts, decide what to draw and model in developing those concepts, and graphically control how drawings and models look when presented

Architectural design is taught primarily in design studios, where students design a great variety of projects. First-year design studio projects are usually small in scope, abstract, and conceptual,

intended to spur imaginative and critical thinking and also nurture graphic skills. In subsequent years, projects become increasingly real, often analogous to what architects do in practice: designing structures in cities, suburbs, or exurban settings. Students also may design towns or urban neighborhoods. Real-world studio projects still can embody symbolic, spiritual, or philosophical pedagogy.

Architectural design studios operate fairly consistently throughout the United States. As few as eight or as many as eighteen students may be assigned to each design studio instructor, the studio critic, and each critic's section may be one of several at a given level within the curriculum. The studio critic may operate independently, assigning his or her own projects and following his or her own schedule. Or the studio may be part of a coordinated curriculum involving several sections, an entire level, or even the entire school. This too can change from year to year within a school.

Design studio critics plan the studio course, select projects, schedule work, critique students, and continually evaluate student progress. Studio courses have the greatest amount of one-on-one student-teacher contact in the curriculum, more than most courses in any university. Usually six to nine credits (typical lecture or seminar courses are three credits), studios meet three or four days each week for four hours or more per day. This means twelve to sixteen hours of studio work and interaction weekly. Students work independently during most of this time whereas the critic makes rounds reviewing work at each student's desk (called *desk crits*). Group reviews, generally referred to as *pinups,* regularly interrupt the routine.

Generally studio design projects increase in complexity as students progress through the program. Complexity depends on the number and difficulty of design issues addressed in a given project, not necessarily on a project's size or cost. A house or exhibition pavilion can be a more complex project than an office building or industrial plant, depending on site conditions and design requirements. Unconstrained design problems can be more challenging than highly constrained ones.

In most programs, beginning-year studio projects concentrate on design fundamentals. Students are introduced to visual composition in two and three dimensions: concepts of geometry, space, form, movement, and functional organization; basic technology; and sustainability. Projects are often theoretical and speculative rather than practical in nature to encourage creative, out-of-the-box thinking and to develop graphic and representational skills.

Projects in subsequent years become more like architecture, although specific requirements and conditions may still be idealized and unrealistic. Projects that illustrate this approach might include small pavilions or kiosks, emergency shelters, vacation homes or retreats (usually in the mountains or the woods, if not on the beach), religious buildings, and modest civic buildings such as a branch library or town hall. Each project presented by the critic introduces students to new design issues and reinforces principles and skills previously learned. One project might emphasize site planning and architectural massing (shaping a building's overall volume on a site), another might focus on patterns of structure and materials, and still another might deal with facade composition, climate, and energy conservation. The student is expected to create and manipulate form—volumes, spaces, surfaces, structures, and landscape—and functions on a given site in response to stipulated design goals and requirements, the so-called project program.

As competency increases, students advance to higher-level design studios, where they explore projects with more complex site and program requirements and with opportunities for more sophisticated investigation of theoretical questions, architectural technology, and urban design. Such projects can include multifamily housing, administrative buildings, educational facilities, theaters, libraries, museums, or transportation terminals. More rigorous site planning may entail design of residential communities, college campuses, transportation corridors, and civic parks.

The final year of design frequently involves a thesis. This typically requires research and preparation in a preceding semester, during which the student selects a topic and project and gathers relevant data. Most thesis work is done independently, unlike preceding design studios in which students work together and receive guidance from their instructors two or three times per week. Thesis students usually have an adviser or faculty thesis committee that periodically reviews their work and progress before final presentations. Some schools require submission of a thesis document, especially at the master's level, with text, photos, and images of final drawings and models.

Architecture schools generally have minimum standards of competency and performance that students must meet before advancing to the next level of design studio or before graduation. Because the design studio sequence is continual throughout most programs, studio sections often include students who did not begin architectural school at the same time. Some students need extra semesters to complete architecture school, either because of academic difficulties or because they had to hold down jobs to earn money to pay for their education.

History

History, the second broad area of study within any architectural program, explores and evaluates the past but also impinges vitally on the present and future. Prospective architects learn about the rich architectural and urban legacy produced over centuries by the world's diverse cultures. Reading texts about architecture and architects as well as visiting and studying cities and buildings of the past reveal design theories, compositional principles, and aesthetic philosophies relevant to what architects do today and will do tomorrow.

The historical evolution of architecture may be approached chronologically, geographically, and thematically. Historians may explore architecture by time periods—decades, centuries, or eras—or by geography—continents, countries, cities, or regions. Thematic analysis can focus on architects, compositional strategies and styles, urbanism, technology, symbology, philosophy, or building types. Each historian has preferred ways of approaching and presenting architectural history but there is substantial commonality in content. Following is a representative list of course content in architectural history:

Surveys of Western architecture from ancient to modern times, typically illustrated with countless projected images

Surveys of non-Western architecture, primarily Islamic and Far Eastern cultures, but taught more rarely than European history

Ancient Western architectural history concentrating on Egypt, the Near East, Greece, and Rome

Early Christian and Byzantine architecture

Architecture of the Middle Ages, primarily Romanesque and Gothic structures in France, Italy, and England

The Renaissance, primarily in Italy

Architecture between the Renaissance and the industrial revolution—the baroque and rococo periods in Europe and neoclassicism in France and England

French beaux arts influence from the eighteenth to the twentieth centuries

US architecture in the nineteenth and twentieth centuries

Modern US architecture

Modern European architecture, usually divided into pre–World War I, between the wars, and post–World War II periods

Russian architecture

Japanese architecture

History of indigenous architectures, usually across diverse regional, cultural, temporal, and technological lines

History of architectural theorizing and philosophizing

History of building technology

History of landscape architecture

History of urbanism and urban design, exploring origins, form, growth, and planning principles of cities, towns, and urban spaces—urbanism and urban design can be an aspect of study in all these history topics

No one school of architecture covers all of these subjects in its collection of history courses, and no student can begin to study but a fraction of the topics on this list. Survey courses, lasting one or two semesters, skim the surface of the past, whereas smaller lecture or seminar courses provide the opportunity to concentrate on the subsequently listed topics. Once in school, you will quickly discover your interests and learn which teachers and courses appeal to you.

Similar to related courses in the humanities, history courses in architecture school consist of assigned and recommended readings coupled with extensive viewing of images selected and projected by the lecturer or seminar leader (who may sometimes be a student in the class). Essays, term papers, and small projects are typically assigned. Depending on the school's location and resources, teachers may lead students on field trips, always an invaluable learning experience. Indeed, field trips are popular in studio and technology courses as well.

Technology

Technology, the third broad area of architectural course work in all professional school curricula, entails analyzing, shaping, and implementing architecture as constructed form. It also encompasses digital methods for studying and representing architectural form. Students learn engineering principles and techniques that influence designs and make designs stable, safe, comfortable, buildable, and sustainable. Technology is not separate or different from the art of design; rather, it is the part of design more closely associated with science and engineering in content and method.

Architectural technology includes multiple areas of study: structural technology; construction methods and materials; building environment technologies—interior climate control, lighting, and acoustics; energy conservation; and computer-aided design (CAD). Some of each is required in all architecture schools, although in differing doses and with widely ranging levels of rigor. Architectural technologies are better understood by aspiring architects who have basic mathematical and scientific knowledge, a reason many schools require beginning architecture students to take introductory math and science courses. This pays off later because architectural technologies, similar to design and history, are covered in state exams for licensing architects.

Structures

Understanding structural concepts and methods is indispensable for anyone who hopes to design buildings. Structure is that part of a building or any constructed form that resists the primary forces of gravity (weight) and lateral forces imparted by wind and earthquakes (seismic forces). These forces act vertically and horizontally but they can cause a structure to flex, bend, twist, vibrate, or even lift up. The structure of a building, its skeleton or frame, consists of foundations and footings, retaining and bearing walls, columns, and spanning members—beams, girders, trusses— holding up floors and roofs. Arches and vaults also can span space. Integral parts of a building's overall structural system, these elements are connected all together to support and stabilize a work of architecture.

Many components of a building are not part of the building's structural system—plumbing, cabinetry, ductwork, and windows, for example. Not so obvious, however, is the role the structural system plays in affecting or being affected by the overall spatial and volumetric form of a building. First, the structure must be designed to work safely and efficiently in supporting and stabilizing the building. Second, the architect must orchestrate the patterns of framing and the patterns of architectural form—volume, space, surface—to create visual and constructional relationships. Here is clearly where structural technology and the art of design unite. Indeed, the architect can use the structural system expressively, creating a visual language of exposed structural elements and details. Or the architect can make the structural system recessive, concealing it from direct view.

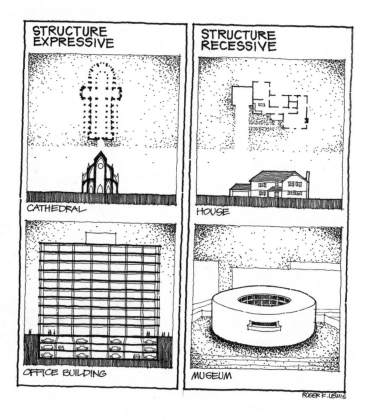

To master this, students in architecture school study statics—
how forces act on bodies in equilibrium—strength of materials—
how specific materials behave under stress—and how fundamental
structural components—beams, trusses, columns, cables, rods,
footings and foundations, bearing walls, and slabs or decks—
behave when forces are applied to them. They learn about tension
and compression, stresses and strains, and about how deflection,
bending, and buckling affect elements of a structure when loaded
or overloaded. They learn about critical connections and joints
between members and about temperature-dependent expansion
and contraction. And they learn how a building's framing system
as a whole can behave when subjected to nature's forces. Such
systems include the familiar wood frame of a house, post-beam-
floor framing typical of office buildings, bearing wall construction,
membrane or tensile structures (such as tents or bridges), thin-
shell structures (vaults, domes), and space frames.

Practicing architects often determine the overall framing
concept of buildings they design but they rely on consulting
structural engineers to calculate all loads and design all load-
bearing elements and connections. Nevertheless, architects must
understand structural engineering fundamentals to effectively
communicate with and guide engineers. This enables architects
and structural engineers to collaborate effectively in making
decisions that affect the look, quality, and cost of a structural
system and the architecture it supports.

Materials and Methods of Construction

Beyond structural systems, architects must know the implications
of using diverse construction materials: wood and other naturally
fibrous products, structural steel, reinforced concrete, masonry
(brick, block, stone, tile) and mortar, miscellaneous metals, glass,

plastics, fabrics, composites, and synthetics such as sealants and insulation. Each material has unique aesthetic, technical, and cost characteristics and the architect must choose materials and systems thoughtfully and knowledgeably. In addition to visual appearance, key properties to consider are strength, durability, workability, weight, resistance to thermal variations and moisture, and cost.

But one other property is critical: how "green" is a material? Responsible architects strive to maximize use of materials that are recycled, renewable, nontoxic, nonpolluting, and locally produced and available, which minimizes the economic and energy costs of transportation. The ultimate goal is to specify materials that help reduce a building's carbon emissions and contribute to making its carbon footprint approach zero.

Structural engineers design structural system details but architects retain primary responsibility for selecting nonstructural materials and designing assembly details for essentially all nonstructural building components. Therefore some schools teach design-detailing courses in which students study control of moisture, control of heat loss and gain, dimensional stability, durability, sustainability related to energy and natural resource conservation, and visual appearance. They produce design drawings showing how materials are used and pieces fit together, how joints and connections are made, and what the dimensions of all assembled components will be. Such drawings depict roof, wall, and floor assemblies, window and door assemblies, guardrails, stairs, cabinetry, and decorative finishing elements.

However, many architecture programs do not invest much curricular time and effort teaching materials and methods of construction. These programs instead rely on design studio teachers and studio projects to introduce and explore materials and methods as part of studio pedagogy. The reasoning is that aspiring architects will inevitably acquire this knowledge when they are employed and work on real projects in architectural offices, during architecture school, and as intern architects after completing architecture school.

Environmental and Energy Technologies

Environmental and energy technologies are concerned with making the built environment safe, usable, comfortable, and green. With the help of engineering and other specialists, architects strive to craft buildings with interior environments that are safe from fire and smoke, ensure thermal comfort, are properly lighted, provide fresh, unpolluted air to breathe, and have appropriate acoustic characteristics. Such buildings must be well insulated to retain heat in winter and keep it out in summer. They harvest daylight and solar energy year-round to reduce the need to buy and consume energy. And to the extent possible, they capture and use waste heat that otherwise would be thrown away.

In addition to tempering the environment and satisfying the senses, architects and their consultants design energy-efficient systems for filtering and distributing air, circulating and recycling water, collecting waste, piping natural gas, and moving goods and people within buildings. These systems are like metabolic networks woven into the rigid, supporting skeleton of a building's body. Architecture students study the basics of electrical systems, plumbing systems, heating and cooling systems, ventilating systems, and conveying systems (elevators and escalators). They learn engineering principles and specific applications, understanding how such systems influence overall building design. Similar to structural systems, architectural designers do not undertake the detailed, quantitative design of environmental control systems but rather collaborate with engineering experts in system selection and design coordination.

Many schools include lessons about architectural lighting, focusing especially on ways of maximizing daylight penetrating into workspaces and living spaces. This can greatly reduce the amount of electric power required for daytime lighting. Students also may study room acoustics, the behavior and perception of sound within spaces, and sound transmission, the passage of sound between spaces or through structures. Proper acoustic design is critical for theaters, classrooms, auditoriums, restaurants, airports, or buildings near loud noise sources. Anyone with functioning eyes and ears knows that the world is full of architecture inside of which seeing and hearing are difficult.

Working Digitally

Virtually every architecture student in the United States uses a computer for design and other course work and for staying

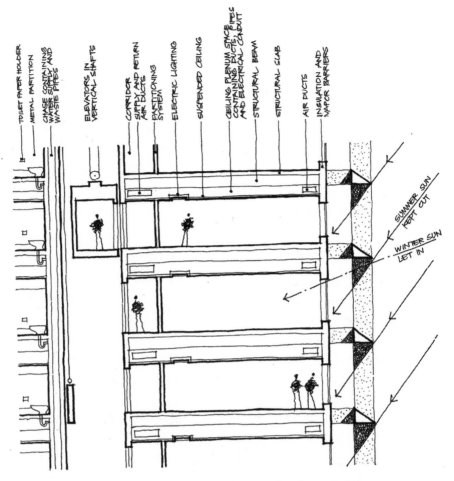

TOILET PAPER HOLDER
METAL PARTITION
CHASE CONTAINING WATER SUPPLY AND WASTE PIPES
ELEVATORS IN VERTICAL SHAFTS
CORRIDOR
SUPPLY AND RETURN AIR DUCTS
PARTITIONING SYSTEM
ELECTRIC LIGHTING
SUSPENDED CEILING
CEILING PLENUM SPACE CONTAINING DUCTS, PIPES AND ELECTRICAL CONDUIT
STRUCTURAL BEAM
STRUCTURAL SLAB
AIR DUCTS
INSULATION AND VAPOR BARRIERS
SUMMER SUN KEPT OUT
WINTER SUN LET IN

Cross-section showing various systems and elements that shape a building
and serve its occupants

connected to the world. Computers are powerful tools for
practicing architects as well as for architecture students and faculty
members. Accordingly, most schools offer CAD courses because
architecture firms today hire only CAD-literate graduates.

Many students entering architecture school already have
acquired basic computer skills. Therefore, CAD courses
concentrate on teaching students how to use specialized, more
advanced software programs to build, modify, and present digital
models of design concepts in addition to delineating and plotting
conventional architectural drawings. Employing continually
evolving software, students can generate realistic perspectives from

any viewpoint and create animated videos simulating movement through, around, and over a proposed design. They can construct, study, readily modify, and represent very complex building geometries and spaces, building facades, structural patterns, natural and artificial lighting conditions, diverse building materials, colors, and surface textures. And students can digitally create abstract visual compositions.

Despite computer power, students and practitioners still must do the critical and imaginative thinking and make all the value judgments necessary to create, develop, test, and communicate design ideas. Those ideas frequently appear not on a computer screen but as freehand sketches. Consequently, many schools insist that students in their first year or two learn to draw and design by hand. And most students come to realize that there are times when pencil and paper or stylus and pad are the right tools.

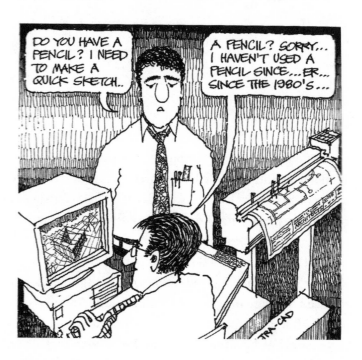

Management

Management embraces topics and courses that prepare students to manage the design process and to conduct the business affairs and operational tasks of architectural practice. Schools vary greatly in the number and variety of such courses taught, with most offering very few. They often rely on courses given in other departments, such as business administration, economics, computer science, or civil engineering, to satisfy students' needs and interests.

However, architecture schools usually teach at least one required course on professional practice to satisfy NAAB accreditation criteria. These courses explain how firms are organized and managed. They delve into the marketing of services, fees and compensation, project management and documentation, contracts, legal and ethical concerns, and construction administration. For example, students may be introduced to building information modeling (BIM), whereby architects and their consultants create a layered, multidimensional digital model of a building with all physical elements and related data about the project displayed and accessible. Integrating the work of architects and engineers, the digital model is thus available in real time to all concerned parties—designers, owners, contractors, subcontractors, and suppliers. BIM enhances documentation reliability and greatly facilitates project coordination, cost estimating, and bidding.

In a few architecture schools, more advanced courses focus on management of construction projects in detail. These deal with planning and scheduling of construction tasks, coordination of building trades and subcontractors, estimating and bidding, materials purchasing, contract negotiating, and cost accounting. However, because of time and resource limitations, many architecture schools have resisted introducing this subject matter, believing that construction management belongs more appropriately in schools of management or engineering.

Several schools offer real estate development programs that examine financing, sources and deployment of capital funding for building, the development process through which buildings are created, the economic characteristics of private and public sector projects, and the role of government in architecture—its regulations, zoning and building codes, tax and investment laws, planning policy, and construction programs. As they near the end of their studies, many architecture students become increasingly interested in real estate development, realizing that they are likely to be working in the real estate world with which they have little familiarity.

Historic Preservation

Preservation of historic buildings, towns, and cities is an important component of architectural education and practice. Preservation sensibility greatly increased in the United States in the wake of ill-conceived twentieth-century public policy that enabled irreplaceable historic buildings and impoverished sections of cities to be razed in the name of urban renewal and progress. Citizens and public officials, as well as architects, finally recognized that such structures are an integral part of our cultural heritage, embodying substantial political, cultural, commercial, and often aesthetic significance.

Preserved, repurposed historic architecture also offers great economic and sustainability value for property owners and their communities. Preserving architecture is a very effective green design and construction strategy. Saving and reusing an existing building conserves all the energy and material resources along with the financial resources already invested and embodied in the building. Increasing numbers of projects undertaken by architects will involve urban and suburban properties with preservation

opportunities. But critical questions arise for architects and
property owners: which buildings merit preservation? Which
buildings are so obsolete and decrepit that they deserve
demolition? How can neglected buildings be stabilized? When is it
appropriate to retrofit, modernize, and even enlarge a historic
building?

Preservation of a historically significant building may be
limited to restoration of the building's original appearance and use
but sometimes it entails adaptation for new uses within its
preserved exterior shell. Thomas Jefferson's Monticello and George
Washington's Mount Vernon are preserved historic buildings

restored to their original condition. By contrast, Boston's Quincy Market is a preserved historic structure adapted for new commercial uses. Sometimes older buildings are preserved, either wholly or in part, and incorporated into new construction that abuts or envelops them. In all projects involving existing architecture or urban fabric, dealing with historic preservation is as much a design challenge as designing a new project from scratch.

Electives

Courses in design, history, and technology are the core of an architectural curriculum but that core should be complemented by electives in other areas of study. Indeed, electives may be required. They furnish credit hours needed for graduation and, more important, broaden professional education. Some architectural courses, particularly in history or technology, can be taken as electives when they are not part of the core requirements. Electives outside architecture may offer the largest and most fertile selection, however, reinforcing the liberal-professional duality of architectural education.

Following are courses and topics most relevant to the study and practice of architecture:

Urban studies and city planning
Landscape architecture
Civil engineering
Geography
Computer science
Art
Sustainability
Biology
Anthropology and archeology
Sociology
Psychology
Economics
Business administration and management science
History
Government and politics
Law

Travel and Study Abroad

Many architecture schools offer optional travel and study abroad programs, usually for graduate students or advanced undergraduate students. These programs can be relatively brief—a week or two during a regular semester, several weeks during summers, or during breaks between semesters—or they can last for an entire semester or academic year. Destinations can be anywhere on the planet, although most programs are conducted in Europe, especially Italy, France, and England. Other favored places are Scandinavia, Spain, Turkey, Russia, India, Japan, and China. Schools may develop programs taking students to more exotic, less popular places in Africa, in Central or South America, as well as Europe or Asia. Language can be an issue, but fortunately for Americans, English is increasingly understood and spoken around the world, especially by students. Nevertheless, some foreign language ability is an invaluable asset when studying abroad.

Travel and study abroad programs vary greatly in content, course work, and credit-hour opportunities. Some may be short-term travel experiences equivalent to a two- or three-credit course in which students earn credits by sketching, photographing, and visually analyzing existing architecture, towns, or cityscapes and perhaps by studying relevant history. Semester-long and year-long programs include design studios, plus additional course work, to equal a semester's or year's worth of work at the home architecture school. Invariably design studios abroad undertake projects in the host country and typically host-country faculty members are invited to participate as lecturers, critics, and reviewers.

To participate in foreign study programs, students usually must bear travel and lodging expenses in addition to paying tuition or other fees. However, many universities offer needy students financial assistance for study abroad programs, which can cost several thousand dollars more than usual tuition and living expenses. If you have the time and can muster the economic resources, study and travel abroad experiences are not to be missed. They are truly unique opportunities not only to see cities and architecture very different from what you see in the United States but also to immerse yourself in and learn about very different cultures. Studying abroad, even for just a few weeks, is intellectually challenging and stimulating, and for some it is life altering. Many students return with new ideas and transformed perspectives—about architecture and about themselves—that they otherwise would never have acquired.

4 Experiencing Architecture School

No outline of the structure of architectural education in the United States can ever reveal what it is really like to be an architectural student. This chapter offers an account of the educational journey, which I hope is the next best thing to being there.

The First Year and Workload Shock

Starting architecture school is a challenge, a mystery, and a surprise—a period marked by extraordinary rates of learning coupled with extraordinary fatigue. No matter how well prepared you are or what you have been told, it will be different from what you expected. The first year of real immersion is when you begin design studio courses along with other architectural courses. You will be very, very busy.

In fact, one of the first shocks is how busy you will be, the workload shock. Few students anticipate the amount of work piled on in architecture school, especially in first year. By tradition, introductory design studios set the initial pace, which is hectic with continual assignments of variable duration. Some require hours, some days, others weeks, often broken down into shorter subassignments. The staccato rhythm of basic design projects demands constant effort, day and night at times, far beyond the credit hours earned.

Workload shock, similar to other assaults on the brain and body, produces positive and negative responses. Negatively, it is tiring and mind numbing. Much of the studio work is labor intensive rather than intellect intensive. Hours are spent drawing, cutting, and gluing. Some hours will seem tedious and others exhilarating. Up moments are later wiped out by down moments as the struggle to keep going and keep abreast, let alone ahead, goes on. Second winds, fueled by bursts of adrenaline and surges of renewed strength and energy, recur with reasonable frequency. If you can tolerate it all, it will toughen you.

Key to coping with workload shock is time management. With the design studio demanding so much time and energy, how does anyone meet other obligations? There seems to be a deadline every other day and some days two or three. Lulls are few and far between. Faculty members will tell you to work steadily and regularly in each subject, allocating your time proportionately to each course throughout the semester, which is easier said than done.

Much design studio work is produced in intense spurts, often just before deadlines. The creative process defies attempts at smoothness, continuity, and regularity. Architects refer to such spurts as *charrettes* (French for *little carts*). In architecture school, a charrette is an intense, uninterrupted period of work prior to a deadline, almost always including at least one all-night stand. In the nineteenth century, at the Ecole des Beaux Arts in Paris, a charrette would arrive to collect project drawings just prior to the final deadline, and students, desperate to finish, would climb aboard the moving cart to add last-minute touches to their drawings—hence the term *being on charrette*. Visit an architecture school studio, especially near a project completion deadline, and you will see students on charrette day and night. Many never go home. Some practically live in the studio in what can best be described as camping-out conditions.

The most sensible attitude for handling first-year workloads is a positive, having-fun, on-to-victory one. *Illegitimus non carborundum,* meaning "Don't let the bastards grind you down!" Hang in, be tough, enjoy the occasional psychic pain and degradation as well as the periodic successes, discovery, and enlightenment. Amaze your friends with your dedication and ability to overcome. Other students in the university will be awed by your commitment and endurance. Rare is the campus where architecture students are not considered the most hardworking, grind-it-out students or where architecture is not considered one of the hardest majors.

You will find little sympathy among most faculty members when you voice complaints about the amount of work you have to do, the overlapping deadlines and exams, the pressures, and the state of your mental and physical health. Their lack of sympathy does not mean that they do not understand or appreciate what you are experiencing. They too have been through it. They know that you are behind in sleep, neglecting your friends or family, in desperate need of a shower, and probably going broke while trying to pay your way through school. They know that your love life is suffering or interfering with your work. But they will tell you it is inevitable, a taste of and preparation for future reality. It is a rite of passage, a deposit on account for the dues anyone must pay to become an architect. The workload and its pressures are a positive stimulus as well as an ordeal.

New Values, New Language

Workload shock is accompanied by value and language bafflement. The latter results from being deluged by a new and often imprecise vocabulary. Only architects and a few architectural groupies really know the lingo, and there are sublingos used only by a few architects and architecture professors. You will first hear the language from your teachers, then from upper-level architecture students. Reading architectural literature also will introduce you to the new language.

Values bafflement is related to language bafflement because values are professed and examined through language. Recognize that all academic and professional fields have elaborately developed, internal value systems, a set of commonly understood principles and criteria applicable to work within the field. This value system, with its concomitant vocabulary, is not clearly written down anywhere. You cannot go out and buy a book titled *Architecture's Value System: How to Judge Everything You See or Hear* or *Words Architects Use and What They Mean.*

The values and vocabulary transmitted in architecture school come as a shock because they are unfamiliar, they are unclear and ambiguous, and their application and meaning are context dependent, changing from professor to professor or semester to semester. Just when you thought you had figured out what your teacher was talking about, new metaphors and references renew your confusion.

Architecture is at once an art and a science. It demands logic, method, rational analysis, and measurable quantification, on the one hand, and intuition, emotion, sentiment, willfulness, and subjective judgment on the other. Thus the beginning student continually faces conflict, uncertainty, and confusion, especially in the design studio where values and judgments that cannot be justified scientifically are routinely presented, debated, and defended. Students discover that design thinking occurs in both sides of the brain and that design teachers expect work demonstrating sound reasoning and aesthetic invention.

Most architecture students have shared similar academic experiences. In high school and college courses, the teacher presented specific material and asked specific questions and the student periodically regurgitated, sometimes with minimum digestion, what was presented. Emphasis was on delivering facts, providing logical answers, or rationally deriving solutions. Students tried to figure out what teachers were looking for. "Tell us what you want!" say students, "and we'll give it to you."

This is generally not how design is taught. Values espoused by design studio critics may seem vague, the pedagogical expectations ill-defined. One day the critic says that it is important to think about efficient and legible circulation and the next day the critic protests that the design is too much like a circulation diagram. Too little color one day, too much the next. Nice proportions, proclaims the critic, but it doesn't work; or it works but the proportions are bad. Be simple, they say; too simple-minded, they say. It has wonderful complexity . . . it's too complex . . . it lacks complexity. Less is more. You can't read the structure. Why express the structure? Too much variety! Too little variety!

Perhaps the intertwining of values and vocabulary is becoming apparent. What about these words we teachers utter so often, so confidently, so critically? What do we mean and what do we really want? How do teachers, much less beginning students, know when

a proportion is bad, or which colors to use, or when there is just the right amount of complexity? Obviously, claim the students, the critics know something—some set of understood but not explicitly communicated values—that allows them to make judgments and know the truth. Why not share it?

Words expressing values pour forth. Buildings are described as *constructs, habitable artifacts, environments, built form, structures,* or *edifices.* They can be *object* (freestanding), *background,* or *in-fill buildings.* The word *space* can refer to a room, a corridor or hallway, a street, a plaza, an attic, an interval, or any void. Space can *flow, penetrate, modulate, expand,* or *contract.* It can be amorphous and open, without clear boundaries, or it can be crisply defined, figural, and contained, with discernible shape and boundaries. A closet or bathroom is a space; so are the mall in Washington, DC, and New York's Central Park.

Familiar building components are favorites for renaming. Windows can become *fenestration, voids* in walls, *oculi, penetrations, punched openings, apertures,* or *cutouts.* Walls become vertical *planes, surfaces, space definers or delimiters, enclosing envelopes, partitions,* or *separators.* A courtyard may be an *atrium,* a *peristyle,* or an *interior open space,* whereas a porch translates into a *loggia,* a *portico,* or a *transitional space.* Corridors are called *galleries, circulation conduits, pedestrian streets, passages, channels, ambulatories,* and *hallways.*

Critics and students like to talk about the visual characteristics of form. Among the nouns and adjectives one hears are the following:

Scale Having to do with the relative sizes of the whole and its constituent parts and in turn their relation to human dimensions. When architects talk about scale, they usually are concerned with design perception—about how small or large something looks within a given context because of its composition and proportions.

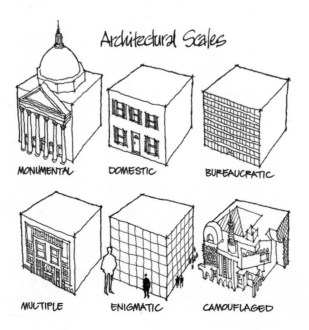

Appropriateness   Whether a design fits or reflects the circumstances of a project. Appropriateness can relate to the scale, style, character, or functional purpose of a design.

Image   The overall look and feel of a place or building

Texture, shape, rhythm, relief, color, dimension   Quasi-objectifiable but very important visual qualities characteristic of architectural form

Metaphor   Refers to architecture that looks like or symbolizes something else. Buildings can be machines; natural organisms such as seashells, birds, and vegetation; or geometric solids—cubes, spheres, rectangular slabs, bars, cylinders, lattices, pyramids, chains, mats, or combinations of these. Metaphoric architectural form can express ideas derived from literature, religion, philosophy, science, or art.

Function   Refers to the role of architecture in fulfilling objectifiable human requirements relating to utility, structural stability, comfort, safety, buildability, and cost. Functional considerations are different from aesthetic ones in that they are relatively quantifiable and typically not ego dependent.

Form, formal, formalistic   Broad terms for the three-dimensional, visual nature and shape of what architects design. Buildings, cities, spaces, structural elements, ornaments, plants, and other objects have *form* and *formal-formalistic* qualities. Form imparts *image.*

Typology   A noun (*typological* is the adjective) borrowed from linguistics and referring to classifiable sets of objects (e.g., building types, house types, room types, street types, bridge types) that share common, identifiable patterns of structure and form, independent of their historical origin, style, or function

Circulation   The patterns and methods of movement within, around, or through an environment—circulation of people, vehicles, and goods horizontally and vertically in buildings, neighborhoods, campuses, villages, towns, cities, rooms, or landscapes. Circulation patterns often constitute the spatial skeleton of many building types.

Unity, harmony, coherence   Denoting in any composition that quality whereby the whole and its parts appear to belong together primarily through visual linkages and perceptible interrelationships, of which there can be many, depending on the eye of the beholder. Compositional unity can be achieved through either analogy or contrast. Without unity, visual incoherence and fragmentation occur. Yet one person's harmony may be another's disharmony.

Layering and layers   Pertaining to visually overlapping elements—
volumes, rooms, wall planes, doorways, sheets of glass, transparent
screens, arches, rows of columns, vegetation, or other objects—
distributed in space from foreground to background, side to side,
or top to bottom so that an observer sees several elements at one
time. Looking down a city street, you see layers of signs, trees,
benches, and parking meters. Building facades are layered with
planar differences to create three-dimensional skins and to cast
shadows, which makes the layering especially legible.

Disparate architectural elements and multiple planes are layered together to
create this cartoonish building's front facade and overall form

It reads   Characterizing an architectural design concept or motif that can be seen and interpreted, that can be "read" like a text or facial expression. Buildings can be read to discover their functions, their two- and three-dimensional compositional patterns, their materials and structure, their cultural sources, and their symbolic content. A Gothic cathedral, an airport terminal, a commercial office building or the New York Stock Exchange are buildings fairly easy to read. If a building design cannot be read, according to some critics, then the architecture student may need to "rewrite."

Hundreds of adjectives season the critical comments of architects, especially when making remarks about students' work. A few are heard often:

Interesting   A word meaning anything from boring, banal, passable, or conventional to provocative, inventive, stimulating, or witty. An *interesting* design rarely merits an A, whereas *very interesting* may be in the A category.

Competent   Similar to *interesting,* it implies that a design is merely okay, workable, or acceptable but not brilliant or revolutionary. Competent is what every architect is expected to be at a minimum.

Convincing   Cropping up regularly, this usually means that a specific design appears to be well thought out and well executed as depicted in drawings and models. *Convincing* says that you have created something believable artistically, functionally, and perhaps technologically.

Ugly   *Ugly* is heard periodically. It really means that the critic does not like the looks of what you have designed, for reasons on which he or she may never elaborate, whereas others may instead find your design . . .

Beautiful   The critic likes the looks of your design, also for reasons that may not always be clear. Remember that in architecture, similar to all other art, much of the perception of beauty is in the eye of the beholder.

Meaningful, meaningless   Judgments about what designs say, represent, stand for, denote, and connote beyond what they actually do or look like. Columns, for example, are vertical structural elements that support loads and play a role in a building's composition. But they could be imbued with additional meaning, perhaps signifying virility, strength, victory, connection between heaven and earth, or any other symbolic notion ascribed to them by their designer or the scholarship of historians. For some teachers and architects, designs that cannot be read and interpreted are deemed to lack meaning. Of course, sometimes the word *meaningful* can lack meaning.

Perhaps the uncertainty and subjectivity of architectural values lead academically minded architects to search for more scientific language, for a more precise set of words and definitions with which to explain design. And with each new batch of jargon and classifiers, the vocabulary list lengthens and the uncertainty and subjectivity persist as always. Thus, beginning architectural students should remember that this is part of the tradition and should not let first-year language shock deter their quest for understanding.

Competition and Grades

Many students who start architecture school never finish, usually dropping out because they feel they lack aptitude. Few students quit simply because of the amount of work, to which most quickly become accustomed. However, there is a keen and discernible atmosphere of competition, intensified by the artistic nature of the work in design studio, and this atmosphere can discourage even the most hardworking student.

Most institutions use grades to indicate how students are doing with respect to the competition within the class or school. This is certainly not unique to architecture. What is unique is that diligence and hard work do not necessarily bring correspondingly high design studio grades. In fact another of the great first-year shocks may occur when a project you have designed with all the blood, sweat, tears, time, and imagination you could summon is judged to be mediocre or worse. And this can happen inconsistently and without warning. You may have received an A or B on your last project, then a C or D on the next one. What should you make of this?

It is all normal. Your design work, not you, is what is being judged. Most students experience the roller coaster of project grading throughout school, and it takes getting used to. Many students have good and bad semesters, good and bad months, weeks, or days. Keep reminding yourself that effort alone is not being assessed in architecture school, that native aptitude and talent are essential and even dominant evaluation factors.

Most faculty members grade students' work in architectural design on a curve, relative to only those students in a section or class, and against broader standards applied to all students. Occasionally every project in a section falls short or, conversely, earns an A or B. Semesters occur during which no one receives an A and others when nearly everyone receives an A. This depends on the critics, some of whom may have unrealistically high standards, as well as on the students.

You must be philosophical about grading, recognizing that grades represent only the combined objective and subjective evaluation of your work at a particular time. They may change as you proceed through school and as your work changes. They neither destroy nor ensure your future career. Once you are out of architecture school, probably no one will ever again see or care about your grades as a student. But one thing is certain: if you do not make the effort to do the work, you will not receive good grades, no matter how gifted you are.

The competition in architecture school is typical of grade competition anywhere else. Once admitted, you are expected to maintain some minimum grade point average (GPA) for continuation in the program. Most graduate schools require a minimum GPA of B (3.0) for graduation. Many programs do not allow architecture students to proceed to the next level of design studio with less than adequate performance in design, even if their GPA is high enough. Consequently students feel pressured to maintain their academic standing but this is usually a problem for only a minority of students in a class.

Wanting to excel, to stand out, to be on top or at least near it is a source of stress and motivation. Competitive pressure is internal and external. Dedicated students push themselves, notwithstanding other influences, reacting to an internal need to achieve. With this comes pushing from external sources—faculty members, fellow students, friends, and family—which can be relentless and unending. Some students thrive on such pressures; others feel substantial anxiety, which can affect their work. The pressures are there, the competition and pushing are inevitable, and you must at least cope with them. Ideally they will help you to do your best and succeed.

Not all student work in architecture school is done solo. Frequently design studio teachers will assign students to work in teams, either for the entire duration of a project or to undertake certain project phases, such as building and sharing a site model, and conducting research. Students may form teams and work together in other courses, such as architectural technology. But team projects in school still engender competition within teams as well as between teams. Regrettably, one member of a team may not do his or her part adequately, always an awkward situation breeding resentment by other team members and making fair grading by the professor difficult. Nevertheless, teamwork experience in school helps prepare students for the realities of practice because most real-world projects are designed by teams, not by one individual.

Pencilphobia

Pencil and paper are still indispensable for architectural design, even in the computer age. And drawing is still the primary medium for initiating and pursuing free-wheeling exploration of design possibilities. Similar to other artists and craftspersons, architects must thoroughly master the use of tools through practice and repetition. Good architects become so comfortable and facile with drawing that they cannot engage in the act of design except with a drawing tool—pencil, pen, stylus, or mouse— in hand. In designing architecture, the mind, body, and tool merge, acting together as one. No one can design simply by thinking and visualizing a work of architecture mentally.

Prior to mastering computer-aided design, students must learn to sketch with pencil, ink, and other media. Indispensable for design, drawing is how architects represent conceptual hypotheses graphically. Some beginning architecture students discover this painfully. They develop a fear of committing themselves and their ideas to paper, a fear of drawing, albeit sometimes an unconscious fear. The reluctance to draw stems from anxiety and uncertainty.

Beginning students quickly learn that without a drawing to look at, critics assume that there is no design yet and nothing tangible to evaluate. Many design teachers refuse to discuss students' design proposals or ideas unless they have been drawn. At the same time, students discover that some teachers may make what seem to be only negative comments when the indispensable drawings are presented. So it is not unusual for a few students to plead pencilphobia as a defense, a way of avoiding the risk of being criticized.

Architectural design is inherently a conjectural, trial-and-error process. Drawings are the primary means by which to hypothesize (to try) and evaluate alternative design concepts, to discover good ideas and purge bad or inappropriate ideas, then to refine and perfect the chosen concept. Design is a continual trial-test-change process. Without this iterative struggle using pencil, paper, study models—and later digitally produced drawings and models—you will not go far as an architectural designer. Therefore draw freely, willingly, and accurately. More design study sketches are always better than fewer. Twenty minutes of thoughtful criticism, even if disapproving, is far more valuable than two minutes of verbal lamentations and regrets.

The Culture and Community of Architecture School

During your first year in architecture school, you will begin to sense that you are becoming part of a school culture and community that is unique to schools of architecture, regardless of the university. The sense of culture and community exists for several reasons. Most architecture schools are small, making it easy to get to know well a large percentage of the students and faculty members within a year or two. Architecture students spend enormous amounts of time working together, day and night, within the school building, especially in design studios. At many schools, students spend weeks or months during summer or other semesters traveling and studying together abroad. Groups of students frequently work on projects in local communities or volunteer to aid distressed communities in need of pro bono design assistance. All this personal interaction promotes social bonding, typically lacking among students in other academic disciplines. And bonding is reinforced by the rigors of sharing a common mission: the challenge of mastering architecture.

Many architects look back on architecture school as one of their most formative and rewarding life experiences, a time when they not only felt intensely stimulated intellectually and creatively but also closest to their friends and academic colleagues. Some liken it to spending several years in boot camp. Most remember the positive experiences, forgetting or suppressing memories of the more arduous or disappointing moments all students faced.

Architecture students not only bond with other students but they also may form affiliations with faculty members they respect and admire, professors with whom they study and work closely. Such bonds are usually based on some combination of personal resonance and shared academic interests. Students usually are drawn to mentors with whom they feel comfortable intellectually and personally, who show concern for their work, or who are close in age. Teachers vary tremendously in comportment and teaching style, and this affects how students relate to them. Some are aloof and distant and others seem easygoing and approachable. Students may never get to know some teachers well and others could be best buddies. Of course, what matters most is how effectively teachers teach—how well they help students realize their potential in the field of architecture.

Despite all the bonding and shared experiences in architecture school, students inevitably develop close friendships and form social subgroups. Motivated by mutual personal or academic interests or by similar social, cultural, and ethnic backgrounds, students naturally seek out and affiliate with fellow students with whom they feel comfortable. Consequently, subgroups of students tend to stick together because they are especially artistic, intellectual, or Internet fixated; Hispanic, Asian American, or African American; foreign or female; older or married; fraternity members or sports enthusiasts.

Another kind of social distillation may exist in many schools. Design is academically the core of architectural education, the curricular endeavor in which native talent is most evident. Therefore students who excel in design, who are perceived as especially inventive and artistically skillful, acquire a certain status in the eyes of students and faculty members. They are the "gifted" ones who set high standards of performance in the design studio. This status may manifest itself subtly but it also can be acknowledged quite overtly. Top design students may get extra attention and even deference from design critics. More respected and willingly indulged by critics, they may get away with breaking project rules—which other students feel obliged to follow—with greater impunity. Other students more frequently ask them for crits. And they usually receive more praise in reviews. Such status is problematic if it results in other students' being short-changed, especially students who excel in areas other than design. But it is simply a fact of life in architecture school: design talent tends to be the most valued asset.

Being Judged—a Rite of Passage

No other tradition in architecture school is as tenacious and enduring as public judgment of student design work, either pinned up on a wall or displayed on a digital screen. Reviews mark the completion of work on a design project or project phase when students present their drawings and models for evaluation. Reviews are typically organized and conducted by the studio critic and may include invited faculty members and outside guests who may be architects or hypothetical clients. Reviews are a significant component of the architect's educational experience and often an open event that fellow studio students and sometimes students from other studio classes attend.

For a typical review, students display and stand next to their work, all eyes on them, and orally present their project to the reviewers. Often the graphic presentation speaks for itself but the student nevertheless is expected to advocate his or her concept verbally and subsequently to engage in dialog with reviewers following the initial presentation. This seems straightforward enough but in fact it is not an educational experience familiar to most students prior to arriving in architecture school.

Imagine yourself preparing for a review. Two concerns preoccupy your every waking moment: (1) Will your drawings and models be sufficiently comprehensible and complete to effectively communicate your concept? (2) Will your design be praised or ridiculed? These are separate but related concerns.

Satisfactorily completing work and meeting deadlines depend on the ability to manage time, organize tasks, make decisions, and produce manual and digital drawings. You quickly learn in the first year of school that displaying an incomplete presentation for reviewers to scrutinize is a bad move. Reviewers will almost always cite students whose work is unfinished, vaguely described, or unreadable, regardless of the merits of the students' creative or conceptual thinking. Critics may even refuse to discuss incomplete presentations, especially if the student attempts to fill in gaps verbally, and they often publicly chastise the beleaguered student.

Reviewers who believe in positive reinforcement might say, "This could have been a great scheme, if only we could have seen all of it," or "One more week and this could have been fully and very successfully developed," or "It's a shame that your presentation doesn't do justice to your idea," or "What we see only suggests its potential quality."

Reviewers who believe in negative reinforcement might say, "You certainly had enough time to finish this project," or "How can you ask us to review so flimsy a presentation?" or "You're never going to make it with presentations like this," or "Why do you

An architecture student presenting her project design to faculty reviewers

expect us to waste our time on incomplete work?" or "The least we expect is completion of the *minimum* required drawings."

Often reviewers lace their remarks with humor and sympathy but just as often with sarcasm and disdain. In anticipation or even fear of being on the receiving end of such critiques, students mount heroic efforts to be or appear to be complete when the deadline arrives. But students vary considerably in their ability to pace themselves, budget time, and produce drawings and models. Those able to expeditiously make design decisions and drawings will finish with relative ease whereas others struggle to finish at all.

The other preoccupation before each review concerns the aesthetic, functional, and technical qualities of the project itself. Will the proposed design be judged marginally acceptable? competent? perhaps good? maybe even outstanding? Quality entails value judgments made by reviewers who invariably have diverse perspectives and biases. You may love your design, and your design critic may love it, but some reviewers might not.

Correctly anticipating response of reviewers to a design is impossible. Response anxiety is intensified because much effort, thought, and creative energy may have been invested prior to the review. You say to yourself, "That's not just my work hanging up there, that's me!" Consequently, you interpret criticism of your design as criticism of you personally. Consciously or subconsciously, you think, "If they don't like my work, then they don't like *me!*" Telling you this is not true—that reviewers evaluate your work, not you as a person—is no guarantee that such feelings will disappear. You know that you will feel good if reviewers seem to like your work and bad if they do not—hence the anxiety.

Another factor contributes to review anxiety for many students: being in the public limelight. There they are, faculty members and students, professionals and peers, focusing on you and your presentation, waiting to see if you succeed or fail. The blood rushes, palms sweat, mouth dries, the words you intended to say never come forth. You worry about appearing foolish, showing anger or embarrassment, fumbling with your notes, perhaps even shedding tears, or defensively arguing with a reviewer who has questioned your efforts and design ideas. For a few students, mundane and insignificant preoccupations may intrude on their consciousness under the pressure of being judged publicly. "How do I look? Fly open? Should I have showered first?" After a charrette, these concerns may be justifiable.

But many students are exhilarated by the review experience. Such students are usually self-confident, no matter what the quality of their work, and they relish the challenge of the review and the opportunity to show their stuff and engage in stimulating discussion. It can be an ego trip if you believe in yourself and your work, even in the face of negative criticism. Those with gambling or risk-taking instincts welcome the unpredictability of reviews, hoping to win yet knowing there is always a chance of losing.

No description of the review ritual would be complete without describing a few of the behavioral characteristics of reviewers: what they do and say and how they interact with students and with each other. Assessing architectural design is a subjective, taste-dependent process. Each reviewer brings to the review his or her own particular agenda, a collection of interests, opinions, prejudices, and idiosyncrasies. Students commonly hear remarks made by reviewers that seem vague, unclear, contradictory, needlessly deprecating, self-laudatory, or irrelevant. Especially amusing, though sometimes confusing to the student, can be debates between reviewers. A debate may begin over the student's work but then evolve into a more generalized disagreement over opposing polemics or conflicting values. Such debates can be very enlightening to those students awake and listening because the arguments always apply to projects other than the one on the wall.

Some reviewers are relatively silent and passive, saving their remarks for propitious moments, or they comment on only the weightiest of issues. Reviewers can intimidate each other, depending on interpersonal chemistry. Some are very talkative and demonstrative, seizing every opening to take the floor. They can dominate the review owing to their verbal wit, prodigious memory and powers of recall, professional prominence, personal charisma, or persistent intervention. Others pontificate about the world of architecture and the human condition, perhaps saying little about the student's work. Or they may offer specific, nit-picking criticism of the student's design.

Still others specialize, talking about only one aspect of architectural design—for example, site planning, structure, energy conservation, or formal composition—to the exclusion of other aspects. Eventually students get to know the faculty members well enough to predict what they will focus on, although they can rarely predict their reactions.

After the review—hearing praise and criticism at the same time, hearing that this is good and that is bad—students may feel uncertain as to whether reviewers approved or disapproved, whether comments were positive or negative. Students wonder what silence on the part of a reviewer might mean, and they cringe whenever the word "but . . ." follows a vaguely complimentary statement. Some reviewers sketch directly on presentation students' drawings to make their point or illustrate an idea. If they are considerate, they draw in pencil, although sketches in ink or colored marker make a more indelible impression. Students strain to interpret reviewers' implicit reactions: their demeanor, facial expressions, body movements, and inaudible utterances. Reviewers cover their mouths and chins, scratch their heads, lean forward in their chairs, get up and walk around while studiously eyeing drawings or models. They continually whisper to one another or pass notes. What are they thinking? Is it plus or minus?

Confusion may be compounded when the student learns from his or her studio critic that, in fact, reviewers thought highly of the project, whereas the student believed the review had been a disaster. But the opposite occurs. A student senses that the review went well, remembering only positive comments, and then, after feeling elation and pride, learns that reviewers thought the work, on the whole, quite mediocre. Of course individual reviewers do not always agree about the quality of student work, and it is not unusual to receive an A or B from one reviewer while another dispenses a C or D. However, most grades cluster. Ultimately, the studio critic is responsible for the grade, reporting it to the student verbally or in writing.

Some architectural students and teachers question the value of public reviews as a pedagogical technique. They argue that they are excessively time-consuming—reviews can last four, five, or six hours, depending on the size of the class and number of reviewers (more reviewers means more time)—and too frequently degrading to students. They claim that reviews are repetitious, with the same comments heard over and over again, and can seem like self-indulgent word games enabling faculty members to put down students. A few believe that public reviews place undue emphasis on presentation graphics at the expense of design substance and conceptual quality.

Although some criticisms are well founded, the public review ritual survives because it accomplishes worthwhile goals. It simulates the reality of architectural practice, in which public presentations to clients, government officials, and civic groups occur frequently. It helps students improve their public speaking abilities. It reinforces the importance of meeting deadlines. It provides a forum for students to see each other's work and for faculty members to see the work of students other than their own. And it encourages and reinforces development of graphic and verbal skills. Most important, intellectual discourse during a lively, thoughtful review is as valuable for students as a lecture or seminar. Insightful reviewers pose vital and probing questions, challenge conventional thinking and assumptions, raise issues perhaps overlooked, and stimulate new and more creative thinking. Review discussions can surprise not only the studio students but also the studio critic.

Like it or not, the architectural review is here to stay. Final project reviews are the ceremonial culmination of each studio design project, the moment when the skills, knowledge, and ideas of the prospective architect are synthesized and expressed. Judging design is also a celebration of design and the art of architecture.

Other Traditions and Experiences

As you might guess from reading about design studio courses and reviews, design activity dominates other course work and activities in most architecture schools. At times the demands of studio, coupled with poor time management, keep students from meeting other academic obligations. Teachers of history or technology courses can count on extensive absenteeism just prior to scheduled design studio deadlines and reviews, particularly at the end of each semester. Or they know that, during charrettes, students attending their classes will either sleep or sit as if in a state of semi-consciousness, eyes open, breathing slowed, swaying back and forth almost imperceptibly in their chairs, hearing and absorbing practically nothing. Occasionally, after extensive sleep deprivation, students may get a second wind that keeps them momentarily alert but this is unusual.

Students also learn to capitalize on scheduling conflicts between courses. A favorite ploy is to explain to your studio critic that you are behind in design, usually evidenced by a lack of drawings, because you had to study for a structures exam or write a history paper. You beg for understanding and compassion for your deficiencies in structures or history because you had to meet a design studio deadline and have not slept for three days. Most students, when faced with the choice, give first priority to design, knowing that a review is pending and assuming that somehow they will catch up on assignments and exam preparation in other courses. Unfortunately, if too much is postponed, they may not catch up until subsequent semesters.

One of the more lamentable architecture school experiences is periodic burnout. Its symptoms are reduced motivation and interest, waning morale, and perhaps a desire to drop out. To understand burnout, recall the intensity and pace of work in the first one or two years of architecture school, when the learning curve is steepest and, for most students, morale and educational gratification run high. Regardless of what occurs in subsequent years, it is difficult for any program to sustain the energy and rate of discovery of the beginning years. Even the trials and tribulations described earlier contribute to the exhilaration and peer-group coherence of the initial year or two. But things change and later burnout is attributable to several of these changes.

Attrition can affect fellow students, especially when friends disappear. Some of the mystery of architecture and design vanishes, making the process seem somehow less intriguing or challenging than before. Students work with increasing independence and less intervention by teachers, and some students miss the boot camp, basic training unity of the beginning year or two. Indeed some miss it because they are unable to perform well without it. Even after a couple years of study, students may begin feeling that architecture is not for them, that it is too competitive or unrewarding. If not excelling, they may feel disappointed, unwilling to be second best, and genuinely lose interest and find new interests. All these changes can produce the same effect: poorer work, cynicism, boredom, and, in some cases, the abandonment of architecture, either temporarily or permanently.

The concentration and commitment demanded by architectural studies make success elusive in the face of competing distractions or obligations. Even talented students take leaves of absence or postpone taking courses when circumstances outside school inhibit their in-school performance. Deferring course work, particularly in design, can be a prudent strategy. No negative stigma is associated with taking extra time to finish architecture school, and it is often advisable for some students. Many successful architects spent extra semesters to complete their education.

For economic reasons many architectural students need to hold jobs while attending school. They may work for architects but some do work unrelated or marginally related to architecture. If such work consumes a reasonable amount of time relative to a student's academic load, employment outside school poses no problem. For example, students carrying a full academic load—fourteen to sixteen credit hours per semester—can comfortably work eight to ten hours per week without jeopardizing their schoolwork.

But students who work half-time—twenty hours per week—or more while trying to perform successfully as full-time architecture students are unlikely to do well. Many try but few succeed. The time and effort demanded in school, especially by design studios, inevitably conflict with job demands. And time and energy expended on a job will detract from the quality of work in school. In the long run it is better to forgo the burden of extra weekly hours holding down a job, even at the cost of incurring debt, than to compromise the quality of your professional education. Cooperative architectural education programs are the one exception. Students enrolled in these work-study programs are employed in architectural offices committed to mentoring students. However, relatively few structured cooperative programs exist in the United States.

Of course, campus life exists outside the architecture studio, of particular interest to undergraduates. The enjoyment and rewards of higher education come partly from experiencing and taking advantage of that life in addition to studying and attending classes. Architecture students do find time to participate in on-campus student activities and organizations, student government, sports, and social and cultural events. In fact, in appropriate dosages, these experiences have educational value for would-be architects.

The foregoing traditions and experiences cannot be fully appreciated without some understanding of those who teach architecture. Therefore, read on because it is the professors—and what they profess—who ignite and stoke the fires of learning.

5 What Professors— and Architects—Profess

Faculty members determine the quality and direction of any architecture school. A school's physical facilities and resources, location, size, and stated curriculum matter but much less than the school's individual professors and what they profess. Most professors share a love of teaching and the stimulation of an academic environment but architecture faculty members' interests, expertise, and personalities vary greatly. Therefore, consider the nature of teachers of architecture, how and what they teach, and why you will not forget some of them long after you finish school and become an architect.

The Professors
Scholars and Researchers

In architecture school, most traditional scholars are historians. Beyond teaching classes, they focus on research, writing books and articles for scholarly journals, and attending conferences with like-minded scholars. They may be interested in specific periods and places, stylistic movements of the past, current design theories, history of technology or individual architects whose work may or may not be well known. They can remember names and dates, and their speaking and writing are amply footnoted. Some faculty members are primarily scholars and researchers with reduced teaching loads, especially if they have procured substantial research funding to help pay their salaries.

Designer-Practitioners

These men and women, many of whom are adjunct faculty members, practice architecture and teach design studios, splitting their time between office and school. Their experience as practitioners influences their teaching. They are simultaneously pragmatic and idealistic, concerned with the act of building as well as the art of design. Teachers who practice may express real-world ideas and points of view while encouraging students to be unconventionally creative. Their design work often influences their students' work. But their work also may be viewed with some disdain by designers who are theoreticians.

Designer-Theoreticians

These teachers engage in little or no practice and rarely in conventional practice. They profess theories and philosophies of design, in class and through writings and lectures, that ignore or transcend practical considerations. They especially appeal to students looking for an intellectualized aesthetic compass. Designer-theoreticians prefer studio problems focused on issues of form and meaning and less on functional, social, technological, or constructional issues.

Student Advocates

Some faculty members identify with or even hang out with students, empathizing and communicating with them, almost as peers. They may be close in age to their students and share their points of view. Often spending a lot of time at school, they serve as sounding boards for student grievances. Their behavior may provoke mixed feelings of disapproval or guilt in other faculty members who do not share their advocacy or who enjoy much less rapport with students.

Student Adversaries

The advocate's opposite, the student adversary, is frequently critical of or at odds with students in the school. Students may perceive such faculty members as acting distrustfully, disrespectfully, and disinterestedly toward them, as being unsympathetic, excessively demanding, or abrasive. Yet despite these perceptions, seemingly adversarial teachers in fact can be effective teachers and, in their own way, may actually have their students' best interests at heart.

Young (or Old) Turks

Some faculty members habitually encourage reform or revolution, continually challenging the institutional status quo. They may disregard rules and conventions for the sake of a cause, making a point of their nonconformity—sometimes subtly, sometimes with great fanfare. Often they are perceived by students as student advocates. Young Turks are not necessarily radicals or anarchists, tendencies clearly discouraged in the halls of academe. To those who resist change or challenge, they are like tiny stones lodged in shoes: they do not prevent walking but their presence is always felt.

Good Ol' Boys and Girls

This subgroup of faculty usually has seniority and, as carriers of institutional memory, enjoys telling stories of "how it used to be." Some may be burned out as teachers, having run out of ideas or become bored with teaching the same courses year after year. Others may help set the tone of the school and influence school policy and management. They routinely gossip and talk shop. The old guard in a school may symbolize permanence and continuity to some, atrophy to others.

Logicians

Logicians cope with the uncertainty and subjectivity of architectural design but are most comfortable with rational discourse. They value intuition and creative invention but have less patience for inconclusive philosophical discussions. For them, projects and problems lend themselves to systematic analysis. Armed with data and methodology, they prefer the approach of the scientist or engineer yet tolerate that of the artist.

Techies

Architecture schools need at least a few faculty members who know how to set up, operate, program, debug, and otherwise keep constantly evolving digital technology—computers and computer software, plotters, printers, milling machines—running smoothly. Techies are of course indispensable for another reason: they teach students as well as other teachers how to creatively exploit digital technology.

Obfuscators

A few teachers employ vocabularies and manners of expression unintelligible to most students. They are hard to understand and tedious to listen to, notwithstanding the significance or depth of what they have to say. Obfuscators, not satisfied with simple, straightforward language, seek richness and complexity in the use of English and equivalent richness and complexity in the thinking that produced the English. Unfortunately this correlation may not always exist.

Zealous Leaders

Heading every school is a dean, departmental chair, or program director, along with appropriate deputies (titled associate, assistant, or something else). They are intensely involved in leading and managing the architecture faculty and shaping the curriculum. Their zeal can be infectious and provide inspiration to teachers and students. But excessive zeal can be obstructive, patronizing, or misdirected. For students, the best leader is one whose zeal is

directed toward advocating and protecting student interests. From the teachers' point of view, the ideal leader does the same for the faculty while protecting academic freedom and ensuring smooth and efficient architecture school operations.

Laid-back Leaders

This leader pursues a laissez-faire policy of management. He or she believes that most faculty members are best left free to stoke their own furnaces, to identify and pursue their own teaching and research interests, and to set their own standards. Laid-back leaders may provide guidance and be active in the life of the school yet maintain a low profile. They often delegate administrative work to assistants, secretaries, committees, and individual faculty members.

Separatists

The separatist is a faculty member who has rejected the "if you can't lick 'em, then join 'em" philosophy and instead embraced the "if you can't lick 'em, then leave 'em" philosophy regarding intrafaculty relationships. Architecture schools may have a faculty member who cannot get along with another faculty member. Or a small faction may find itself at odds with other factions. To cope with this situation, separatists may avoid those colleagues with whom they disagree. The source of conflict may be ideological or political, usually related to academic issues. Teachers may disagree about architectural ideologies, methods of instruction, course content, administrative policy, or curricular direction. At the extreme, having become dogmatic and unreasonable, they retreat from the battlefront to safeguard their domain of opinion.

Inscrutables

Some professors are introverted and relatively shy, characteristics that may be less apparent in the classroom or in the company of close companions. Inscrutable ones are sometimes hard for students and faculty to get to know because they are stoic and less gregarious, revealing their thoughts and feelings quite sparingly. They seldom lower their guard or expose themselves emotionally. Inscrutability can be a defense or a wise offense whenever silence is appropriate and appreciated.

Venerable Heroes

Many schools have a professionally well-known faculty member, either permanent or visiting, who inspires adulation and emulation. Such heroes may be famous because of their work as designers, historians, critics, or authors. They may be innovators or trendsetters, rebels or reformers. Whatever their claim to fame, they tread the halls of academe as special citizens. Students await and anticipate their every utterance, hoping that it will be of profound significance. Few contradict or challenge them except with deference and diplomacy. They can be idols in architectural education—at least until they lose their edge or fall out of fashion.

Whatever their individual characteristics, expertise, and interests may be, full-time architecture faculty members have substantial duties outside the classroom and studio. In addition to pursuing their research, writing, or creative activities, they are expected to serve on various architecture school and campus committees, regularly advise students, and attend periodic faculty meetings. Not surprisingly, some take service obligations more seriously than others. In any case, a professor must compile a strong record of achievement and excellence in all three areas—teaching, research, and service—to become tenured.

Increasingly architecture schools depend on part-time, adjunct faculty members hired to teach required and elective courses. Their contracts can be of any duration. Most adjuncts are either practicing architects or engineers willing to spend some of their time teaching without a permanent university appointment. They usually have no duties in an architecture program other than teaching their respective courses but they generally are poorly compensated for their time and receive no employee benefits. Motivated primarily by the intellectual stimulation teaching provides, many adjuncts are in fact very effective teachers. And an adjunct's characteristics and expertise can be the same as the full-time professors.

Some -Isms and -Ologies

Listen long enough to any faculty member at any school of architecture and you will eventually comprehend what he or she is professing. I refer not to the specific subject matter they teach but rather to the more general philosophy, cause, interest area, or movement to which they subscribe, no matter what courses they are responsible for.

Any teacher offering instruction in a given subject, such as architectural history or design, inevitably brings to the subject his or her own beliefs and values about culture, social behavior, politics, economics, and of course aesthetics. For some, this set of beliefs and values may be organized into a formalized, personal ideology that continually influences opinions and actions including what is conveyed to students in the classroom. Even a course that appears to be value free and nonideological, such as structural analysis or drawing, may be accompanied by subtle expressions of the teacher's personal philosophy. Thus teachers can be very influential, transmitting more than objective information and techniques.

Architects and architectural educators cultivate and embrace ideologies because it's impossible to create good architecture without taking a theoretical or philosophical position about design. This is the attribute of architecture that differentiates it so notably from engineering or other fields in which most decisions are based on commonly accepted scientific principles and standards, quantitative data, methodological protocols, and measurable performance.

Consider engineering. After sufficiently defining the problem to be solved (ventilate a space or make a faster microprocessor, for example), an engineer sets about designing a system to solve the stated problem most efficiently. Design efficiency is measured by applying specific evaluation criteria such as least cost, highest yield, least weight, greatest speed or strength, fewest number of parts, least energy consumption, or easiest fabrication. Some value judgment enters into the selection and weighting of criteria because engineering design requires trade-offs between conflicting advantages and disadvantages. But most engineering decisions are made objectively and dispassionately, with designs tested through performance evaluation. And the engineer does not depend on some personal design philosophy to solve the engineering problem successfully.

The architect, similar to the engineer, may seek to "optimize" building performance, as if buildings could be solutions to well-defined problems. But making architecture, being more than engineered construction, is an ill-defined problem. For any given site, client, budget, and functional program, countless designs can be devised to acceptably meet all requirements. Indeed, no matter how precisely one defines the design problem, there is always an array of feasible design possibilities and variations worth considering. How, then, does the architectural designer decide which option to choose? Inventing and refining options is the art, rather than the science, of architecture, the part of design that demands more than engineering methods.

The built environment provides shelter and space for human activity but architecture also affects our feelings and emotions, engaging our senses and intellect. The ancient Roman architect Vitruvius, considered Western civilization's first architectural theoretician, wrote that good architecture must provide commodity, firmness, *and* delight. Thus architecture has long been interpreted and taught as a form of applied art expressing generative aesthetic philosophies, theories, and meanings. The challenge of learning and practicing design stems from the ever-expanding range of possible philosophies and ideologies, none of which can be conclusively proved right or wrong.

What, then, are some of the -isms and -ologies professed by architecture school faculty members and architects that affect architectural education and practice? Most pedagogical philosophies and teaching approaches relate to one or more of the following:

Formalism
Functionalism
Historicism
Technology
Deconstructivism
Symbology
Sociology and psychology
Methodology
Ecology
Sustainability
Regionalism and vernacularism
Urbanism

None of these exist in isolation; each can combine with one or more of the others. But itemizing them facilitates understanding what and how professors teach architecture. At the same time, they help explain what practicing architects believe long after being taught.

Formalism

In biology, *morphology* is the study of the form and shape of organisms. An organism is, by definition, a whole entity or biological system that is contained and bounded. In architecture, by analogy, we can talk of morphology with respect to building form. Unlike natural organisms, architecture is human made and takes its form, in part, through an act of will. Although many forces act on the designer and the design, they nevertheless are insufficient to generate an inevitable, natural form that is the "right" form. The willful design act is thus indispensable, which obliges the designer to bring a philosophy or theory to the act of architectural form making.

Formalists explore and exploit geometries and visual patterns to create spaces, structures, surfaces, and volumes of buildings. These geometries and patterns can unify often complex buildings into organic wholes by making all parts of a building appear to belong together compositionally. Sources of such geometries or patterns may be quite arbitrary. They may be based on the forms of natural organisms, structural modules with repeated dimensions, a system of proportion, preexisting site geometries and patterns, or idealized mathematical relationships not readily perceived. Conversely, some formalists intentionally pursue disunity and fragmentation as a compositional strategy by juxtaposing dissimilar elements. Rather than pursuing unity through analogy, they seek to celebrate dynamic visual contrast.

Examples of formalism abound. The plans and facades of villas designed by the sixteenth-century architect Andrea Palladio, which have greatly influenced domestic Western architecture, exemplify the use of mathematical proportioning to achieve harmony and visual interrelationships among building volumes, rooms, facades, and details. Ratios established among widths, lengths, and heights of elements—interior spaces, courtyards, and facade components (columns, pilasters, entablatures, cornices, and pediments) permeate the entire design. Often architects of the Renaissance and Roman builders before them developed elaborate systems of proportioning derived from musical harmony ratios in

the belief that such ratios were natural and that what was natural
for the ear must be natural for the eye.

The use of planning grids represents another common strategy
of formal organization. Employed universally in modern office
buildings, this method of planning in fact can be found throughout
history: in the layout of towns and cities, Roman camps, early
Christian churches, and mosques built throughout the Islamic
world. Some grids are not rectangular. Grid networks can be based
on triangles, hexagons, and even circles. The East Building of the
National Gallery of Art in Washington, DC, designed by I. M. Pei, is
composed throughout using a triangular planning grid with angles
derived from the angles of the museum's site.

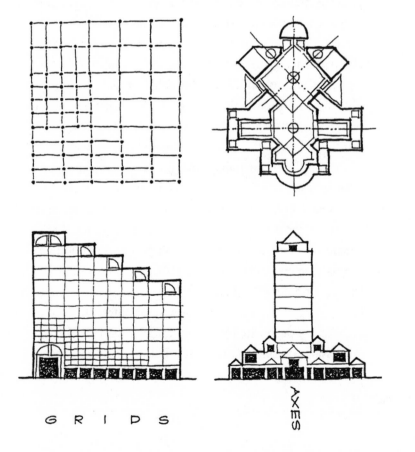

GRIDS   AXES

Akin to grid-based design, axis-based design uses one or more axes about which a composition is centered or arranged, frequently with observable symmetry and balance of elements straddling the axes. The visual terminus of an organizing axis or other points along the axis may be marked by an appropriate physical element such as an arch, a building entrance, a portico, a tower, or a sculpture. But there also can be axial asymmetry. Thomas Jefferson's design for the campus and rotunda at the University of Virginia illustrates well the use of symmetrical axiality. Le Corbusier's design for the government center at Chandigarh, India, illustrating asymmetrical axiality, uses mixtures of grids, proportioning systems, and rhythmic patterns to generate the plans and facades of the government center's buildings.

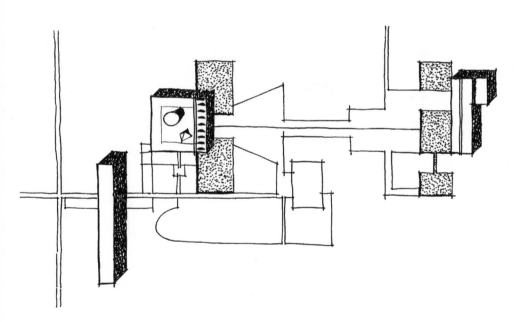

Site plan of the Chandigarh, India, capital complex, designed by Le Corbusier; from left to right, the Secretariat, the Assembly Building, and the High Court

The Chandigarh buildings reveal still another formal tenet important to many designers: the virtue of the recognizable geometrical solid in the architect's kit of parts. Cubes, pyramids, cylinders, cones, and spheres are the basic, irreducible building blocks. These "ideal," or Platonic, volumes are universally recognized, are mathematically and precisely describable, and can be combined with one another or repeated in an infinite number of ways: cutting parts of them away, perforating them, slicing them open, fusing them together, and stretching or distorting them. Yet this design strategy is no better or worse than other strategies. It simply represents one option for composing architectural form.

Functionalism

Quite a few architects and teachers of architecture view functionalism as the most fundamental form determinant. Often they are pragmatists eschewing aesthetic fantasy and speculation. Their guiding ideology is to make buildings that "work," that efficiently accommodate the uses intended, that are structurally stable, environmentally responsible, cost-effective, and, by virtue of being functional, also attractive. Functionalism can complement formalism but does not begin consciously with the willful act of producing form only for form's sake. Rather, functionalists generally believe that if the architect succeeds at making a building that works, without overtly striving for artistic effect, then the building will be intrinsically artful.

Functionalism emphasizes the client's program and budget, project site, user needs, climate, and other design constraints as determinants of architectural form. Accordingly site conditions, circulation and space requirements, building codes, and construction methods are stressed as decision-making considerations. Designs are evaluated pragmatically. Style is assumed to be derivative, the inevitable result of rational decisions about massing, spatial organization, structure, materials, fenestration, and proportioning. To many, functionalism is synonymous with modernism.

For architecture students, functionalism is one of the easiest philosophies to understand and apply in design studio. It seems to be analytical, logical, straightforward, an extension of the kinds of thinking and problem solving experienced earlier in primary and secondary schools and in life in general. It comports well with US utilitarian culture. It does not rely on highly abstract or intellectually arcane theories of design. It is transferable readily from project to project as a design strategy. It can guide the design of a toll booth as well as of a hospital or museum. It is always contemporary because it does not preclude the architect's willful application of up-to-date stylistic embellishments.

But pure functionalism can short-change or overlook architecture's nonfunctional qualities—psychic, emotional, intellectual, visual—that are difficult to quantify in a list of functional requirements. Architects may consciously impart these qualities but they may instead appear by accident or as an afterthought. Whatever the source, these qualities transcend functionalism and make buildings more than just buildings that work. Many inspired architects, although not perceived as functionalists, indeed practice functionalism, but always in combination with some other aesthetic philosophy.

Historicism

Architectural history always has been a source of design inspiration. Studying the past reveals not only what has occurred but also teaches lessons about what might occur or recur in the future. There are different ways to relate to history in making architecture. You can look for compositional patterns, transcending specific periods, styles, or places, which may be applied when and where appropriate for creating modern architecture today. For example, you might admire Palladio's exploitation of juxtaposed, solid volumes and do likewise in a contemporary structure but without replicating Palladio's stylistic motifs and details.

Or you could treat historic buildings as replicable models for designing in the present, believing that architects of the past already have designed and built suitable prototypes sufficient for today's world. All that's needed is to update the models. Hardly a century has passed since the ancient Greek and Roman eras without a period of classically inspired historicism in architecture, when architects looked back admiringly at their predecessors and emulated or reproduced their predecessors' work, motivated by nostalgia and genuine adoration for bygone styles.

Historicism, like formalism, is ultimately subjective. It reflects taste or sometimes the lack of it. It can be faddish and transitory, inappropriate and dysfunctional, inefficient and costly. But where an act of will is needed, it provides guidance and resolution. Think about the many periods and styles of Western architecture—Greek, Roman, Gothic, Romanesque, Renaissance, Victorian—with revivals based primarily on surficial attributes of ornamentation. Think of all the wonderful places and cultures offering models: Italy, France, Germany, Holland, England, and Spain.

Historicist philosophy suggests that rather than trying to invent new architectural forms, we should adopt *and* adapt the forms, building traditions, and perhaps even attitudes of the past. Contemporary design by a historicist may replicate buildings of the past or borrow pieces of buildings from the past and, through distortion or graphic transformation, adapt them for new uses and buildings.

Although architects always have vacillated about the role of history, sometimes repeating it, sometimes adding new elements to it, the US public is fundamentally historicist in its design preferences. Most US homes, furniture, building decoration, housewares, and textiles are traditional in style, that is to say, historicist. We harbor a tenacious, untutored reverence for an idealized past, much of which was not even ours. Modern design has never been popular or widely accepted, except for machines such as airplanes, autos, computers, mobile phones, and appliances.

Historicists and antihistoricists populate architecture school faculties. The former avow the validity and universality of historical precedents, encouraging students to look to the past for design solutions and stylistic motifs transferable to the present. The latter, typically in the majority, advocate the study of history

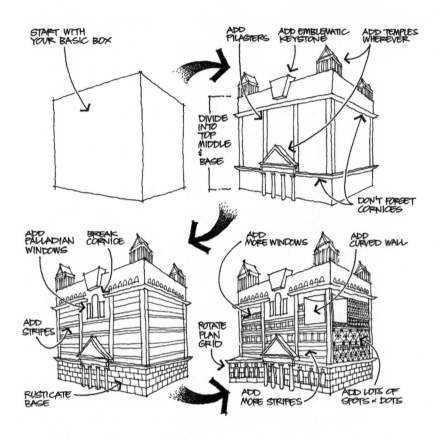

as a source for concepts and compositional principles. To them, building styles and types of the past are products of specific historical pressures incomparable to pressures of the present. They learn about history but their aim is to search for new forms of architectural expression without literally reproducing or transmuting forms that, to them, belong to a different age.

Most "modern" architects do not apply historical motifs and ornamentation to new buildings. They argue that (1) such elements are useless and often costly; (2) building technologies today differ significantly from past technologies, which greatly

influenced the form and appearance of historic architecture; (3) historicist or revivalist buildings are too often ersatz and impure, an affront to buildings and architects of the past; and (4) historicism is a cop-out, a way to avoid meeting the demands and creative design opportunities of the present and future.

Historicists rebut by asserting that buildings should be historically reverential and referential not only to remind us of other times and places but also to continue upholding time-honored, two-thousand-year-old architectural traditions. Even mediocre talents, they argue, can design halfway decent buildings

by using classical architectural language—its grammar and vocabulary—as their template and kit of parts. Historicists like cornices and pediments, fluted columns and Corinthian capitals. Abstract, formalistically driven designs that ignore the past are deemed "meaningless"—too alien, too slick, too self-referential and impersonal, too denuded of familiar ornamentation. Of course, not every architect or teacher is either a historicist or antihistoricist. Many recognize that reality is too complex for constraining labels and narrow ideologies.

Technology

Technology always has fascinated architects. The engineer in us, stimulated intellectually and manually by the workings of things mechanical and constructed, likes figuring them out. But technology also has been a source of aesthetic invention for architects, not just an end in itself or a means to an end. Technology can inspire and generate architectural art as much as any other generative source. Architects who profess technology are not engineers. Many approach design intuitively and qualitatively, avoiding computational involvement, which they leave to engineers. Yet they are moved by the craft and precision, the quality and interplay of materials, the complex and visually elegant details that reflect the application of building technology. Architectural possibilities have been expanded even more by digital technologies.

Construction technology encompasses numerous systems defined by the roles they play within a work of architecture:

Structural systems—structural elements and connections
Enclosure systems—roofs, curtain walls, partitions
Mechanical systems for heating, cooling, ventilation
Plumbing systems for distributing and recycling fluids
Solar energy systems
Electrical systems
Illumination systems, including daylighting
Acoustic control systems
Conveyance systems—stairs, elevators, escalators, ramps, walkways
Telecommunication systems
Security systems
Life-safety systems—fire and smoke protection and suppression
Furnishing systems

Associated with all these systems are specific materials and physical components that can be used and manipulated by designers to provide the intended technical service and to achieve willfully created artistic effects. Every year, the construction materials industry manufactures new products, usually pursuant to technical and market research. Many new products are slightly modified or refined versions of existing products but some may be truly innovative—and often expensive when first introduced. Architects try to keep up, hoping for appropriate opportunities to specify something new and ideally renewable that they believe will look and perform better.

Innovations of special interest to architects—professors and practitioners—are new structural systems and components; high-performance glass, curtain wall systems and windows through which water, air, and summertime solar radiation cannot pass; durable, impermeable roofing and roof membrane systems; better insulating materials and stable, moisture-proof sealants; and improved exterior cladding materials—metal panels, masonry, wood, and composite siding. These products help make buildings smart and sustainable. Without innovative materials, not only would green strategies such as vegetated roofs and energy-efficient exterior walls be unfeasible and ineffective but also the carbon footprints of buildings wouldn't shrink significantly.

Along with high-performance materials and assemblies, smart buildings benefit from state-of-the-art engineered systems, with energy-conserving and energy-generating equipment that contribute to sustainability and ensure indoor health and comfort. For example, many sites are suitable for geothermal heat exchange, whereby heat pumps more efficiently collect heat in winter and reject heat in summer by using ground water from multiple wells instead of air. Harvesting sunlight more efficiently, state-of-the-art photovoltaic solar energy collectors are more flexible physically and also more affordable. Buildings become even smarter if fitted with data-collecting devices linked to computers that monitor and control systems and equipment. Such devices can sense and respond to patterns of indoor occupancy and use, electrical demand, water and gas use, and climatic variations. Thus a building's dispersed, digital brain power can further increase operational efficiency and energy conservation. Some really smart buildings, generating more electrical energy than they consume, can sell and send their surplus energy back into the urban electric power network.

Architects understandably exploit technology, using and celebrating it expressively. The most commonly professed aesthetic strategy is visually exposing a building's technological components: structural skeleton, members and connections; mechanical and electrical system elements—ductwork, plumbing, conduits; and various machines, such as elevators. Displaying the usually hidden guts of buildings, architects may use color to heighten awareness of exhibited components and show their functional interrelationships. This strategy also can save money by avoiding the cost of concealing—using suspended ceilings, for example—exposed systems and system components.

It's possible to design an entire building to reveal how it is built. This is not a new idea. The skeletal components of Greek temples, Gothic cathedrals, Native American teepees, and sports stadiums are quite visible. Many modern commercial and some cultural buildings also employ this strategy. You can see continual layering of vertical tubes—elevators, stairs, ducts, structural columns—supporting multiple layers of floor-ceiling "sandwiches" composed of trusses, beams, joists, ductwork, conduits, and pipes, with the overall building volume usually enveloped by a pre-engineered curtain wall, a skin literally hung on the structure.

Yet technology can get out of hand when architects treat buildings only as machines. If the technological bias is not balanced by other biases, such machines can fail to respond to human needs not enumerated in technical specifications and lists of functional goals. Sometimes designers see buildings *only* as giant systems—steel or concrete skeletons, networks of ducts, pipes, and electrical conduits—serving inhabitable spaces. Great architecture transcends such a singular interpretation of how or why it was created.

Deconstructivism

In the 1980s, a controversial, arcane architectural design theory appeared and gained a foothold in the halls of academe as well as in the profession and the media. Borrowing liberally from the field of literary criticism and the esoteric writings of French and German philosophers, a number of architectural practitioners and teachers suggested that buildings could and should be "deconstructed." The "decon" thesis proceeds from the fundamental premise that the perceived substance and meaning of any work of art depends as much on the observer's experience, point of view, and circumstances as on the artist's intent and context when the work was created. It further denies that a work of art needs or possesses a predetermined, intrinsic, immutable structure. It asserts that, in art, there are no rules and strictures, no right or wrong, only limitless interpretative possibility.

Importing literary criticism theory into architecture, deconstructivist architects—the decon label was seen as yet another example of imposing society's rules—saw it as an intellectual justification for challenging and rejecting conventional principles of design composition, both traditional and modern. Their aspiration was to invent a new, autonomous architecture liberated from constraints of aesthetic style and normal design and construction practices. The modern condition, they argued, demands an exploration, acceptance, and celebration of the realities of society's chaos and imperfection. Let buildings express ideas of disorder and confusion, collision and conflict, ambiguity and uncertainty. Accordingly, decon architecture visually embodies all of these attributes. And decon architects freely pursue their highly personal design interests, impulses, and whims, much like an avant-garde painter or sculptor might, unfettered by tradition.

Of course, decon quickly became yet another stylistic design label. Many decon buildings look as if suddenly frozen in the process of exploding or imploding, collapsing or shattering apart, melting down or dissolving. Some critics refer to them as *train wreck architecture.* Walls, ceilings, columns, and beams may not be orthogonal to each other. Surfaces may be tilted, curved, or warped. Diversely shaped volumes may be arbitrarily juxtaposed. Many elements may seem purposeless, functionally or structurally gratuitous. Disparate elements and materials may collide with each other, fusing together or blasting each other apart like three-dimensional collages. And they are prone to leaks. Yet because of their dynamic visual complexity, they are provocative and newsworthy simply because they are radically different, unorthodox, disdainful of architectural norms. Ironically, most decon buildings can be designed and constructed only by using sophisticated CAD software. For these reasons, decon ideology can be very appealing to architecture students naturally seduced by decon's computer-generated forms.

Symbology

One of the most controversial but persistent philosophies of design teaches that architecture is a medium, similar to poetry or painting, for the transmission of messages. Architecture can communicate ideas or information that the designer-author wishes to express and convey through building. Some believe this is the highest plateau of design achievement and meaning in architecture. It is not sufficient only to provide shelter, facilitate work, produce a return on investment, or look good. Architecture must transmit something meaningful to the senses and minds of those who interact with it, who "read" it. For the French, this is *architecture parlante* (architecture speaking).

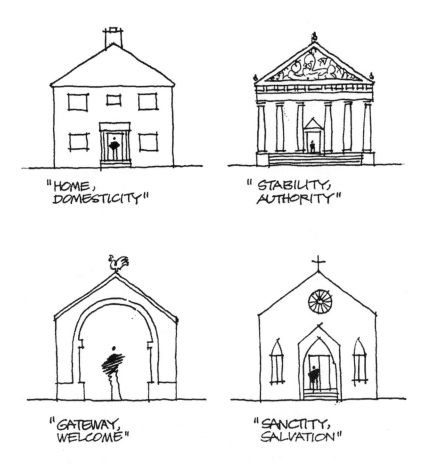

"HOME, DOMESTICITY"

"STABILITY, AUTHORITY"

"GATEWAY, WELCOME"

"SANCTITY, SALVATION"

There is no limit to what architecture can say and symbolize. Buildings can be designed to be mystical, to represent spiritual or theological concepts of which Gothic cathedrals are a splendid example. Architecture can be rhetorical, preaching specific beliefs or causes through particular use of styles, ornamentation, and forms. For example, Roman classicism and neoclassicism were embraced by fascists and communists in Europe in the 1930s as the style of architecture best suited to express to people the fundamental dignity, nobility, and correctness of their respective governments and political philosophies. The same styles in the capitalistic United States were considered especially appropriate for banks, state capitols, and federal buildings in Washington, DC.

Metaphoric architecture abounds. Buildings can represent other buildings in other places. In the early years of the US republic, the Parthenon, symbol of Greek democracy, was a source of architectural inspiration. Buildings can symbolize nature, people and their activities, struggles and victories. The Washington Monument and Eiffel Tower are symbolic structures. The former, modeled after an Egyptian obelisk (obelisks have been fashionable for centuries), memorializes a man but symbolizes a nation. The latter, demonstrating the achievements of engineering, has become the universally recognized symbol of Paris. Eero Saarinen's air terminal buildings at Kennedy and Dulles airports symbolize flight by appearing to be in flight. Cantilevered over Santiago Calatrava's seashell-like Tenerife Auditorium in Spain is an immense, breaking wave.

Buildings can generate responses in observers through symbolic association. They can make us feel secure by being like nests or wombs—intimate, cozy, human scaled, soft to the touch. They can make us feel small and humble by being like giants: huge, heavy, hard, overpowering. Buildings can be endowed with wit and humor, as evident in many architectural follies, or they can be apocalyptic, similar to many deconstructivist edifices. The most common form of message delivery through symbolism is the use of historical allusions and references in buildings. Such architecture may say, "I am unquestionably a new building, but because much modern architecture is so sterile, I offer you transformed architectural motifs and elements from the past to which you can better relate: an Ionic column here, egg and dart molding there, multipaned double-hung windows." Similar to historicism, this approach reveres traditions from the past but uses them symbolically rather than literally, avoiding replication.

In its own way, much of the architecture produced by the anti-traditional modern movement was symbolic, even though many thought it devoid of meaning or symbolism. After World War I, architects in Europe, and later in the United States, believed that a new architecture was needed to express the spirit and values of what they perceived to be a new age. This new age was heralded by new social and political orders (primarily socialism and democracy), new technologies and machines, and new economics.

For these architects, this meant new, unprecedented building functions and building types, and building on a much greater, mass-production scale. Symbolizing the aspirations of the new age through architectural expression seemed logical and inevitable.

To achieve this, modernist architects abandoned traditional motifs to look for a new symbolic language. The new age implied efficiency, standardization, and repetition. It was to be a machine age but also an age of expanded individual freedom. Buildings became less ornate, plainer in detail, simpler in form, more systematized in their appearance. Still others, exploiting new materials and construction methods, became exuberant and complex in form, symbolizing the freedom of expression enabled by the new age. Historical styles no longer seemed relevant. The new symbology was predicated on principles of functionalism and technology: buildings should look like what they are and what they do, expressing their function and mode of construction.

Modernism today is neither a rebellious movement nor a specific style. It merely categorizes architecture that does not literally replicate historic buildings or motifs. Most architects and architecture professors are modernists who believe that buildings should express ideas and use symbolism in ways that can be appreciated by anybody anywhere.

Sociology and Psychology

Most US universities offer introductory courses in sociology and psychology, and many architecture schools advise students to take them. After all, because architects design environments for people, they should have some understanding of human motivations and behavior. Moreover, exploration and knowledge of human behavior have increased substantially. Taking note of this, some architectural educators have tried to teach design based in part on sociology and psychology. Except for a few years in the 1960s and 1970s, however, study of human behavior has never been a mainstream research or pedagogical interest for design faculty members or architecture students.

Nevertheless, because an essential purpose of architecture is to accommodate human activity and respond to human needs, architects routinely consider how occupants and users of designed environments will feel and act, even if their research is limited to anecdotes and their own observations. Design for special population groups—the elderly, the very young, the hearing or sight impaired, the learning disabled, the hospitalized, the homeless, the imprisoned—requires particular knowledge of user characteristics. Architects today can design facilities more effectively for these populations thanks to extensive information gained through experience and research about individual and group behaviors.

Decades ago, Congress passed the Americans with Disabilities Act (ADA) because citizens finally realized how many architectural barriers exist for people with physical impairments, those whose mobility, vision, or hearing is limited. This legislation was attributable to sociological studies and to advocacy by the disabled, who demonstrated that many public buildings were partly and sometimes completely inaccessible to people in wheelchairs. Today ADA goals, requirements, and design techniques are as familiar to architects as zoning ordinances, building codes, or any other routinely applied standards. An even more far-reaching concept, universal design, aspires to make everything accessible to everyone.

Senior citizens obviously appreciate accessibility. But social scientists will tell you that seniors also prefer to furnish their own apartments and surround themselves with their personal mementos, furniture, and belongings. Elderly residents like to sit and look outside, to watch activity in neighboring spaces or abutting streets. Further the elderly are especially sensitive to temperature, tolerating thermal variations, drafts, and humidity much less than younger residents. For the architect designing a dwelling for elderly users, such factors suggest an apartment with ample wall space for furniture and wall hangings, large windows for bringing in daylight and looking outside, and high-performance insulating glass to reduce heat loss, drafts, and thermal discomfort. Still, no amount of computer time, research, or user interviews can alter the fact that, as always, the architect must mediate finally among these potentially conflicting requirements, ultimately making subjective value judgments about geometric form, proportions, materials, and details.

Sociological and psychological research also deals with perception and stimulus-response relationships that can inform architectural design decisions. For example, many architects rely on personal taste or follow fashion trends to select colors. But some, knowing that certain colors provoke specific kinds of reactions, select accordingly. The effects of noise, levels of illumination, and thermal comfort are increasingly well known and influence the design of office buildings, dwellings, museums, schools, churches, and factories. The need for privacy affects the design of workplaces, hospitals, and housing. Again, the architect still must mediate among conflicting objectives, willfully devising an aesthetic strategy.

Methodology

A few teachers profess methodology as an end in itself. Focusing on how one produces rather than on what one produces, methodological architects and teachers are interested in process and its management per se. Professed methodology can relate to design, CAD, administration, project management, finance, and business development.

Using diagrams, work schedules, tables, charts, and data surveys, methodologists are into decision theory, digital modeling and simulation, cost accounting, value engineering, marketing, and personnel management. By mastering the process by which work is produced, they argue, the quality of the work product will be automatically enhanced and efficiency and cost savings will be achieved. Improved methods equal improved products.

Allied with other compatible philosophies and willpower, methodology helps cope with architecture's uncertainties and complexities. But similar to any of the -isms and -ologies already cited, excessive preoccupation with the how at the expense of the why can lead to compromised results. No matter how rational our approach to architecture, we still need wisdom and inspiration derived from human values and personal convictions, which vary with time, place, culture, and circumstances.

Ecology

As inhabitants of the natural environment, we tend to think of ourselves at odds with nature, expressed in often-heard phrases: *man against nature, against the sea, against the elements,* or *don't fool with Mother Nature.* It's the forces of nature from which buildings separate and shelter us. Therefore architects are concerned with how their designs relate to nature, sometimes using nature itself as the generator of building form.

Buildings exist within multiple ecosystems. The atmosphere above the earth's surface contains gases, water vapor, and particles. Climate—air, wind, atmospheric pressure, precipitation, temperature, humidity—is the natural result of the interaction of the sun with the earth's ecosystems. The hydrosphere is composed of oceans, seas, lakes, rivers, and aquifers on and below the earth's surface. The lithosphere is the earth's crust of soils, minerals, and rock formations at and below the surface. Pervading all of these is the biosphere, animal and plant life native to each region of the earth.

Nature's elements, however, do not tell how to design a work of architecture until humans intervene. That intervention manifests itself somewhere between two extremes. At one extreme is architecture thoroughly integrated with nature, married to a region's landscape and a specific building site. This kind of building echoes the form and character of the site. Exemplifying this on every continent except Antarctica are indigenous settlements and dwellings built on prairies, steppes, deserts, hills, cliff sides, forestlands, and underground. These buildings are almost indistinguishable from the earth and environment in which they sit.

Architects inclined toward nature profess not only respect for ecology but also physical design that draws form-making cues from the specific ecology at hand. Such designs, shaped by landscape and climate, use indigenous materials and are minimally destructive of the land and life-forms found there. High priority is given to saving trees, minimizing excavation or filling of land, avoiding interference with the natural flow of water, and employing the sun and wind to temper the constructed environment.

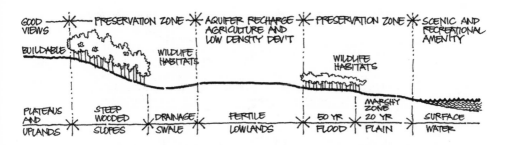

At the other extreme are buildings that stand in sharp contrast to the natural setting, in no way emulating or blending with the natural environment. Architecture and site coexist in an equilibrium of juxtaposition and complementarity, each asserting itself against the other without yielding unreasonably. There is no attempt to camouflage or be unobtrusive. Usually such buildings stand as dominant objects, marking the ground where civilization has tamed nature. The Taj Mahal in Agra, India; the Villa Rotunda in Vicenza, Italy; and Dulles Airport in northern Virginia are such buildings.

Sustainability

Whether a building merges with or dominates its site, another ecological consideration impels architects and educators: sustainability. Sustainable design and construction means consuming fewer natural resources; using renewable and recycled materials; capturing and recycling water, including storm water and wastewater; and attaining optimal energy efficiency to reduce a building's carbon emissions and its carbon footprint. The ultimate goal of sustainable building is to minimize adverse effects on the earth's climate and natural environment. Clearly sustainability, functionalism, and technology are interrelated.

Architecture demands huge investments of materials, energy, and money for construction and operation. Extracting from the earth, processing, manufacturing, transporting, installing, finishing, and maintaining every item in a construction project, from roads to roofing, has an environmental cost. Consequently, by assessing and reducing these costs for a given design, architects can contribute to enhancing the ecological health of planet earth. For many architects and professors of architecture, sustainable design has become an ethical and practical imperative.

Many architecture schools offer sustainability course work and design studios in which sustainability is a primary theme. Some

schools engage in funded sustainability research activity. It is virtually certain that some of the faculty members at the architecture school you choose or that you attend now are serious advocates of green architecture. Ideally, designing buildings to be sustainable will be as natural and routine as designing buildings to be accessible, structurally sound, and waterproof.

Regionalism and Vernacularism

Architecture professors as well as practitioners have long been interested in the many ways diverse cultures and peoples inhabiting different regions of the world have built settlements and structures for themselves without the benefit of professional designers. Architects admiringly study how building form, ancient and modern, has been influenced and sometimes ingeniously shaped by tradition, anthropological factors, and natural conditions—regional geography, climate, geology, vegetation, and agriculture. Thus a region's vernacular architecture can be primitive, quaint, aesthetically rich, or structurally complex.

Whatever a region's vernacular looks like, exploring and understanding it when designing new architecture in the region teaches indispensable lessons: about how native people behave and function, about their beliefs and desires, about how they efficiently use scarce resources and interact sustainably with their natural and human-made surroundings, and about the unique architectural language and vocabulary characterizing a region's vernacular traditions. This is why so many architects and architecture students travel: to discover, document, and draw inspiration from not only architectural monuments but also indigenous built form, whether in the Americas, Europe, Africa, the Middle East, or Asia.

Urbanism

In cities and their suburbs and in newly urbanized or redeveloped areas, a multitude of other forces come into play that render a philosophy of environmentalism or sustainability, taken alone, inadequate to the task of design and urban growth. Accordingly, urbanism encompasses a broad range of goals and principles applicable to design or redesign of urban fabric and the architecture and public spaces comprising urban fabric. Subscribed to by many architects, some of whom specialize in city planning and urban design, urbanism is predicated on the fundamental belief that good cities, good neighborhoods, and good urban spaces are the ultimate manifestation of good architecture.

Proponents of urbanism teach that great towns and cities are vibrant centers of life, the locus of commerce and trade, governance, habitation, cultural activity, education, recreation, entertainment, and production. A well-designed urban environment facilitates and encourages the interaction of people from all walks of life; accommodates diverse modes of transportation; has a variety of building types, some civic and monumental, some quietly in the background; has identifiable neighborhoods with a mix of housing; has within it a hierarchical network of streets ranging from boulevards to alleys, punctuated by public squares and parks; and is walkable. Dwelling types exhibiting a wide range of size, style, location, and cost are a hallmark of urbanism, as is development at densities higher than most suburbs and exurbs. Good urbanism intermixes residential, commercial, cultural, and recreational uses rather than segregating these uses into separate zones or city districts.

Architects who are urbanists often point to European cities and towns as models, although they also extol the virtues of

eighteenth and nineteenth century US towns. Using examples such as Paris, Rome, Amsterdam, Savannah, or Charleston, they admire the traditional street patterns, public spaces, and pedestrian friendliness of these places: spacious avenues; piazzas, civic squares, and public gardens; intimate, narrow streets and passageways; venerable old buildings (churches, town halls, palaces, museums, stately as well as modest dwellings), some serving as visual landmarks in the urban fabric; well-proportioned courtyards within and between buildings; intense sidewalk activity, including shopping, eating, and drinking; rhythmic arcades or colonnades lining streets and plazas; and frequently a common palette of building materials, giving unity and variety to what otherwise might be a visually chaotic collection of individual structures. They like places where pedestrians and bicyclists coexist successfully with automobiles.

Urbanists condemn much of suburbia and metropolitan sprawl, citing among their ills visual formlessness, automobile dependency, absence of public transit, single-use zoning, social isolation and alienation, and lack of a sense of place or community. The characteristics of sprawl include congested, unattractive commercial strip highways, excessively wide subdivision streets, and unfathomable, circuitous road networks. Also condemned are previous planning and urban design principles that have been widely discredited, although not discarded. Much US zoning law still embodies the modernist, utopian ideas about cities that held sway between the 1920s and 1970s. During that period, especially after World War II, prevailing urban theories led to strict separation of land uses into zones and enclaves interconnected by high-speed freeways, with low-density land uses spread across vast metropolitan regions.

Urbanism in recent decades, similar to the historic preservation movement, has sensitized many architects, directly influencing how they design urban buildings. Prior to the 1970s, most architects were taught to design a building as an autonomous object to be shaped or sculpted at will by the architect, largely ignoring the urban context of the site. Building form was constrained only by its budget and functional program, zoning regulations, available technology, and the client's demands. Relating visually to the size, scale, geometry, materials, and details of surrounding buildings was at best a secondary consideration. But architects began to appreciate the importance of context,

recognizing that a building could harmonize with its context, either by analogy or by contrast. Of course, contextualism can be overdone when an architect literally replicates neighboring buildings, which may not be worthy of replication, just to fit in.

Urbanism is fueled in part by romanticism and nostalgia for an idealized past, and some who profess urbanism also profess historicism. But most architects and urban designers agree that many parts of modern cities and suburbs have been badly crafted and are often dysfunctional, with something of value lost during the twentieth century. Without rejecting technology, the private car, or economic reality, urbanists espouse principles that promise to enhance the vitality, livability, and sustainability of US cities and neighborhoods. Driven in part by humanitarian motives, many also focus attention on design that improves urban settlements in

other countries, especially places suffering from the effects of natural disasters, economic deprivation, or war. Around the globe, designers have helped plan and build livable refugee camps using temporary, low-tech shelters, such as tents or lean-tos, or somewhat more permanent but inexpensive prefabricated dwellings.

Urbanism in practice—urban design methodology and urban development—is now being affected in positive new ways by advanced information technologies that collect, process, and respond to voluminous data about urban patterns, systems, and buildings. Geographic information systems (GIS) enable detailed mapping of a metropolitan region, graphically showing layer by layer a city's many attributes, current conditions, and dynamic growth trends—physiographic, geologic, hydrologic, demographic, sociological, economic, climatic, architectural, historical, and cultural—invaluable for planners and architects. The "smart cities" concept is predicated not only on having access to much more information but also on creation of responsive, more proactively managed urban environments and systems. Widely deployed, today's digital sensors can observe, monitor, and in real time control: public transportation networks to improve mobility and relieve congestion; electric power distribution and consumption to conserve energy; and water and sewer systems to prevent flooding and pollution. Being green at the urban scale is as important as designing green buildings.

You, the reader, must now ponder these abbreviated observations about what professors—and architects—profess. If still moved by the prospect of becoming an architect, the next chapter will help you select professors through the choice of a school.

6 Architecture Schools: Choosing and Being Chosen

General descriptions of architecture school curricula and professors are revealing. But how does one select, get admitted, and prepare for architecture school?

Preparing for Architecture School

No matter what kind of architecture program seems appealing, most schools demand similar kinds of academic experience, knowledge, and abilities: aptitude in drawing and graphics; creative talent evidenced by work in art or design; aptitude in basic mathematics (algebra, trigonometry, geometry, introductory calculus) and science, particularly physics and ecology; computer skills; verbal aptitude as evidenced through reading, writing, and oral expression; and some cultural interests and awareness.

Whether through course work or extracurricular initiative, any experience creating two- or three-dimensional art is beneficial to the prospective architect. Contrary to popular assumptions, mechanical drawing courses in high school or vocational school are not the most valuable kind of graphic experience prior to studying architecture. Indeed, these courses can be hindrances if they lead to "mechanical" thinking that emphasizes drafting techniques rather than visualization, freehand sketching, and creative composition.

Freehand sketching experience and ability are more valuable than drafting skills at the outset of architecture school. Courses in painting, drawing, or sculpture or exercises that focus on perception and depiction of form and space are recommended over drafting or mechanical drawing. Experience in the visual arts, whether abstract or representational, creative or applied, develops visual thinking essential to being an architect.

Visual thinking and sensitivity also may be developed by looking at and reading about architecture. Those who have taken the time to travel and visit buildings and cities, and to think about them, will be a step ahead. You do not necessarily have to travel far because you interact with architecture every day, no matter where you are. Thousands of books about architecture have been published, and design is regularly a topic of articles in journals, newspapers, periodicals, blogs, and architecture-oriented websites.

Because architecture is so integral to the history of civilization and so directly concerned with human activities, studies in the humanities are valuable preparation for architectural education. History courses are particularly relevant, as are courses in literature, English composition, and foreign languages. All these courses nurture and hone skills of observation, analysis, and expression that are of great value to architects. Even studying music is appropriate; for Renaissance architects, music was a "mathematical art" with rules of harmony and consonance applicable to architectural composition.

In addition to the humanities, introductory courses and readings in the social sciences—economics, sociology, psychology, and anthropology—are pertinent to the education of an architect. Excursions through the fields of humanities and social sciences can continue during architecture school but time will be limited so it is wise to pursue them before embarking on three or four years of intense architectural concentration.

Finally, before starting architecture school, visit an architect's office and talk with architects in practice. You will get a sense of the physical environment in which architects work, what they do from hour to hour, and the kinds of projects they produce. Many will freely offer advice about the profession, schools, other firms, and even other careers.

Choosing Schools

This is a big decision. You must consider many factors in choosing which architecture schools to apply to and then, if admitted, which one to attend. As a first step, go to the NAAB website (www. NAAB.org/architecture_programs) to peruse the list of accredited architecture schools in the United States, after which you can begin to explore websites of schools that interest you. And all the while, keep in mind pertinent criteria.

Location

Where is it? City, suburb, town, or country? A school's location is vital because it partly determines the school's ambience and relationship to the larger world. Schools in cities have access to cultural activities and become urban cultural resources themselves. City schools have urban design laboratories at their doorsteps. They can directly engage the city's urban design issues, even influencing policy and helping solve real city problems. Urban schools can readily draw on the resources of the city, inviting people from the city into the school to teach, lecture, or evaluate work. The University of California at Berkeley, the University of Utah in Salt Lake City, Rice University in Houston, Washington University in St. Louis, Harvard and MIT in Cambridge, Yale in New Haven, the University of Pennsylvania in Philadelphia, and Columbia University in New York City are city-based schools with strong urban ties.

Other schools reside in more idyllic settings on campuses located away from cities, often in college towns—for example the University of Virginia in Charlottesville, Cornell in Ithaca, or the

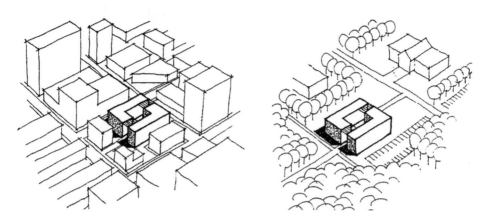

An architecture school in an urban setting—or a suburban setting

University of Michigan in Ann Arbor. Students at such schools face fewer off-campus distractions, although being located away from major cities is not necessarily urbanistically disadvantageous. Students in suburban or exurban schools can engage urban design problems with vigor but they have farther to go to tap into urban resources. The greatest difference between schools located in or out of cities concerns the quality of extracurricular life. Boston, New York, San Francisco, and Chicago have more movie theaters, performing arts venues, museums, restaurants, clubs, shops, bookstores, libraries, and other universities than college towns.

Program Type

Which program is most suitable? Do you plan to study architecture at the undergraduate or graduate level? If you are entering college as a freshman knowing that architecture will be your major, you have to make a choice. Do you want to pursue a five-year, professional BArch degree, the most direct and economical route to a professional degree but also the most intense with the fewest general education and elective options? Would it be more prudent to pursue a four-year BS or BA degree, majoring in architecture, and then go for two or three more years of graduate school to earn the MArch degree? This option takes longer and is more expensive but it offers greater flexibility for taking more electives, exploring other fields, changing majors without losing time, maturing, and perhaps taking time off to work between undergraduate and graduate studies.

Answering these questions may depend on your educational background, age, economic resources, work experience, and other factors not related directly to program type. However, keep in mind a practical consideration: most graduate architects now receive master's degrees as their *first* professional degree. This is an advantage in initially finding a job and getting higher pay, especially in government employment, over peers holding BArch degrees.

If you begin your architectural studies as a graduate student, consider the organization and duration of the MArch curriculum. How many calendar years will it require (make sure to count semesters)? Programs offering a three-year master's degree may require at least two summers of studio work because fully accredited programs often take seven to eight semesters to complete. Be wary of schools promising graduate students with no previous architecture school experience a master's degree in fewer than three years. If a thesis is required, most graduate programs take closer to four years to complete.

Reputation

A school's reputation is not unimportant. Schools have reputations, deserved and undeserved, and such reputations influence who attends and, to some extent, what becomes of them as graduates. Of course there are different kinds of reputations but most are academic in nature. People think of universities such as Harvard, Yale, Princeton, Cal Tech, Columbia, Cornell, and MIT as academically first rate, with top students and faculty, high admission and grading standards, fat endowments, and distinguished alumni. But most universities have schools, departments, or programs with individual reputations that exceed the reputation of the university as a whole or, conversely, do not live up to the university's reputation. This is often the case in public universities where specific disciplines have been well supported. Nonacademic reputations are related to quality-of-life characteristics—small, big, personal, impersonal, socially oriented (parties, fraternities, sororities), or pastoral—that are usually independent of strictly academic reputations. For example, a university may have a reputation as a party school yet also have many outstanding academic departments.

The potential risk in choosing a school based on a university's reputation is that the architecture school's reputation may not be deserved. Architecture schools experience turnover in faculty, frequently tinker with their courses and curricula, and periodically modify their goals and approach to design teaching. The departure of one or two key professors can make a big difference for a school if its reputation depends primarily on those teachers' reputations and abilities to attract students. Or a dean and faculty may adopt a new educational direction inappropriate for some students. For these reasons, there is a long history of architectural programs at very good universities fluctuating in quality, even from year to year. Therefore prospective students must be certain that the university *and* the architecture school within it have reputations that reflect current conditions to the extent that reputation is a factor in selection.

Many architecture schools at state universities have top-quality programs taught by first-rate faculty members, with excellent resources and physical facilities. Often overlooked or underrated by superficial attempts to compare schools (such as the rankings compiled annually by *U.S. News and World Report*—see commentary in the afterword), these programs may be not only financial bargains but they also produce graduates who excel and lead the profession. Long gone are the days when you had to have an Ivy League diploma to succeed as an architect.

Ultimately you will be a graduate of the institution you choose to attend, a lifetime member of a network of alumni. This accounts in part for the real difference between universities: the students and the alumni they become. The selectively chosen student body at Yale, for example, is likely to encompass a greater percentage of very intelligent, high-achieving students than the student body at a state university. Thus a Yale graduate, even with a mediocre academic record, may succeed because he or she belongs to the Yale network, and because many people and institutions place great value on origins, credentials, and network memberships. Nevertheless, for substance, you must dig deeper than networks and reputation. You must get firsthand, up-to-date information.

Resources

Does the school have a strong combination of tangibles—funding for faculty and operations, classroom and studio space, library, digital facilities, equipment—necessary to run an outstanding architecture program? These are questions asked by the NAAB when architecture schools are accredited, and prospective students should ask them, too. You can ascertain some of this by exploring a school's website but you also should visit the school and talk to its dean, chair, admissions director, faculty members, and students.

What is the student-teacher ratio, particularly in studio courses? Ideally each design studio professor should have no more than sixteen students, twelve to fifteen is desirable, ten to twelve is ideal, fewer than ten would be a luxury, and more than sixteen generally would be excessive, unless there are graduate teaching assistants.

Is there sufficient support staff—administrative personnel, librarians, IT specialists, curators, graduate assistants—to support the program and keep the place operating smoothly? Lack of staff can seriously impair the effectiveness and administration of an architecture program. Despite the amount of information available via the Internet, a good architecture library is still invaluable. Ask students about their school's collection of slides, digital images, and videos and the availability of audiovisual equipment. These are essential to any architectural program of quality.

Look at the physical environment where you will be spending great amounts of time. Is there sufficient space for layout tables, exhibition, and group reviews? In addition to studios, there should be spaces for conducting seminars and design reviews and an auditorium for lectures, films, or video presentations. Is there a public exhibition gallery associated with the school? Are conference rooms and offices adequate for faculty members and staff? Even the quality of lighting and acoustic environment are worth noting. There should be an adequately sized, well-equipped shop with digital laser cutters and 3-D printers for making physical models, a photographic studio with appropriate lighting for photographing models, digital plotters for printing large-format drawings in color, copy machines for reproducing drawings and other documents, a lab for testing materials and experimenting with structural assemblies, and plenty of storage for student work. Only a visit to the school will fully answer questions concerning resources and reputation. Facilities vary from school to school but all of them should exist or be accessible in some form. Many architecture schools have their own, separate buildings on campus and others are embedded more impersonally in university megabuildings or building fragments left over from earlier times. The latter are sometimes the softest kind of environment to work in; aging buildings do not imply program senility.

Cost

The cost of education has become so high that few can disregard it as a school selection factor. There is a point of diminishing returns in paying high tuition fees for educational quality and diploma reputation. Spending twice as much does not increase educational worth or career payback twofold. Therefore every student and family must carefully weigh the value and benefits of educational expense against other alternatives, including pursuing educational alternatives outside the traditional university. There is little choice today about attending architecture school if you want to be an architect but there is a choice as to cost. The primary choice is between public and private universities. The quality of publicly supported state universities has grown steadily, despite diminishing state funding support and cyclical pressures of economic recession. Although tuition has been increasing, generally state universities have not experienced threatening drops in enrollments, in part because tuition rates at private institutions have risen faster and are still much higher than at state schools.

Thus students should compare tuition and living costs at schools they are considering. They also should ascertain availability of student financial aid and loans. Many universities offer substantial scholarships, fellowships, and teaching or research assistantships (for graduate students) that can significantly reduce tuition outlays. But each university differs in its student aid strategy, and these choices should be closely scrutinized.

Students

Who attends the architecture school you are considering and
what kind of students are they? Ideally, students in a school are
socioeconomically diverse but also geographically diverse, coming
from various US cities, regions, and states and also from various
countries and cultures abroad. Never underestimate the impact on
program quality attributable to student diversity as well as student
abilities. Good students are attracted to what they perceive as good
schools and programs; they want to be with esteemed mentors and
peers. This is a distinct advantage enjoyed by schools with strong
reputations that attract outstanding students and faculty members.
But there are always outstanding students in every architecture
program, students who would excel wherever they might enroll.
It then becomes a matter of percentages and ambience. At state
universities, a large percentage of the student body will be of
average academic ability. These students establish the academic
ambience and generally perceived student intellectual level within
the institution and its classrooms.

Yet this does not mean that programs and faculty at state
universities are inferior. In fact, they may be superior, perhaps
lacking only in reputation. The outstanding student at a state
university may stand out even more. But on the whole he or she
will find the campus intellectual climate somewhat less stimulating
than it would be at a highly reputed private university. This is
less consequential for architecture schools because they control
admission to and retention within their own programs, applying
standards of performance frequently more stringent than those of
other campus disciplines. Thus even at many big state universities
filled with students just passing through, the intellectual climate in
the architecture school can be quite heady.

Faculty

An architecture school is no better than its faculty but you cannot judge the quality of a school's faculty just by perusing a website or a listing of each professor's degrees and universities attended. You must inquire. There are many sources: students already in the program, graduates of the program, practicing architects who know the faculty and program, other teachers in other departments or schools, and the faculty members themselves, most of whom are quite willing to tell you how good they are. But what do you want to know? What do the faculty members teach and how do they teach it? Are they dedicated to their work? Do they show concern for their students and for what they are learning? What do they do outside the classroom or studio: practice, conduct research, write and publish, travel, lecture? Have they gained local, regional, or national recognition or reputations individually? Are people stimulated by listening to them? Do they demand the best of their students and do they invest time and energy preparing to teach? Are they in touch with the real as well as the academic world? Above all, are they continuing to grow intellectually and learn themselves, to innovate and question while professing fully and competently the subject matter for which they are responsible? A number of architecture school faculties include individual members who are well known far beyond the campus. They are usually architects, architectural historians, or theoreticians who have gained national or international reputations for their work or ideas. Teaching is often only one of several activities in which such faculty members engage. Their status as academic or professional celebrities is believed to bring comparable status to the institutions where they teach. Indeed, their presence does draw students because students can easily imagine and anticipate that some of the master's aura and insights will be transferable. For example,

Colin Rowe, well known as a teacher and urban design theoretician in architectural circles, drew graduate students for years to Cornell. Louis Kahn's studio at the University of Pennsylvania attracted and produced hundreds of disciples during the 1950s and 1960s. It was not their course syllabus that drew the students but rather their personal design philosophies, approach to teaching, and star quality. Regardless of other program characteristics, the presence of a known and respected faculty member can be a great asset to a school and its students. Yet there can be danger in chasing stars. Frequently their time and commitment to teaching and interacting with students are limited. Off-campus interests and obligations may keep them away from the classroom or studio or may compete for their attention even when they are there. They may teach only a small number of students in advanced courses, perhaps only one semester per year, so that relatively few students in a school's population ever study with them. And occasionally these superstars are less than super as teachers. They may have grown stale, bored, and boring or espouse philosophies or ideas that no longer seem relevant or applicable. In any event look closely at who is getting top billing and get reviews from currently enrolled students and recent graduates.

Prospective architectural students having specific interests related to architecture should seek schools with faculty members who share and pursue those interests. Try to discover who is focused on issues that interest you, such as urban design, historic preservation, sustainability, affordable housing, landscape design, interiors, construction, digital methods, or history, to name a few areas of specialization and research. There could be no one sharing your interests, something you need to know before making a choice.

These questions will never be fully answered until you are actually in school but you will get some sense of a faculty's quality by probing a bit. Unfortunately most students rarely know what their faculty is all about before enrolling in an architecture school, and a few are not so sure even when they finish.

Program Ethos

A key characteristic differentiating one architecture school from another is a school's dominant pedagogical ethos. Collectively an architecture dean and like-minded faculty members can and often do promote specific design philosophies and principles, certain kinds of problems and projects, and even certain ways of thinking about and looking at the world. Even while satisfying requirements that all schools must meet to maintain professional degree accreditation, a school of architecture can have its own spin, its own discernible tone and orientation.

At Syracuse University, for example, the architecture school was led for years by Dean Werner Seligman, an architect who stamped his imprint indelibly on a generation of Syracuse students and faculty. Seligman's strongly modernist design attitudes, language, and graphic approach permeated the school, in keeping with master-apprentice traditions prevalent in Europe. Diversity in design thinking was minimal. Faculty members taught and students designed à la Seligman, and studio projects naturally reflected Seligman's powerful tutelage. Similar circumstances prevailed for decades after World War II at the Illinois Institute of Technology (IIT) in Chicago, where Ludwig Mies van der Rohe, who had emigrated from Germany, was the resident guru. Students came to IIT to learn how to design like Mies, despite the presence of other faculty members, and anyone uninterested in Miesian design would have found it pointless to be at IIT.

Other schools focus differently. After World War II, urban design as a distinct subdiscipline of architecture was pioneered by Harvard University. MIT's architecture program always has traveled in diverse topical directions, with periodic shifts. At various times MIT has emphasized urban design, sustainability and energy conservation, construction technology, housing and community design, CAD methodology, and design visualization. By contrast, Princeton's school of architecture focused for decades primarily on aesthetic form making, on intellectual speculation and verbalization, worrying little about constructability. Despite its program's theoretical tendencies, Princeton's design faculty members often have been celebrated practitioners.

Notre Dame's architecture school revived classicism and pedagogical traditions of the Ecole des Beaux Arts. At Howard University, where many students are African American or come from other countries, design studios often explore projects associated with economically disadvantaged communities in US or foreign cities. Other schools push technology-inspired, constructivist, and deconstructivist design, treating architecture as purely an art form with less explicit concern for technological, social, or economic issues. Still others, such as the University of Maryland, focus on urban design and architectural design together, coupled with studies in architectural and urban history. A few schools, still allied with engineering colleges, offer programs geared to engineering and construction but their numbers have diminished.

Before selecting a school, ascertain its pedagogical ethos, being mindful that schools sometimes change directions within the course of only a few years. Query students, faculty members, and architects to get a clear and current picture. Knowing about program ethos and direction is crucial because you may find it difficult not to pursue that ethos and direction once you begin your academic journey into architectural practice.

The Admission Process

You've looked at architecture schools, asked lots of questions, and decided where you would like to study. How do you get admitted? What is the application process like? Each architecture school has its own system for processing applicants and provides online application forms and guidelines. Nevertheless, there are several things to do and keep in mind when applying, independent of particular school requirements. These involve little extra efforts demonstrating clearly your strengths and the merits of your application.

The Portfolio

Many schools require submission of a portfolio showing examples of creative work. Portfolios typically contain images depicting the applicant's efforts in art, design, drawing, or photography. Some schools may accept portfolios in digital form. How well your portfolio is designed, its look and graphic quality, always gets the admission committee's attention and can make a positive first impression. Seldom can an admissions committee predict future performance from an applicant's portfolio content but if the portfolio effectively conveys the sense that the applicant might already be thinking like an architect, it can convincingly sway the admissions committee, even more than design achievements illustrated within. Of course, the better the design work, the more positive the impression.

Interviews

Many schools do not require a personal interview for admission. Disregard this nonrequirement. Go there anyway, not only to learn about the place but also to meet at least one or two faculty members concerned with admissions. You are, after all, building a case for yourself. Convey to your interviewer your interest,

motivation, background, and qualifications and do so with
sincerity and enthusiasm. Be engaging. Establish a dialog in which
you learn about the program, the faculty, and the interviewer
(remember that architects like to talk about themselves) while the
interviewer is learning about you. A few positive notes jotted down
by that interviewer and placed in your application file can have
great impact on an admission decision.

Reference Letters

All schools ask that you request teachers or others who know
you and your work to send letters attesting to your character,

skills, and academic qualifications. These letters can be very decisive but of little impact if they come from personal friends or relatives whose credentials or objectivity are doubtful. To make reference letters count, ask the writers to focus on your educational and professional achievements, your work habits, and your creative potential. The best letters are from employers and teachers who knew you well as a worker or student. Citation of specific accomplishments, abilities, and outstanding personal characteristics will be most helpful to admissions committees. Finally, it is always a good idea for the writer to explain briefly his or her relationship to you: where, when, and in what circumstances.

Grades

There is no way around it—grades are very important. Apply with the highest grade point average you can muster. However, grades are not everything, and softness in course grades can sometimes be overcome by strengths elsewhere, especially portfolios, letters of reference, and exam scores or experience. It is not unusual for architecture schools to admit students with less-than-stellar academic records but who show great potential through a combination of experience and creative talent exhibited in their portfolios. This is particularly true of applicants who have been out of school for a while.

Essays

A short essay or written statement, dreaded by some students, is often a component of many admission applications. Schools pose similar questions for you to address: why do you want to study architecture? Why this school? What experiences have you had that significantly affected you? I have read many such essays and statements and frankly most are of little value in assessing a prospective student's qualifications and potential. Essays and statements often are neither insightful nor well written—too long, rambling, and repetitive. Consequently, your writing should demonstrate four things: that you have something relevant and interesting to say; that you can think and organize your thoughts logically; that you can express yourself clearly, succinctly, and perhaps poetically; and that you are able to write in English using reasonably correct grammar, spelling, and punctuation. What you say may be less important than how well you say it.

Exams for Admission

For admission, generally universities require the Scholastic Aptitude Test (SAT) for undergraduate programs and the Graduate Record Exam (GRE) for graduate programs. Neither exam measures aptitude or skill directly related to architecture but they do show basic academic talent and suggest how students can be expected to perform. Some preparation for these exams is possible, including guidance in the art of exam taking. If you feel uncertain about your examination prospects, consider enrolling in test-training programs and courses that target admission exam performance.

Timing

Because university schedules usually call for classes (and the academic year) to begin in the fall, the admissions process must commence almost a year earlier. Most application deadlines occur in mid- to late winter, and students are usually notified between February and May. Therefore applicants should visit schools no later than the previous fall, then prepare their portfolios and application forms prior to submission deadlines. Examination dates should be verified and exams taken prior to the spring admissions review. Only in special circumstances do schools accept late applications. If you go for an interview, make sure it is before the admissions committee meets to consider applicants.

Financial Aid

When you apply for admission, indicate your interest in financial aid directly on your application and in a cover letter as well. Many universities use standardized financial assistance applications processed separately from admissions applications. Fellowships, teaching assistantships, and work-study positions for graduate students are typically allocated in spring and summer. Therefore, let the school know of your interest in being considered for any or all of these. Also check availability of university scholarships and fellowships, which may not be administered by the architecture school.

Education has become so expensive that many students, to supplement scholarship funds, must borrow money to pay some or all their college costs. Most universities have low-interest loan programs to help cover these costs, with loan interest and principle repayments deferred until after graduation. Students also can obtain education loans at below-market interest rates from commercial lending institutions, thanks to federal, state, and sometimes local government loan guarantee programs.

Admission Odds

To how many schools should you apply? Presumably the more you try for, the higher the probability of being admitted by at least one. However, this strategy has practical limits of cost and time. I suggest the "rifle" rather than the "shotgun" approach. Apply only to those schools, perhaps three or four, in which you are genuinely interested and add one or two more as backup choices. Your backups should also be schools acceptable to you but for which admission is somewhat less competitive.

If you find yourself on a waiting list, be optimistic because schools admit more students than they can actually enroll but then may fall short in enrollment a few weeks later, having expected more to accept admission. This is when they turn to their waiting list. If you are on a waiting list, stay in touch with the school about your continued interest in attending. Help them keep you in mind.

If you cannot attend your first choice school, you can begin studying architecture at your backup school, complete one or two years in good standing, and then transfer. But this entails certain risks. First, without a strong record to support your transfer application, you still may not gain admission. Second, if admitted as a transfer, you may lose some course credits or even a semester or two in making the transfer between schools with programs not equivalent in content and quality. Third, to your pleasant surprise perhaps, you may prefer to finish your architectural studies where you started, having lost your desire to transfer to the school you originally preferred. This happens often because students settle into a program, become comfortable with familiar territory, and conclude that the backup school was better than they had expected.

Once admitted, reply to the school as soon as you have made your decision. There is usually an admission acceptance deadline because it is critical to the school's planning to know how many intend to enroll in the coming year. If you need an extension while awaiting notice from other schools in which you are more interested, write to request the extension. This is also the time to pose any still unanswered questions about financial aid, assistantships, and transfer or advance standing credits. Don't be surprised if some of these issues cannot be resolved until you arrive in the fall.

Feel positive about yourself because an architecture school wants you but recall that the tough phase of architectural education is only just beginning. The next several years will be exciting, frustrating, mind expanding, enigmatic, amusing, tedious, exhausting, exhilarating, and outrageous all at the same time. Choosing and being chosen is still just one of many milestones on the road to becoming an architect.

7 After School, What?

Successful completion of architecture school is a significant accomplishment and milestone in the career of any architect. The years of intense study and demanding work at times seem unending. Not all who start graduate. And although graduation signals the end of formal schooling, it is by no means a signal that your architectural education is complete.

In fact, as challenging as architecture school is, what follows graduation can be more challenging. Graduate architects face new choices and hurdles that may not have been well understood while in school. Every subsequent career path is a continuation of the architect's education, even if it does not entail traditional architectural practice. Therefore it is essential to look ahead and be aware of the options, remembering that education now simply shifts from the schoolroom to the workplace.

Internship
The majority of graduate architects, whether possessing a BArch or MArch degree, go from architecture school to architectural offices. These first few years of work are the internship years. The term is appropriate, clearly implying that the recently graduated architect is still being trained, still learning, still a student. In many cases, however, interns have already acquired office experience working during summer vacations and part-time during the academic year.

Architectural interns, similar to new arrivals in most professions, work hard because they are energetic, eager to produce, and hungry for new knowledge. They are the ones often asked to work the longest hours, in part because their hourly salaries are always less than more experienced architects. Intern compensation is also relatively low because most interns are inexperienced technically and when assigned new and unfamiliar tasks with steep learning curves require more time to accomplish such tasks.

Architectural internship is somewhat like the internship physicians serve after completing medical school: lots of work, long hours, little compensation. It can be justified as a way of getting paid for still being a student. States require a specified period of internship before becoming eligible for licensing as an architect. However, the architectural profession has never institutionalized its internship program like that of the medical profession, which has developed a national, competitive, computer-based system for evaluating and placing medical school graduates. Architectural interns still must make their own way, searching for and taking a job wherever they can find it. Consequently, obtaining and completing an architectural internship is solely in the hands of the intern.

Architectural employment is highly volatile and dependent on the economy, with demand for new graduates fluctuating year to year and even month to month. A continuing, systematized internship program would require steady sources of employment, a unified process of intern-firm matchup, and rigorous methods of evaluation. Economic uncertainties, coupled with the propensity of architects to resist consensus on practically anything, particularly concerning their pocketbooks and their freedom of action, make the internship essentially a series of employment relationships established between individual interns and individual firms.

However, internship requirements and standards have been standardized, thanks to the National Council of Architectural Registration Boards (NCARB). It developed the Intern Development Program (IDP), now adopted by virtually all state registration boards for licensing. The IDP entails creating and maintaining a permanent file for each intern but the intern is responsible for documenting his or her accumulated experience with each employer while maintaining contact with an IDP adviser, who must be a licensed architect. Interns are expected to accumulate stipulated, minimum amounts of time and experience performing diverse tasks. Considered integral to architectural practice, these diverse tasks are specifically defined and categorized by the IDP. Each of the intern's employers must certify that the intern satisfactorily performed the work in each category for the amount of time indicated and earned the points claimed. Thus the IDP goal is to ensure that every intern masters the full array of skills required for licensing.

To receive a license to practice architecture and use the title *architect*, states require an accredited professional architecture degree, the equivalent of no less than three full years of diversified internship experience, and passing the state licensing examination. Fortunately, accumulated internship time does not have to be with one firm or within one state. Thus new graduate architects compete for jobs in the marketplace that will provide the mix of experience and training needed. Many graduate architects change jobs frequently during those initial years, whereas others stick with a single firm, perhaps hoping to become a senior employee or partner. Some work for small, edge-of-survival firms and others for large, established ones.

Graduate architects can acquire a great variety of skills and knowledge during internships, depending on the number of jobs held, type and size of firms worked for, type and size of projects designed, and responsibilities assumed. Some architectural interns are exposed immediately to a wide range of practical experience, including management experience. This is most common when employed during internship years by relatively small firms (five to ten professionals). However, most small firms do not have the opportunity to design projects large in scale and complexity.

Graduate architects who work for large firms may gain substantial experience focusing on specialized aspects of large projects but may not have the opportunity to gain the breadth of experience possible in small offices. Concentration and specialization often characterize the role of the intern architect in large practices, whereas diversification and generalization characterize many small practices. Additionally, large projects generally take longer to design and build than small projects, so over a three-year period, one might work on only two or three projects in a large firm but six or eight in a small firm. The intern in the large firm might never grasp the totality of a project and the integrative design processes that are more apparent and accessible to the intern in the small firm. However, the young architect in the small office may not acquire the depth of experience achievable in bigger offices or have access to the range of expertise, methodologies, and resources found in many large, well-established firms.

One other critical variable related to firms is the willingness of senior architects—associates or principals—to spend time and energy teaching intern architects they employ. Active teaching encompasses adequate discussion and explanation of design and technical issues, demonstration, exposure to clients and consultants, and, above all, delegation of responsibility without supervisory neglect. For the newly hired intern, senior architects are the surrogate mentors and professors left behind in architecture school. Therefore architectural offices sensitive to intern needs ensure that young architects, still eager to learn, acquire the knowledge and master the diverse skills necessary not only to satisfy internship requirements and pass the licensing examination but also to practice architecture successfully.

Some candidates approach the licensing examination never having designed and built in steel, concrete, or wood. Some have had little on-site construction experience or have never written specifications. Others may have found their internship years devoid of any substantial client contact or project management and contract administration responsibilities. Unfortunately, this reflects a reality of day-to-day practice in many firms that use personnel to the firm's best economic advantage. If an individual is very good at doing sophisticated CAD work, designing construction details, or negotiating with contractors, there is great temptation for the firm to regularly assign such tasks to that individual. Having mastered modeling software, an intern can find herself chained to a computer without ever having the opportunity to perform the many other tasks architects must accomplish. This is the downside of specialization in architecture.

Therefore, graduate architects should choose employment very thoughtfully, even if jobs are in short supply. The years of internship are extraordinarily formative. They not only prepare you (or fail to) for licensing and independent practice, they also establish directions and attitudes that may shape much of your future career as an architect. Begin your career working for a mediocre architect and you may acquire mediocre habits of thought and production, no matter what your aspirations. Work in an office where good design is paramount and you are among talented designers and you are likely to be inspired to develop your own talents more fully. In fact, many outstanding firms have been founded by architects who worked for firms founded by a previous generation of architects, a generation that wisely nurtured its successors and disciples.

What would be the ideal internship experience? Working for a small- to medium-sized firm doing high-quality design work, being assigned and successfully undertaking a multiplicity of tasks from conceptual sketching to producing contract documents to inspecting construction, and receiving a regular and adequate, if not generous, paycheck.

Becoming a Licensed Architect

The process of becoming licensed as an architect is another mini-ordeal on the way to becoming a full-fledged practitioner, and similar to graduation from architecture school, it too is a milestone. Once licensed, you can offer personal architectural services to clients or become owner of a firm. The common track to becoming licensed as an architect in the United States and being able to legally use the title *architect* is as follows:

1. Obtain an accredited professional architectural degree (BArch or MArch).

2. Complete a state-required minimum internship, usually three equivalent calendar years of architectural office experience.

3. Apply for and pass a state-administered architectural licensing exam, following which the state issues a certificate of registration and license to practice architecture.

For most applicants, the licensing examination itself is an ordeal. Why bother testing architects who already have survived architecture school and received their professionally accredited diploma?

Architects must be licensed because design and construction of buildings affect the public's health, safety, and welfare—especially safety. To protect the public, government is empowered to regulate by law the actions and practices of individuals—architects and engineers as well as doctors, attorneys, and accountants—who offer professional services on which public health, safety, and welfare depend. States want to ensure that anyone claiming to be an architect meets certain minimum qualifications concerning professional competency. Further, because of variability in educational standards, states have chosen to administer their own tests for competency. There are no federal, county, or municipal licenses for architects.

Some states have their own unique definition of what constitutes three years of internship. Some states grant internship credit for time spent teaching, doing research, or conducting postprofessional degree studies in advanced graduate programs. Others are stricter, demanding that the three-year internship be composed entirely of architectural design practice in the offices of licensed practicing architects. A state-by-state inquiry will reveal the qualification policy of each state. However, most states have adopted NCARB's IDP standards, making it easier for aspiring architects to understand what is needed to satisfy qualification requirements.

Over the years, the NCARB exam, adopted by most states as the standard licensing exam, has changed many times in form and content. In its continuing effort to improve the quality and reliability of its exam, NCARB has experimented with and used successive examination approaches that inevitably drew criticism from practitioners, teachers, and licensing candidates for various reasons: too long, too technical, too subjective, too ambiguous, too conceptual, too practical, too irrelevant, and . . . too easy or too hard. Indeed, since the first edition of this book was published in 1985, the NCARB examination format has changed several times. And after this edition has appeared, the exam will change again.

No matter when you take the exam, always obtain up-to-date qualification and testing information from NCARB (http://www.ncarb.org/Becoming-an-Architect) and the state from which you seek licensing.

NCARB's standardized examination, the Architectural Registration Examination (ARE), is currently a multidivision, computerized test. The ARE is supposed to be efficient, accurate, reliable, and fair. It is designed to distinguish more clearly among candidates who pass and those who fail. It reportedly can make sharper distinctions because all questions have been pretested, are of average difficulty, and are not easily answered by guessing. Moreover, a candidate can attempt one, several, or all divisions of the examination throughout the year at one of the NCARB's many authorized, computer-based testing centers.

Each division of the exam contains several discrete sets of questions, with each set providing comprehensive coverage of the subject matter in the division. As candidates complete the initial question sets, the system monitors their answers. If a candidate clearly is passing or failing, the system stops administering that exam division. If a passing or failing pattern is not clear, the system continues with additional sets of questions for that division until a clear passing or failing pattern is detected. Thus candidates do not necessarily answer the same number of questions.

As of 2012–13, the examination had seven divisions:

1. Programming, Planning, and Practice
2. Site Planning & Design
3. Building Design & Construction Systems
4. Schematic Design
5. Structural Systems
6. Building Systems
7. Construction Documents and Services

As the list shows, the ARE is broad in scope and places great emphasis on architectural technology as well as design. Examination candidates who qualify to take the exam usually study for it by enrolling in refresher seminars oriented toward the exam or by reviewing their own books, notes, and materials. Practice questions and graphic vignettes for the exam are available via the Internet. It is not uncommon for candidates to pass some divisions of the exam and fail others, and most states require reexamination for only those parts failed. Some states require that a candidate succeed in passing all divisions of the exam within some limited number of sittings; otherwise, he or she must retake the entire exam. The NCARB imposes no limit on the number of examination pass attempts.

Historically, passing the twelve-hour design section, along with site planning and structures sections, were the exam's major stumbling blocks. But today's exam does not test aesthetic talent or presentation skills but rather a candidate's ability to deal with issues and satisfy criteria relating to programmatic, organizational, building code, life-safety, structural, and environmental needs. Today some candidates, perhaps shaky in handling quantitative problems, may struggle with the more technical exam divisions, but with good preparation, these too can be mastered.

Having passed the exam and become licensed, one may use the professional title *architect* and legally offer architectural services and certify drawings. States require that professionals periodically renew their licenses, without further examination. However, earning continuing education credits each year is required for maintaining and renewing architectural licenses in most states. States also grant licenses by reciprocity to architects licensed in other states, recognizing the equivalency of other states' licensing standards. NCARB issues a national certificate to architects licensed by NCARB examination in any state, and this certificate can expedite licensing in other states. For many architects, the licensing exam has another significance: it may be the last examination ever taken.

Past NCARB surveys have shown that after licensing, more than 90 percent of licensed architects were involved in some form of architectural practice and about 4 percent in teaching. Over half work in architectural firms with fewer than ten employees. By contrast, although a majority of the AIA's junior members are pursuing traditional architectural careers, roughly a quarter of them do not follow the school-internship-licensing career path. Thus we can infer that although most licensed architects proceeded directly from school to practice, working primarily in small- to medium-sized firms, many graduate architects travel different routes or take side trips.

Continuing Education

Architects never stop learning, partly because there is so much to learn and also because knowledge and standards evolve: new design theories, new work methods, new management practices, new computer applications, new construction materials and techniques, new building codes and regulations. Similar to all other professions, architects have an obligation to clients and the public to keep abreast of developing knowledge and evolving standards applicable to architectural practice. Consequently, architects continue pursuing education throughout their careers.

Continuing education can be formalized, as it is in universities, with organized classes and instruction. Many structured, continuing education programs—short courses, lectures, seminars—are sponsored by the AIA, by architecture schools, or by trade associations and professional organizations concerned with life safety, environmental protection, sustainability, digital technologies, building technology, construction industry products, historic preservation, urban planning, and real estate development. Or an architect can earn continuing education credits informally, achieved through self-testing by reading articles and studying technical literature.

To ensure that its members maintain and regularly update their practical knowledge, the AIA has adopted a continuing education system (CES) for evaluating and reporting continuing education activities. It requires members to verify their professional development by documenting continuing education "learning units," creating a record of time, effort, and subject matter related to specific educational activities. The CES identifies critical areas for continuing education—for example, public health, safety, and welfare—but the system is nevertheless flexible, allowing each architect some choice in selecting his or her own learning objectives. Because states require continuing education credits for license renewal, the AIA's CES report serves as a transcript.

Further Studies

Some architectural students, as they near the end of their primary architecture school education, desire further, more advanced schooling. Graduate architects also return to school to pursue new areas of interest and research after being in practice for several years. There can be several reasons for such postprofessional degree graduate work:

- To gain additional design expertise in a specialized architecture graduate program focused on topics such as urban design, housing, community planning, sustainable design, and digital methods

- To study design with special teachers, who serve as mentors for younger architects. Aware of and admiring the work, methodology, and aesthetic philosophy of a particular professor at a particular school, graduate students may spend a year or more working with that professor, not necessarily to learn a particular skill or acquire specialized knowledge but rather to gain deeper insight into the professor 's unique, creative way of thinking about and approaching design.

- To acquire new or greater expertise and to conduct research in architectural subspecialties other than design, such as history and criticism, building technology, or construction management

- To shift into fields closely related to architecture, such as landscape architecture, city planning, interior design, or graphics

- To change fields substantially, perhaps shifting from architecture to business, law, engineering, real estate development, or public administration

Postprofessional degree study enhances knowledge, capabilities, and career potential. In the competitive marketplace, advanced degrees are clearly an asset and they may be indispensable in some areas. For example, most universities will not appoint or promote faculty members who do not hold the highest degree offered in the faculty appointee's discipline or field of expertise. Federal and local government agencies give credit for advanced degrees in determining employees' salaries and positions. However, in traditional architectural practice, holding an advanced, postprofessional degree is much less critical to an architect's future; practical skills, talent, and personal characteristics are much more important. Statistically a small minority of all graduate architects pursue further graduate study after completion of architecture school and receipt of their first professional degree, whether a BArch or MArch.

If postprofessional studies are of interest and you are looking at various graduate schools, consider the same variables that affected your choice of a first professional degree program, described in the previous chapter. Also note that in pursuing further studies in architectural design you probably will receive a second, specialized master's degree, not a doctorate, because doctoral degrees generally are not awarded in architectural design. Doctorates related to architecture usually entail scholarship and research focused on architectural history and theory or architectural technology.

Traveling

No architect is ever fully educated until he or she has traveled beyond the borders of home territory. In particular, traveling in Europe, from which so much of our Western architectural heritage derives, is a must-do, an educational experience not to be postponed. And if time and money permit, traveling to more exotic parts of the world—Japan, India, the Middle East, North Africa, and Latin America—is equally enlightening and stimulating. Fortunately, many architecture schools conduct study abroad programs during summers and sometimes for entire school semesters or years, offering aspiring architects unique opportunities to see and study towns, cities, buildings, and the cultures that produced them.

Any architect who has traveled will tell you that no amount of viewing images online or looking at pictures in books can match educationally the firsthand experience of walking the streets of Rome, Paris, Barcelona, Istanbul, Beijing, or Kyoto. There is no substitute for analyzing, sketching, and photographing on your own the promenades, piazzas, villas, palaces, temples, churches, civic buildings, housing settlements, and marketplaces on other continents. Touching architecture directly, from the most ancient to the most modern, is the only way truly and wholly to understand it. If you cannot travel while you are an architecture student, make sure you travel soon after finishing your studies, and continue to travel throughout your career.

In fact, US architects also should see as much of the United States as possible. Although much of our architectural heritage originated in Europe, there is a diverse US architectural heritage resulting from transplantation, reinterpretation, amalgamation, and invention of urban and architectural antecedents. Explore Boston; New York; Philadelphia; Washington, DC; Miami; Chicago; Los Angeles; and San Francisco. Visit historic US towns:

The Galleria in Milan, Italy

Charleston, South Carolina; Savannah, Georgia; Annapolis,
Maryland; Alexandria, Virginia; and urban settlements first
laid out by the Spanish in the Southwest and Far West. Equally
important, travel to sense fully the scale and diversity of the
expansive North American landscape, to understand not only

US architecture but also how that architecture has been placed—sometimes well, sometimes badly—on the land.

Travel before settling down too permanently because nothing impedes traveling like an excess of obligations at home, wherever that may be. Commitments to a job or practice, to a spouse, to children, or to a mortgage can stymie traveling opportunities. Constrained vacation schedules, tight work schedules, financial limitations, and domestic duties can all get in the way of a summer in Europe or a year abroad.

Traditionally young architects always have traveled abroad to study the architectural and artistic heritages of other countries, filling sketchbooks and digital memory chips with images of humble and monumental environments. A young architect can even live and work abroad, absorbing far more of other cultures than is possible as a tourist. US architects continue to have such opportunities. They can seek overseas employment with either foreign or US architectural firms, which design increasing numbers of projects in Europe, Asia, Latin America, and Africa. They can work for government agencies or join the Peace Corps. They can compete for travel fellowships available to architects, mostly for European study and travel. Architects who teach can seek Fulbright lectureships and teaching exchange fellowships, which permit them to spend considerable time abroad. Regardless of the method by which you travel, it is an experience that forever influences your attitude as an architect and citizen. Time abroad broadens immeasurably.

Teaching

"Those who can, do; those who can't, teach," according to George Bernard Shaw. Although this may be somewhat true in other fields of education, it doesn't apply to teaching architecture. In fact many professors both "teach" and "do" architecture.

Teaching architecture is an attractive career option for those so inclined and qualified. Universities require architectural design and technology faculty members to have at least master's degrees. Architectural historians usually hold PhD degrees. Most universities allow architecture faculty members to consult and engage in private practice, and those who practice or consult can significantly augment their teaching income. Conversely, their steady teaching income makes it easier to begin and sustain practices, especially as economic circumstances in the construction marketplace vary. Although academic salaries earned by teachers of architecture are modest compared to those in professions such as medicine, law, business, engineering, or computer sciences, they generally are comparable to salaries paid to professors in the arts and humanities. Perhaps most surprising, architecture professors' salaries can be comparable to the incomes of architects in full-time practice, particularly in smaller firms.

Many talented architectural graduates begin their teaching careers soon after completing advanced graduate studies. They may have already gained some teaching experience as graduate teaching assistants before finishing school or they may have completed school and spent several years in practice. Initial appointments are at the level of instructor, lecturer, or assistant professor and they may be adjunct, part-time appointments made annually or full-time, tenure-track appointments. The latter normally entail a multiyear, renewable contract. After a defined period, typically five or six years, a tenure-track assistant professor must be formally reviewed for tenure and promotion by departmental and campuswide tenure committees.

Tenure review encompasses evaluating three areas of achievement: teaching, research—or original creative work—and service to the university, the profession, and the public. Formal review for tenure leads to one of two outcomes: the university can grant the professor tenure, in effect guaranteeing permanent employment, or it can deny tenure, obliging the faculty member to leave after the following academic year. Clearly the tenure-granting process puts substantial pressure on architecture faculty members to build their case over a relatively short period of time. Given the longer professional gestation period needed by architects—in comparison to scholars in other field—to establish themselves, many architecture professors, especially design faculty members, have difficulty qualifying for tenure, no matter how talented and hardworking they are. If life were fair and academic institutions were prudent, tenure-track design faculty members would be evaluated differently than faculty members in other disciplines.

Architecture schools hire new, younger design faculty members for tenure-track positions who show academic and professional promise through achievement in scholarship and practice. Recruiting committees look for strong academic records, compelling portfolios showing work independently designed or built, awards for work or work exhibited, documented original research, articles written and published, participation in design competitions and scholarly conferences, outstanding references, and evidence of teaching ability. Some schools expect architectural design faculty members to be licensed and encourage unlicensed design faculty members to become licensed through some form of professional practice. Nevertheless, many design professors pursue tenure through research, writing, and service rather than practice. In any case, getting tenure today depends on having a strong record of demonstrated excellence in research, publication, and design practice, more so than on teaching excellence.

Teaching offers many significant benefits, not the least of which is a steady diet of intellectual discourse and stimulation. Faculty members are continually challenged by students and colleagues. New ideas and information flow readily back and forth, not only between academics but also between academics and practitioners. Teaching allows time and opportunity for research, theoretical speculation and exploration, and writing. Good teachers act as exchangers, bringing their personal research and practice into their teaching and their teaching into their research and practice. And, of course, teaching is its own reward, offering the great satisfaction of seeing students learn, discover, create, and grow, in part due to the efforts of their teachers.

University teaching can become problematic: budget and salary cuts or inadequate compensation in the absence of supplemental income, especially affecting professors who have families but are not practicing architects; demands and stress of seeking tenure and not getting it; administrative complexities, inefficiencies, and logistical breakdowns endemic to universities; potential for boredom and burnout arising from too many repetitions of courses and subject matter, which in turn can bore students; and intellectual stagnation arising from insufficient activity outside the classroom or studio, a condition commonly afflicting teachers who do nothing but teach or have been teaching the same material for too long. Most of these problems, however, can be mitigated by positive benefits or avoided altogether through the efforts of helpful colleagues, wise mentors, sensitive administrators, and supportive spouses.

Work in Related Fields

Throughout this book, *practicing architecture* refers to professionals directly responsible for the aesthetic, functional, and technical design of buildings, building complexes, or new communities. Design is the core subject in almost every architecture school, the core topic of almost every architectural magazine. Yet many would-be architects discover, either during or after graduation from architecture school, that design per se and traditional architectural practice may not be their cup of tea. They may reach this conclusion because of limited talent, lack of interest and motivation, newly discovered interests, or a desire to make more money.

But they also may realize that architectural education, with its unique curriculum and approach, has prepared them well for other endeavors. Consider the breadth of subjects studied: manual and digital drawing and modeling; mathematics, science, and engineering; project and firm management; history; humanities, and social studies; and, above all, design, that complex and integrative activity demanding research and analysis, critical thinking, imagination, invention, conflict resolution, and constructive synthesis. Architecture students, regardless of their talent, learn how to work really hard, to engage in rigorous analysis and reasoning, to hypothesize and organize. These are invaluable skills in almost any field. Therefore, no matter what leads them away from architectural design, graduate architects enjoy numerous career choices that capitalize on their architectural education.

Landscape architecture, urban planning, historic preservation, interior design, furniture design, engineering—structural, civil, and environmental—and sustainability are fields closely related to architecture. They all involve design of physical constructs for human use and occupancy and all intersect with architectural practice. They also share many of the same methods and tools, common cultural histories, and similar aesthetic, technical, and functional goals. Similar to architecture, each of these professional fields has its own educational prerequisites and its own body of knowledge, theory, and methods that can be appreciated and mastered by someone trained in architecture. Indeed there are landscape architects, urban planners, historic preservationists, interior designers, and engineers who studied architecture first, just as there are architects who initially mastered another field.

Related less closely to architecture in methodology and goals, but powerfully affecting design of the built environment, are construction contracting and management, real estate development, finance, and marketing. These are not design professions, nor are they constituent parts of architectural practice, but architecture, viewed as a business product and treated as real estate, is their concern.

Construction contractors erect buildings, purchasing and assembling all the labor and materials needed and coordinating the work of subcontractors and suppliers in accordance with drawings and specifications prepared by architects. But architects, similar to contractors, work for building owners or real estate developers. The latter identify markets, generate programs and operational plans, acquire property, obtain financing, hire designers, negotiate contracts with construction contractors, build improvements, and then lease, sell, or occupy the improved property. Owners and developers, not architects, usually have the final say, along with investors and bankers who provide funds for purchasing or developing real estate. Graduate architects who occasionally enter these fields soon discover that, first, nonarchitects exercise more control over the development process and product than architects, and, second, that financing buildings can be much more economically rewarding than designing them, if not as much fun.

Finally, many architects pursue government service and public administration. Federal, state, county, and municipal government agencies are responsible for regulating, building, and managing a great amount of US real estate. This includes all types of facilities, from national parks, military bases, and embassies to office buildings, hospitals, laboratories, housing, and public infrastructure. Architects have a vital role to play within government at all levels, overseeing this vast network of property and, equally important, ensuring that new or repurposed construction is well designed and maintained.

Sometimes architects in the public sector act as initiators and designers, developing proposals and design concepts. Government architects may even prepare detailed construction drawings and specifications for projects. More often they act as reviewers, regulators, or project managers, overseeing design and construction activities performed by outside contractors or consulting architectural firms. Or they may become managers of governmental bureaus, divisions, or departments concerned with generalized policies and procedures rather than specific projects or properties. "Citizen architects" increasingly enter the public realm to become civic activists, appointed officials, or politicians who run for office and win elections. They no longer practice architecture but as architects in government or public service they have opportunities to influence public policy and make decisions that can have profound impact on architects and architecture, especially when they assume the role of client.

Architects in government may miss out on the highs and lows of practice, the joys or sorrows of self-employment and self-expression. They certainly will not get rich. But they do enjoy the benefits of stable, steady employment, paid vacations, insurance and health programs, and sometimes important policy-making responsibilities.

Abandoning Architecture

Lovely as it is, costly as it was, architecture is regrettably abandoned by a number of graduate architects, usually for one or more of the reasons specified previously. They also may abandon the field out of disillusionment or frustration. They might go back to school and study law or business, sell insurance or lumber, or drop out entirely to spend their time sailing in the Aegean.

In almost all cases, the benefits of architecture were felt to be insufficient to justify the burdens.

It would be interesting to compile and compare abandonment statistics for diverse professions. Architecture might be high on the list, similar to many nonprofessional liberal arts fields pursued enthusiastically by students, only to be abandoned later because of a weak marketplace for jobs or personal circumstances. The laws of supply and demand certainly contribute to abandonment impulses in architecture, arising when too many architects compete for too little work. However, those who completely leave architecture probably do so with mixed feelings and a sense of loss.

Recalling the external impediments and inequities that architects know to be real, often inescapable, and beyond control makes it easier to deal with and rationalize such feelings. But the feelings arising from lost opportunity, stifled creativity, and unrealized aspirations are harder to deal with. The intellectual and emotional payoffs of design exploration and invention, the fun of building, the delights of visual composition, of space and form—these are the potential rewards left behind that few other careers can provide.

III

Being an Architect

8 The Building Process and the Architect's Role

Architecture as a regulated profession is relatively new yet there have been architects for as long as humans have built settlements, with little distinction between designers and builders. In ancient cultures and languages, the same word was used for *architect* and *builder*. Erecting structures from foundation to roof was an integrated craft. The master mason or master carpenter could design, assemble labor and materials, estimate costs, and oversee construction. Thus the first people to provide shelter for themselves and for others became, in essence, the first architects. Anyone able to conceptualize, draw geometric forms, and construct such forms without subsequent collapse was an architect.

The industrial revolution changed the building process. New materials, new machines, new engineering techniques, and new building requirements made it increasingly difficult for any one person or organization to master every facet of building design and construction. Specialization was inevitable. New and technically complex structural systems demanded expertise beyond that of a master mason or master carpenter. The proliferation of highly specialized subcontractors redefined the role of the general contractor, whose own labor force built less and less of the building. The complexities of construction increasingly became matters for experts complementing the efforts of the architect.

The first school of architecture in the United States was established at the Massachusetts Institute of Technology in 1868, and architecture was soon recognized as a learned and governable profession when states enacted legislation for licensing architects. Since then, the practicing architect's territory has evolved, becoming at once broader in types of projects but increasingly circumscribed in professional responsibility. Today, architects design buildings, aggregations of buildings, entire towns, and parts of cities but they do so as leader of or key player on a large team of highly specialized engineers and other design consultants. The more specialized the project, the more specialized consultants are needed. In addition to the architect, a project team may include civil, structural, mechanical, and electrical engineers; landscape architects; interior and graphic designers; experts in lighting, acoustics, security, building code analysis and interpretation, traffic, and transportation; and, depending on the project type, specialists focusing on health-care facilities, performing arts design, historic preservation, retailing, and structured parking.

DEVELOPMENT PROCESS PARTICIPANTS

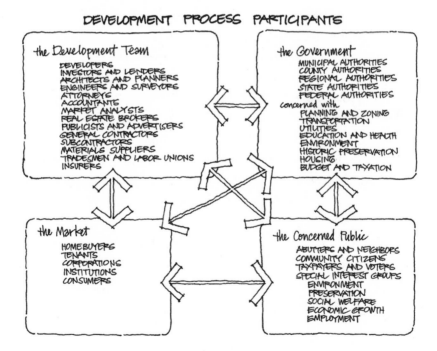

the Development Team
DEVELOPERS
INVESTORS AND LENDERS
ARCHITECTS AND PLANNERS
ENGINEERS AND SURVEYORS
ATTORNEYS
ACCOUNTANTS
MARKET ANALYSTS
REAL ESTATE BROKERS
PUBLICISTS AND ADVERTISERS
GENERAL CONTRACTORS
SUBCONTRACTORS
MATERIALS SUPPLIERS
TRADESMEN AND LABOR UNIONS
INSURERS

the Government
MUNICIPAL AUTHORITIES
COUNTY AUTHORITIES
REGIONAL AUTHORITIES
STATE AUTHORITIES
FEDERAL AUTHORITIES
concerned with
PLANNING AND ZONING
TRANSPORTATION
UTILITIES
EDUCATION AND HEALTH
ENVIRONMENT
HISTORIC PRESERVATION
HOUSING
BUDGET AND TAXATION

the Market
HOMEBUYERS
TENANTS
CORPORATIONS
INSTITUTIONS
CONSUMERS

the Concerned Public
ABUTTERS AND NEIGHBORS
COMMUNITY CITIZENS
TAXPAYERS AND VOTERS
SPECIAL INTEREST GROUPS
ENVIRONMENT
PRESERVATION
SOCIAL WELFARE
ECONOMIC GROWTH
EMPLOYMENT

Nevertheless, the traditionally unique role of architects in society is generally well understood. Architects are artists and technologists whose design talents yield buildings with beauty, stability, utility, sustainability and, it is hoped, cost-effectiveness. The successful architect presumably is hardworking and creative but he or she also is expected to possess extensive engineering knowledge, organizational and managerial ability, political sensitivity, legal acumen, negotiating and marketing skills, economic and accounting know-how, and even social influence and business connections.

Nevertheless, this all sounds generalized, not specialized. If architects are obliged to be so professionally ambidextrous, why are they no longer traditional master builders? The answer is best given by exploring the process through which buildings are created and identifying all the participants in that process. The role of those who practice architecture, the art and science of building design, will then be clear and comprehensible.

How Projects Get Built
Need
The old saw, "necessity is the mother of invention," tells why most building projects get started: recognition of an unmet existing or future need. For projects intended to generate profits for project developers and owners, economists characterize such need as market demand. For most nonprofit, institutional, cultural, and governmental projects, need is attributable to noncommercial human activities, desires, and motivations. In all cases, no project comes to life unless some number of people, perhaps with differing perceptions and goals, agree that there is a real need for whatever is to be built.

In architectural parlance, project needs are usually expressed as a written program or brief. The program document embodies in detail specific project aspirations, goals, and requirements that, if met, will adequately fulfill the identified need. Thus a well-written program generally includes a thorough description of functional, aesthetic, social, cultural, and other objectives; a list of all operational activities to be accommodated; written descriptions and graphic diagrams showing functional and spatial interrelationships; an associated menu of rooms, spaces, and related floor area requirements (measured in square feet or square meters); special technical, furnishing, and equipment requirements; and any other stipulations affecting the project's design.

The process of design can commence once the project need is verified, the program is established, front-end funding has been obtained, and usually after the project site has been selected. The diagram that follows illustrates this building process, although not from the point of view of the architect. Instead, it shows the process from a position of neutrality, giving no special weight to any particular segment. The diagram is somewhat simplified yet comprehensive and it includes steps that may be inapplicable to certain kinds of projects. It also does not show time and activity durations in a proportional way because these vary widely from project to project. The important dimensions of the diagram are the number and interrelationship of activities.

Site

Along with definition of project need comes the site, the place to meet the need. Few projects can be contemplated without a place to put them. Nevertheless, a project may be envisioned before a site is chosen and conversely a site may be in hand before the need to improve it is established. The architect's client undertaking development of a project must eventually have control of the project site prior to construction by either owning it or leasing

The Development Process

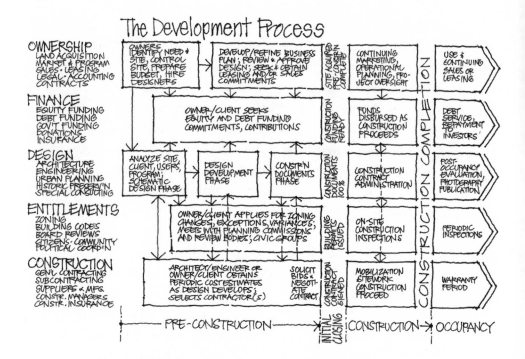

| OWNERSHIP | | | | | |
| LAND ACQUISITION | OWNERS IDENTIFY NEED & SITE, CONTROL SITE, PREPARE BUDGET, HIRE DESIGNERS | DEVELOP/REFINE BUSINESS PLAN; REVIEW & APPROVE DESIGN; SEEK & OBTAIN LEASING AND/OR SALES COMMITMENTS | | CONTINUING MARKETING, OPERATIONAL PLANNING, PROJECT OVERSIGHT | USE & CONTINUING SALES OR LEASING |

it from its owner. Sometimes the architect's client has owned the project site for a long time but frequently the client only has a contract to acquire the site, be it a small lot, an old building to be remodeled, or a parcel of several acres.

The selected site must be surveyed and thoroughly analyzed. Surveys document the site geometry and all existing physical conditions: property boundaries; topography; vegetation; structures; easements; rights-of-way, roads, and utilities on or abutting the site; soil and seismic conditions (rock formations) ascertained through test borings; and hydrological features and conditions. All these data are indispensable for the architect and consulting engineers, who must make crucial design decisions about creative use of the site and location of new construction because many sites encompass areas unsuitable for building.

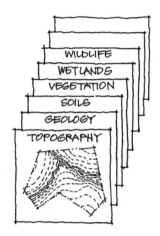

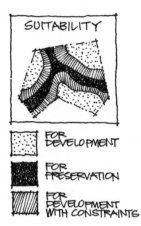

Development Costs and Financing

With project need and site identified, the architect's client must then assemble the resources and expertise required to transform ideas into reality. The essential resource is of course money to pay for all of the costs incurred in project development: site acquisition costs; site surveys and analysis; architectural, engineering, and other design fees; legal and accounting fees; project administration costs; market or needs analysis costs; financing fees and interest on construction loans: advertising and public relations expenses; selling and leasing costs; insurance premiums; costs of obtaining regulatory entitlements—zoning approvals and building permits; and construction costs for all the labor, material, and equipment needed to build. These expenses will be incurred for any project, from building a house to building a new town.

All costs must be covered by project financing, a critical piece of the development puzzle. Without financing, nothing can be built. There are two types of financing: equity funding and debt funding. Equity funding represents at-risk monies that the client invests out-of-pocket or from the pockets of investment partners or development company stockholders. If an income-producing project fails, the at-risk equity invested may never be recovered.

Debt funding comes from institutional lenders—banks, insurance companies, pension funds, credit unions, or real estate investment trusts. The client, as owner and borrower, has a legal obligation to repay the debt, plus interest, within a specified period of time, evidenced by a promissory note and mortgage document. As security for the loan, borrowers typically pledge the real estate—land and improvements—as collateral, and sometimes they may be required to pledge additional assets as loan collateral. The term *mortgage* refers to a loan specifically collateralized by the real estate for which the loan is used. Loans are generally obtained through mortgage brokers or investment bankers, who act as intermediaries between institutional lenders and borrowers. Federal, state, city, and county governments sometimes make loans directly to owners to develop special kinds of projects deemed to be in the public interest, such as low-income housing or job-creating industrial or commercial facilities.

Citizens lend money directly to government agencies by purchasing bonds, which are IOUs issued by state, county, and municipal governments to finance various public projects such as schools, hospitals, highways, or other kinds of infrastructure. Interest on such bonds is usually nontaxable. Ultimately citizens supply the money for all construction, private or governmental, because funds invested in real estate derive mostly from individual savings entrusted to lending institutions. If people did not save, there would be no pool of capital available for debt financing and very little construction would occur. Indeed, 75 percent or more of the costs of privately developed projects are typically paid for with borrowed money. Thus the availability and cost of credit in our economic system is inexorably linked to the building process and directly affects the welfare of architects.

Not all projects depend on the credit market and loans. For noncommercial projects developed by nonprofit institutions, funding comes from endowments, capital campaigns generating pledged donations from contributors, foundation and corporate grants, sale of marketable assets, or government agency budget appropriations. Most museums, performing arts centers, government and other civic buildings, religious structures, and public education facilities are built without mortgage financing.

Virtually all funding of such projects is equity, with little or no debt financing involved.

Design and Design Approvals

As the client wrestles with the intricacies of raising capital for building, the architect begins studying and developing fundamental project design concepts. As a definitive design crystallizes, the architect must increasingly take into account hundreds of potentially conflicting factors: detailed program requirements, site conditions, construction budget constraints, and regulatory criteria—not to mention the aesthetic tastes and idiosyncrasies of architect and client. Zoning ordinances, building codes, and environmental regulations govern building uses and densities, building configuration, engineered systems performance, life-safety provisions, and parking, usually prescribing in what is legal and not legal on the project site. Accordingly as project designs become definitive, they are reviewed by multiple agencies of government, which are solely responsible for granting final approvals and permits to build, commonly referred to as *entitlements.*

Yet citizens or civic groups indirectly may have a say, especially if a project entails public hearings to consider desired zoning or master plan changes or requests for special exceptions or variances. Citizens may oppose new projects and associated changes for a variety of reasons: anxiety in general about change that increases density, land use, or building heights; concerns about traffic congestion and parking; worries about property values and neighborhood character; potential overloading of existing infrastructure, especially public schools; perceived threats to historic resources; and sometimes dislike of proposed architecture. Another reason for opposition, usually unstated, is fear that a proposed project will bring into the community people who are "different," a code word for those of lower socioeconomic status.

Thus building permit department reviews prior to construction are only part of the entitlement process. In many counties and municipalities, there can be several review boards and board hearings, plus endless community meetings. And each reviewing entity may have its own unique schedule, procedures, and design criteria. Usually, seeking entitlements is carried out as a team effort, the team consisting of designers, client, client's attorney, and other expert consultants such as civil and

transportation engineers, economic analysts, and environmental
scientists. Obtaining project entitlements can entail enormous
amounts of time, patience, dialog, persuasion, and sensitivity,
and it can be very costly. Extended delays are not unusual for
controversial projects, many of which rest quietly unrealized in the
file drawers of architectural offices.

Engineers and Other Design Consultants
Engineers play a critical role in the design process. As the architect
develops a building's overall form and three-dimensional
geometry, structural engineers analyze load-bearing portions of

the building—the skeletal frame, footings and foundations, walls, floors, and roofs—specifying components, dimensions, types of material, and connection details for the entire structural system. Likewise mechanical engineers begin designing the building's heating, air-conditioning, ventilating, plumbing, and electrical distribution systems once the architect has provided a preliminary design that approximates the intended, final architectural product.

Based on topographic, boundary, soil, and other surveys provided by licensed land surveyors, the architect prepares a preliminary site plan from which civil engineers can begin site work design: clearing, excavation, and topographic regrading; layout and construction details for roads, bridges, parking lots, walkways, and bike paths; storm water management systems, including drainage inlets and catch basins, manholes, storm water pipes, dams, retention areas, and bioswales; water supply and sanitary sewer systems; and other site utilities or structures. Their engineering work clearly depends on the proposed location, shape, and size of buildings. In the case of residential and industrial subdivisions, sometimes civil engineers, rather than architects or landscape architects, prepare preliminary site plans from which final engineering proceeds.

In addition to engineers, architects and their clients regularly hire landscape architects. Some landscape architects prefer large-scale projects (urban and suburban master plans, highways, residential subdivision layouts, plazas, and parks), their services overlapping with civil engineers and architects. But many practice at the smaller scale of gardens and building landscapes. More horticulturally oriented, the latter concentrate on selection, layout, installation, and maintenance of diverse plant materials (trees, shrubs, and ground covers), along with water features, masonry walls and terraces, fences, walkways, outdoor furnishings, and exterior lighting. The architect may call on the landscape architect to provide a complete landscape plan for a building site or only to advise about basic plant material selection. Very few architects are sufficiently knowledgeable about horticulture and local ecology to assume this responsibility, although they usually make basic decisions about overall site layout.

Other specialized expertise frequently supplements the usual structural, mechanical, electrical, civil engineering, and landscape architecture services. Projects such as theaters, schools, hotels, hospitals, embassies, museums, airports, parking garages, and occasionally houses can pose unique technical challenges. Acoustical engineers, for example, deal with control of sound, its quality, and its transmission, reflection, and absorption. Lighting consultants are concerned with illuminating interior and exterior environments, using daylight and electric lighting. They focus on the aesthetic quality, intensity, deployment, and distribution of ambient as well as task lighting. There are consultants for theaters, kitchens, health-care facilities, security, information technology, signage and graphics, building code interpretation, and life-safety issues. Sustainability and environmental consultants help project design teams in making buildings greener and more energy efficient and also in obtaining sustainability certifications. Whatever the project, it is always the architect's responsibility to coordinate and be conversant with the work of these disparate design consultants.

Finally comes the interior designer or decorator, with whom potential design conflict frequently exists from the architect's point of view. Hardly an architect breathes who does not consider himself or herself to be a qualified interior designer (some architects refer to interior *desecrators*). It is a lopsided struggle because architects can do interiors but interior designers cannot do architecture. This struggle has further played out in a territorial dispute between architects and interior designers, generally

considered unqualified to do work affecting the structural system or other building systems. Modifying architecture naturally was deemed the sole design province of licensed architects, who feared that interior designers, if licensed, might be able to offer services that only architects could offer legally. In any case, usually the client, not the architect, retains interior designers to specify interior cosmetic finishes and furnishings, without changing the architecture. What can make life difficult is a lack of clarity as to where architectural design stops and interior design begins. Nevertheless, fruitful collaborations occur.

In custom residential and commercial projects such as office buildings and hotels, owners frequently hire interior designers to help select furniture and upholstery, carpeting, paint colors, wall coverings, window treatments, lamps, decorative accessories, and occasionally artwork. Consequently the architect's work stops at shaping the building and spaces within to contain and serve as background for the interior designer's layers of decor. Similar to any other consultant group, there are talented and less talented interior designers, some of whom are also architects. For the building architect, the best tactic is to design interior spaces that are visually compelling and resistant to decorative excess and then to persuade the client to consider the interiors an integral part of the architecture.

You might now be wondering about the legal and financial relationships between expert consultants and the architect and other participants in the building process. Most expert participants operate as independent consultants, either retained by the architect as subcontractors or hired directly by the client. Consultants hired by the architect are responsible to and compensated by the architect. This relationship gives the architect more control over the actions and decisions of consultants because the consultants must rely on the architect not only for direction but also for payment of their fees, clearly giving the architect economic leverage.

However, the architect assumes legal and financial responsibility for the work performed by such consultants because, from the client's point of view, the architect is furnishing the services, there being no direct relationship between the client and the consultants. Further the architect, not the client, is obligated to pay for the consultant's services, and unless the consultant agrees otherwise, the architect must compensate the consultant even if the client fails to compensate the architect. Prudent architects usually insist that payment by the architect to the consultant be contingent on payment by the client to the architect.

When consultants work directly for the client, the architect may lose some control over what the consultant does, but only if such control is voluntarily relinquished. If the architect establishes and maintains an effective working relationship among all parties, this form of contractual relationship can be advantageous to everyone. The architect is better off because he or she does not assume the responsibility, legally or financially, for the work of other experts, work that the architect is usually not qualified to perform. And the consultants' fees are paid directly by the client without going through the architect. Nevertheless, under either arrangement, it is the architect's job to coordinate all design services, a task greatly facilitated and made more reliable through the use of advanced design methodologies such as building information modeling.

Some design firms combine architectural and engineering (A/E) services under one organizational umbrella. Their staffs may include not only architects but also landscape architects, urban planners, interior designers, structural engineers, mechanical and electrical engineers, civil engineers, and construction cost estimators. These groups of in-house experts play their respective roles to some extent as if they were independent professional consultants. Because they all work for one firm, project coordination and communication are facilitated, although occasionally internal disputes and competition for control arise. Nevertheless, to clients, it offers one-stop shopping for building design services. Some of these firms even offer construction management, market analysis, and real estate project feasibility services along with comprehensive A/E design services. The only thing they do not offer the client is financing. Partly because of their size and multidisciplinary service approach, the United States' largest A/E firms, although a small percentage of the nation's architectural firms, design a large percentage of the nation's construction.

One other kind of consultant has come into being in recent decades, thanks to the Internet and enhanced telecommunication capabilities: geographically remote architectural service firms that provide cost-effective and time-saving production services. Firms in China, Southeast Asia, India, North America, and elsewhere can create diverse design products—perspective renderings, videos, construction drawings, digital and analog models—more cheaply and often faster than undertaking the work locally or in-house in the United States. An architectural firm in Boston, New York, Washington, Chicago, Los Angeles, or Seattle, especially if very busy, can send digital data files to distant locations anywhere on the planet. When outsourced work is completed, remote service providers can instantly send back completed drawings in digital form to be immediately reviewed, plotted, and presented. Of course, the remote service provider may not do everything perfectly but that occurrence is diminishing as technologies improve.

Brokers

Several types of brokers—go-between agents who help buyers find sellers or, more usually, sellers find buyers—may be involved in project development. Mortgage loan brokers help borrowers find lenders. Real estate brokers help property owners sell property or assist developers find and acquire property for development. Other real estate specialists concentrate on leasing, putting together landlords (lessors) and tenants (lessees), and some assist owners of leased property in managing such property.

All brokers and property managers earn fees for their services, usually a percentage of the selling price or rents received. Architects are frequently surprised and chagrined by brokers' fees, which for a given project can exceed architects' fees for what appears to be significantly less work, less difficult work, and work entailing much less financial risk. This differential reflects the relative market value our economic system places on each service, not necessarily the cost or uniqueness of the service.

Attorneys

Some projects are legally complex because of ownership structure, financing, or regulatory complexities. From the client's viewpoint, the array of legal relationships defined by written or verbal contracts complicates the development process but is unavoidable and at times indispensable. Attorneys draft contracts and provide ongoing legal advice necessary to cope with business and legal complexities, especially related to taxes, throughout each step of project development. Some attorneys are very effective, serving as deal makers, whereas others can impede progress, turning into deal breakers. Inevitably architects have to interact with somebody's lawyer, if not their own.

Attorneys also frequently play a major role in the entitlement process, when project implementation requires petitioning for a zoning change, special exception, or variance. They may formulate the entitlement process strategy and manage preparation of special studies and testimony for public hearings conducted by zoning and planning commissions, city and county councils, and official review boards. To cultivate favorable opinions and positive action by elected and appointed public officials, many attorneys also engage in behind-the-scenes and presumably legal lobbying, which can be quite effective in obtaining approvals.

Construction Contractors and Managers

Of all the relationships and contracts, none is as critical to successful project realization as those between owner and general contractor. Construction is the largest single development expense. Direct construction costs, along with land costs and loan interest, can account for as much as 90 percent of total development expenses, with the balance composed of fees, taxes, insurance, marketing, and administrative overhead.

The role of the construction contractor is paramount, not only because this is the most costly contract but also because the efficacy and quality of construction have great impact on the economic, technical, and aesthetic outcome of the project. Architects are very concerned with construction and those who perform it because the realization of their design and their client's satisfaction depend substantially on how well builders build.

Except for very small, simple projects, such as enclosing a screen porch or building a patio, several construction firms, in addition to the general contractor, are required to carry out the work. Specialization has been taken to its limit in the construction industry. Virtually no general contractor can perform all of the tasks required to build a project, even a modest one. Thus general contractors depend on a collection of independent subcontractors to perform specific pieces or phases of the construction work. They further depend on dozens of separate suppliers to furnish hundreds of different materials and pieces of equipment.

For example, just to build a house, although a general contracting firm would probably have its own supervisory, carpentry, and unskilled labor force, it nevertheless would depend on the following subcontractors, labor trade specialties, and suppliers to fully execute the construction contract:

Site clearing and excavation
Site utilities
Masonry
Concrete
Plumbing
Heating, ventilating, and air-conditioning
Electrical
Lumber and millwork
Structural steel
Miscellaneous metals
Doors and windows
Glass and glazing

Roofing
Lighting fixtures
Drywall and plaster
Painting
Tile work
Flooring
Paving
Landscaping

For larger, more complex structures such as office buildings, schools, museums, art centers, hospitals, or transportation terminals, the list would expand to include the following:

Foundation sheeting and shoring
Steel mills, shop fabricators, and erectors
Concrete precasters
Glazed curtain walls and storefronts
Elevators and escalators
Specialty suppliers (security systems, audiovisual equipment, signage, etc.)

General contracting is a kind of brokering operation. A contractor studies the architects' and engineers' project drawings and specifications; distributes them as digital files or hard copies to prospective subcontractors and suppliers, who submit cost estimates and bids for furnishing and installing everything within their respective work scope; and then, after totaling all labor and material costs, adds a fee to cover the general contractor's overhead and profit. This produces a lump sum amount representing the direct cost of project construction.

In some projects the contractor is selected during the early design phases, working closely with the architect and client to monitor probable construction costs, and a final construction

contract is negotiated as detailed drawings are completed.
This process can save time and potentially money because the
contractor participates in making cost-affecting design decisions.
Many times, however, it is in the client's interest to solicit
competitive bids from several general contractors. Although this
process takes more time than the negotiated contract approach,
it can yield the lowest price if the construction market is soft
and contractors are reasonably competitive and anxious to bid.
Prudent owners and architects usually award the contract to the
lowest bidder who is financially and technically qualified.

No matter which contractor selection method is employed,
the initial lump sum construction cost often exceeds the project
construction budget. Because most project budgets are relatively
inflexible, architects, clients, and contractors undertake value
engineering (VE), a euphemism for prudent, sensitive cost
cutting. VE methodology entails combing through drawings and
specifications to scrutinize in detail all aspects of a building's
design. The VE team searches for anything and everything that
can be acceptably eliminated, changed, or reduced in quantity and
quality to save money and meet the budget, yet without unduly
compromising the project's overall quality and value—thus the
term *value engineering*. VE can affect all of a building's systems
and materials but it doesn't necessarily affect a building's overall
aesthetic form. However, if the cost overage is sizable enough, the
building as a whole may require major surgery.

Once a contract is signed, the general contractor orders and
purchases the needed materials, executes subcontracts, organizes
and coordinates suppliers and subcontractors, and, in effect, sells
the project to the owner at a marked-up price. Construction is
supposed to be carried out in strict accordance with the architect's
plans as approved by the client and by government agencies and

project lenders. However, general contractors, similar to every subcontractor and supplier, have one primary business motive: to make a profit. Therefore their goal is to buy low and sell high, putting them into periodic conflict with the architect and owner, whose objective is to get the most for the money from the contractor. This is why project owners, architects, and contractors are usually separate entities linked together only by contractual agreements, with the architect being primarily responsible for protecting the client's interest and simultaneously being fair to the contractor. In fact during construction, the architect has an obligation to resolve disputes objectively between owner and contractor, even if it means siding with the contractor.

Occasionally an owner will decide to hire a construction manager (CM) instead of a general contractor. A CM acts as a consultant, performing essentially the same bidding, supervisory, and coordination functions as a general contractor but usually without a legal obligation to deliver the project pursuant to a single contract for a single, lump-sum price. The CM, acting as an agent, negotiates with all the subcontractors and suppliers on behalf of the owner, who consequently signs dozens of separate contracts. This relationship does not always prove favorable for either the owner or the architect. With so many contracts to administer, the management and accounting burden is much greater and the architect is often forced to spend excessive amounts of time on coordination and documentation during construction. Further, because there is no general contractor with overall project responsibility, it is easier for items to fall through the cracks of responsibility between subcontractors.

Role-Playing

Different roles in the building process may be played by a single individual or entity. For example, an architect's client may act as general contractor. Developers who build housing or commercial projects may have their own construction contracting department, design department, financing brokerage, real estate brokerage, property management department, or accounting and legal staffs under one corporate roof. Other developers are literally one-person operations, requiring only up-to-date telecommunication and digital devices; a long list of loyal subcontractors, suppliers, and consultants; and perhaps minimal working capital but lots of borrowing potential.

Similarly architects may step out of their design role by buying
property, raising money, constructing or renovating buildings, and
then selling or leasing them for a profit (or loss). Again, similar
to a corporate entrepreneur, the architect can assume the roles of
developer and borrower, contractor, marketer, and investor, as well
as designer. Nevertheless, each separate role must be played. Each
demands certain, distinguishable know-how and action. And each
may draw on widely divergent talents or capabilities in the person
assuming the roles. Also conflicts of interest can arise in playing
multiple roles, such as when architects act as general contractors
for their clients—this was once considered unethical by the
AIA. Today full disclosure of financial interests by the architect
is presumed to mitigate conflicts of interest and satisfy ethical
concerns.

Project construction cannot begin until all of the proverbial ducks are in a row. Adequate funds must be ready to flow; property control or ownership must be finalized; architectural and engineering design documents must be completed and approved by all authorities, with building permits in hand; construction contracts must be negotiated and signed; insurance must be in force; preleasing or presales conditions imposed by lenders must be met; and other minor but essential tasks must be finished. Unless all preconstruction necessities are checked off, construction cannot proceed. It is not uncommon to reach the point of commencing construction only to be stopped, sometimes indefinitely, because one of these contingent necessities remains unsatisfied. Architects have drawings in filing cabinet drawers and digital data storage containing completely documented projects that remain unbuilt because financing fell through, zoning changes were denied, title to the property became clouded, or citizen-sponsored lawsuits tied up the developer for years beyond the time when the project was economically feasible.

The construction period can last for months or years, depending on project size and complexity. House remodelings are notorious for taking as long to complete as constructing a new home or office building. Delays can occur because of labor strikes, material and labor shortages, adverse weather, unforeseen subsoil conditions, errors or changes in design, lack of funds, or poor construction planning. Some projects, such as hospitals, college campuses, and transportation facilities, seem to be under construction forever. During construction, the architect's role shifts from design to design clarification and modification, review and approval of shop drawings, periodic observation of the contractor's work and work progress, attending construction site meetings, occasional meetings with inspectors having jurisdiction over the project, and regular interaction with the client.

Users and the Community

End users rarely have contractual relationships with the major participants in the development process but users are virtual clients for the architect. They are the ultimate consumers of architecture, the community of people who finally see, admire (or dislike), touch, occupy, live in, and move around or through the finished product. Included are neighbors as well as people who visit, shop, work, or reside in buildings. They are the collective constituency for those who design and build. Building codes and zoning regulations protect them, not the architect, owner, contractor, or lenders.

Many users and community citizens care a lot about architecture, about how it looks, functions, and fits in. Abutting property owners are especially concerned about the design of buildings to be constructed next to or near their building. They understandably worry about how new architecture might

adversely affect views, privacy, access to sunlight, and
microclimate, as well as local traffic and parking. Some will fret
about economic impact and a few about aesthetic style. These
concerns go beyond just complying with zoning and building code
regulations, seen by citizens as minimum requirements that must
be met and for which designers therefore get little credit.

Consequently, responsible architects always take into account
the virtual, nonpaying clients sitting invisibly at the conference
table whose interests need to be represented and advocated.
Neglected users, slighted community citizens, or upset neighbors
may seek recourse as if there had been a contract. They can
organize protests, generate negative publicity, withhold rent, even
file lawsuits that blame the architect as well as the owner and
contractor. Do not forget the end user and the general public.
It may even be wise at times to include representative users and
concerned neighbors at the design conference table.

9 How Architects Work

The AIA standardized agreement between an owner and an architect describes the architect's services and responsibilities using well-chosen words and ordering of paragraphs. Ideally a description of services should tell us what we want to know about the work architects do. In this, the AIA document falls short but it does provide an outline we can fruitfully flesh out.

Basic architectural services for a project consist of five phases. The architect's work products—the deliverables—are indicated for each phase. Each phase may seem distinct but in practice phases overlap, especially the three design phases.

Phase 1   Schematic design (SD): Analysis of owner's program, site and site context, and budget; functional relationship diagrams; initial gestural sketches and design ideas; conceptual site plans, massing studies, preliminary floor plans and sections, elevations, and perspective sketches; conceptual physical and digital study models; outline specifications and preliminary estimate of probable construction cost

Phase 2   Design development (DD): Further development of schematic design; definitively establishing project size, geometry, and expressive architectural character; honing in on key dimensions, primary technical systems, and materials; more precisely delineated site plans, floor plans, sections, and elevations; constructed perspectives; more exact, larger scale physical and digital study models; updated outline specifications and estimate of probable construction cost

Typically, to explain project goals and scope, clients present SD or DD documentation prepared by the architect when submitting a proposal and application for financing or when petitioning governmental authorities for zoning changes, variances, or special exceptions. Likewise, SD or DD documents often are shown by clients to citizen groups and journalists interested in or concerned about the proposed project.

Phase 3   Construction documents (CDs): Finalized working drawings and specifications—modeled and documented digitally— depicting the entire, fully engineered project; exact building geometry, dimensions, all materials and finishes, all essential construction assembly details, and necessary construction notes needed to obtain construction bids and for review by government agencies prior to issuing building permits

Phase 4   Bidding and negotiation: During and after completion of construction documents, assisting the owner or client in finding, screening, and selecting qualified general contractors interested in bidding; answering contractor inquiries during estimating and bidding; reviewing construction bids; value engineering and modification of drawings and specifications to meet cost goals; helping negotiate final construction prices and terms prior to awarding contracts

Phase 5   Construction administration (CA): Representing and assisting the client in administering the construction contract, which includes responding to contractors' requests for information (RFIs); issuing approved design change orders; checking shop drawings prepared by fabricators; selecting colors or other previously unspecified items; periodic construction site visits to review the contractor's work; preparing site visit reports and completion of "punch lists"; reviewing and certifying contractor's requests for payment; mediating disputes between contractor and owner

Beyond these five phases, the AIA contract goes on to describe additional services, usually excluded from basic services, which may be provided if the client wishes and the architect agrees. Additional services can include economic feasibility studies, detailed cost estimates, interior design (furniture and furnishings), measuring and documenting existing structures to prepare as-built drawings, obtaining LEED (Leadership in Energy and Environmental Design) or other sustainability certifications, and special design or engineering consultation usually beyond the scope of basic architectural design work.

This summary of services is more or less chronological, proceeding from initial exploration of architectural ideas, to exact delineation of what is to be built, and finally to execution of the project. This is what most practicing architects do and generally how they do it. But this definition of services paints a broad-brush picture and does not disclose in detail what actually goes on in an architect's office from hour to hour or even on a daily, weekly, or continuing basis. Nor does it address how architectural offices are structured and managed.

To understand the nature of architectural practice, consider the specific activities common to all architectural organizations, small or large, private or governmental, domestic or foreign. The following chart shows functions and tasks characterizing architectural practice. To fully convey the significance of this chart, activity classifications need a bit of explanation.

Manual and Digital Drawing

Drawing refers to graphic representation of designs produced either by drawing on paper by hand or by drawing digitally on a screen or tablet using a mouse-directed cursor or a stylus. Different types of architectural drawings are particular to each phase of service.

DAY-TO-DAY TASKS in ARCHITECTURAL PRACTICE — PRIMARY FUNCTIONS	AMOUNT OF TIME REQUIRED TYPICALLY FOR EACH TASK				
	DRAWING	WRITING	READING RESEARCH	MEETING TALKING	CALCULATING
RUNNING the OFFICE					
CLIENT RELATIONS	almost none	large amount	fair amount	large amount	almost none
MARKETING	small amount	large amount	fair amount	large amount	almost none
FIRM MANAGEMENT	almost none	small amount	small amount	fair amount	fair amount
DESIGNING PROJECTS					
PROJECT MANAGEMENT	almost none	fair amount	fair amount	fair amount	fair amount
SCHEMATIC DESIGN	fair amount	small amount	fair amount	small amount	fair amount
DESIGN DEVELOPMENT	large amount	small amount	fair amount	small amount	fair amount
CONSTRUCTION DRAWINGS	large amount	small amount	fair amount	small amount	fair amount
SPECIFICATIONS	almost none	large amount	fair amount	small amount	small amount
CONSULTANT COORDINATION	almost none	small amount	almost none	fair amount	almost none
COST ANALYSIS	almost none	almost none	fair amount	small amount	large amount
CLIENT PRESENTATIONS	fair amount	small amount	almost none	fair amount	small amount
GOVERNMENT REVIEWS	small amount	small amount	small amount	fair amount	small amount
CONSTRUCTING PROJECTS					
BIDDING & NEGOTIATION	small amount	almost none	small amount	large amount	large amount
CONTRACT ADMIN' (OFFICE)	small amount	fair amount	fair amount	large amount	large amount
CONTRACT ADMIN' (FIELD)	almost none	small amount	almost none	large amount	small amount

Legend: • ALMOST NONE ▪ SMALL AMOUNT ▬ FAIR AMOUNT ▬▬ LARGE AMOUNT

During schematic design phases, conceptual drawings done by freehand are sketchy, quick, diagrammatic, at times abstract and impressionistic. Soft pencils, marking pens, charcoal, chalk, or colored pencils are used freely, along with inexpensive rolls of thin yellow or white tracing paper, which allows overlays of previous drawings to be made readily.

Among the designer's primary tools at this point is the architectural scale for measuring dimensions. If only three things were available with which to design a work of architecture, they would be pencil, paper, and scale. Even when exploring still unformed concepts, good designers make scaled sketches, whether drawn by hand or digitally. To further explore design concepts, architects also make simple, small-scale study models quickly crafted using cardboard, wood, plastic foam, or clay. Tiny, abstract models, perhaps only inches high, can effectively capture and convey an overarching project idea.

After schematic design is completed and approved by the client, architects continue to refine their design and prepare design development models and drawings, more precise and larger in scale than schematic drawings. But almost all DD models and drawings are produced digitally. Digital study models take time to construct, but once constructed they can be viewed, studied, manipulated, and edited endlessly. When the design crystallizes, the digital model of the definitive design forms the basis for the evolving BIM.

Many types of drawings can be generated from the digital model. They can be plotted and rendered with tones, textures, shade and shadow, color, and a variety of line weights. Artfully composed perspectives, axonometrics, and orthographic views— plans, sections, and elevations—can be projected on a screen or printed for presentation at reviews and meetings or for publication. These drawings convey to nonarchitects the essential imagery of a design and are intended to evoke positive feelings, to entice and persuade. Often firms make presentation drawings during subsequent phases or even after projects are built, if they were not required prior to the construction drawings phase. Much time spent producing drawings in architects' offices is consumed by creation of detailed construction documents derived from the

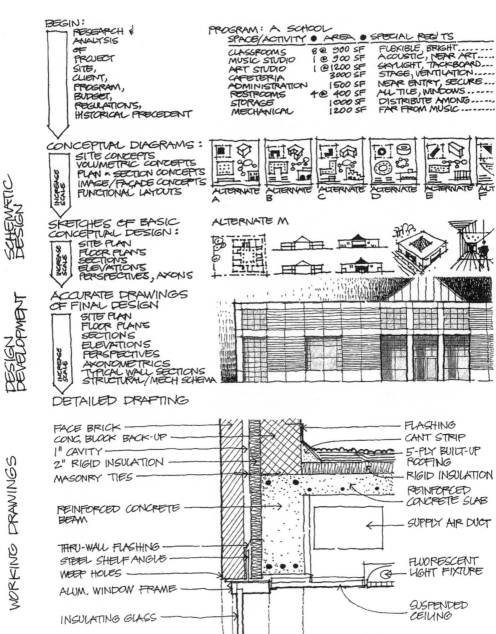

BEGIN:
RESEARCH &
ANALYSIS
OF
PROJECT
SITE,
CLIENT,
PROGRAM,
BUDGET,
REGULATIONS,
HISTORICAL PRECEDENT

PROGRAM: A SCHOOL

SPACE/ACTIVITY ●	AREA ●	SPECIAL REQ'TS
CLASSROOMS	8 @ 900 SF	FLEXIBLE, BRIGHT.........
MUSIC STUDIO	1 @ 900 SF	ACOUSTIC, NEAR ART.....
ART STUDIO	1 @ 1200 SF	SKYLIGHT, TACKBOARD....
CAFETERIA	3000 SF	STAGE, VENTILATION.......
ADMINISTRATION	1500 SF	NEAR ENTRY, SECURE ...
RESTROOMS	4 @ 400 SF	ALL TILE, WINDOWS .....
STORAGE	1000 SF	DISTRIBUTE AMONG......
MECHANICAL	1200 SF	FAR FROM MUSIC..........

SCHEMATIC DESIGN

CONCEPTUAL DIAGRAMS:
SITE CONCEPTS
VOLUMETRIC CONCEPTS
PLAN ≈ SECTION CONCEPTS
IMAGE/FAÇADE CONCEPTS
FUNCTIONAL LAYOUTS

INCREASE SCALE

ALTERNATE A   ALTERNATE B   ALTERNATE C   ALTERNATE D   ALTERNATE E   ALT F

SKETCHES OF BASIC
CONCEPTUAL DESIGN:
SITE PLAN
FLOOR PLANS
SECTIONS
ELEVATIONS
PERSPECTIVES, AXONS

INCREASE SCALE

ALTERNATE M

DESIGN DEVELOPMENT

ACCURATE DRAWINGS
OF FINAL DESIGN
SITE PLAN
FLOOR PLANS
SECTIONS
ELEVATIONS
PERSPECTIVES
AXONOMETRICS
TYPICAL WALL SECTIONS
STRUCTURAL/MECH SCHEMA

INCREASE SCALE

DETAILED DRAFTING

WORKING DRAWINGS

FACE BRICK
CONC. BLOCK BACK-UP
1" CAVITY
2" RIGID INSULATION
MASONRY TIES

REINFORCED CONCRETE
BEAM

THRU-WALL FLASHING
STEEL SHELF ANGLE
WEEP HOLES
ALUM. WINDOW FRAME

INSULATING GLASS

FLASHING
CANT STRIP
5-PLY BUILT-UP
ROOFING
RIGID INSULATION
REINFORCED
CONCRETE SLAB

SUPPLY AIR DUCT

FLUORESCENT
LIGHT FIXTURE

SUSPENDED
CEILING

digital model of the project. Creating construction document data files is the most labor-intensive and sometimes tedious phase of the architect's work. It necessitates extensive coordination within the architect's office, a process facilitated by database management programs. Only two or three architects are needed to take the design lead and work on the project during the conceptual design phase. But several architectural staff members may spend many months in front of their computers completing the digital model and all the detailed working drawings for building permits, bidding, and construction. In a set of printed construction drawings, there can be ten or fifteen sheets for very small projects and scores of sheets for large projects, plus all the engineering and other technical drawings, which can exceed the number of architectural drawings.

The following menu of drawing types and drawing content typifies a set of architectural working drawings describing fully the design of a building.

Prefatory sheets   Index of drawings; site location; applicable zoning regulations; building code standards; bidding instructions; general notes to contractors and subcontractors; list of abbreviations; graphic legend showing materials

Site plans   Location and footprints of buildings and other structures (e.g., retaining walls, bridges); topography and grading; erosion control; below-grade and above-grade utilities; storm water management systems; paving; landscaping

Building floor plans   Location, configuration, identification, horizontal dimensions, and material indications at all levels for spaces, rooms, and corridors; exterior and interior walls and partitions; columns; windows, doors, and other openings in walls; built-in cabinetry, equipment, and appliances

Building sections   Vertical cuts through the building at appropriate places showing roof and floor structures, including structural elements beyond cutting plane; interior spaces, rooms, and corridors; exterior and interior walls and partitions; doors, windows, and other openings in walls and partitions; suspended ceilings; floor-level elevations relative to exterior grade elevations; and all necessary vertical dimensions

Exterior elevations   Orthogonal views of all sides of the building exterior showing overall building shape and massing; location, configuration, and visible details of doors, windows, and other openings; facade decorative elements; visible assembly joints; material types, patterns, and colors

Interior elevations   Orthogonal views showing detailed composition of visible walls, partitions, or other surfaces within interior spaces and rooms, such as entrance lobbies, baths, kitchens, libraries, classrooms, auditoriums, galleries, theaters, ballrooms, and concert halls

Reflected ceiling plans   Composition of ceilings and ceiling surfaces, viewed as if looking at a mirror on the floor, to show acoustic ceiling tile grid patterns or other ceiling finish patterns and materials; exposed structural elements; skylights; catwalks; electric light fixtures; HVAC registers and ductwork; layout of exposed pipes; and sprinkler heads

Details   Large-scale, dimensioned plans, sections, and elevations showing all essential architectural details and component assembly conditions, such as how a window fits into a wall or a railing attaches to a floor (structural, mechanical, and electrical engineering details are shown on drawings prepared by consulting engineers); stairs and stair enclosures; elevator and escalator treatment; interior cabinetry and millwork; built-in exterior and interior ornamentation; and other architectural components

Schedules   Tabular schedules showing the type, size, location, quantity, and other key attributes of doors and windows; rough and finish hardware (e.g., locksets and hinges for doors); interior materials and finishes for walls, ceilings, and floors; appliances; light fixtures; plumbing fixtures; and miscellaneous specialty items

Architectural drawings in a full set of construction documents are complemented by drawings prepared by engineers showing the complete design of all site work; complete design of a building's structural, mechanical, plumbing, and electrical systems; and complete design of all other specialized systems within the building. Using the digital model of the project, architects must constantly check their own work as well as that of others to ascertain that all building components are shown, correctly specified, and dimensioned consistently. This ensures that no essential item is omitted and that components will fit together at the construction site as they appear to fit together in the digital model. Use by all parties of a single digital model and common design database— BIM—have made coordination easier and more reliable.

Working drawings are typically covered with notes that are an integral part of building design drawings, explaining and specifying what cannot be shown graphically. They identify components and materials or instruct contractors to perform specific work in accordance with the notation or with a referenced construction standard. For example, one note might identify a material as *concrete,* whereas another might stipulate how each batch of concrete is to be tested before placement. Often such notes are contained in specifications written and printed separately from the drawings.

The need to write titles and notes on drawings drafted by hand once motivated architects to master the art of manual lettering. Perfected by hours of practice drawing lettering guidelines and struggling to make a well-shaped *S, B, R,* or *M,* the hand printing of an architect is often recognizable. But the need for this skill has disappeared because architects now type drawing titles and notes on computer keyboards.

Firms tend to optimize productivity by employing people who work fast and effectively in at least one area of activity. Because the greatest percentage of a firm's staff time and labor goes into production of complex digital building models and construction documents, firms prefer to hire architects who have CAD mastery and also are knowledgeable about construction. One or two senior design partners, responsible for generating fundamental design concepts, can keep scores of junior partners, associates, and staff architects busy at workstations in front of computer screens. Therefore, young architects hired by any but the smallest architectural firms are likely to work less on conceptual design and more on design development and construction documents. Although it is essential to spend several years early in your career learning the art and craft of detailed design for construction, it may not be your life's ambition.

However, sometimes young architects with exceptional design and graphic talent are hired expressly to be conceptual designers. Concentrating on schematic design and design development phases of project work, they may have little opportunity to learn how to produce technically detailed construction drawings and specifications. If an intern has the ability to make beautiful sketches and presentation drawings, firms are tempted to keep the intern doing what he or she does best. Still other young architects discover that they have personal skills and inclinations that make them practical "field" types, enabling them to be very effective in handling construction contractors and job-site problems. Such architects may rarely produce drawings.

Physical Models Built Manually or Digitally

Few competent architects design a project of any size or consequence without using scale models, especially physical models for studying a design during schematic and design development phases. Physical models greatly help an architect visualize a form and make design choices. Such models also greatly help clients, some of whom have difficulty interpreting drawings, visualize and understand a design. As architecture students know, making analog models is very time and labor intensive, depending on the complexity of the project and size of the model. Anyone who enjoys using his or her hands, who derives pleasure from crafting something carefully and beautifully, will be a good physical model maker. No matter how fast or careful, model builders must have patience, steady eyes and hands, a concern for edges and joints, strong glue, and a sharp knife.

Sophisticated, computer-controlled machines have made physical model making significantly easier and less time-consuming. Once a design is delineated digitally, these robotic machines can analyze and produce relatively complex models. Laser-cutters and 3-D printers create thin slices of material, layer by layer, which are then laminated together to produce an intricate form. Milling machines can cut into and carve solid blocks of materials to shape disparate elements of a larger model, subsequently assembled using the separately milled elements.

Some firms have their own model shop and use young, in-house architects or professional model makers to construct physical models for study purposes and for public presentation. But many architecture firms contract with specialized model-making

companies that are in the business of producing large-scale models for architects, in particular detailed presentation models. Such models, typically showing a project's final design, are usually beautifully crafted and finished, often with extensive detail and internal lighting. Some models can be partially disassembled or have removable sections allowing views of the model's interior.

Architects also build virtual models digitally that eliminate the need for manual craftsmanship. Building a computer model can take less time than crafting a real, three-dimensional model, although a digital model displayed two-dimensionally on a screen can never match the tactile qualities of a physical model constructed of real materials. Nevertheless, computer models are extraordinarily useful. Sophisticated modeling programs allow generation of unlimited, mathematically correct perspective views from any viewpoint. By assigning specific attributes to each element and visible surface of a digital model, unlimited combinations of colors, patterns, textures, and materials, including glass, can be represented, thereby yielding realistic images of the design. Designs can be studied under diverse exterior daylight conditions depending on sun position, time of day, and season of the year. Electric lighting options can be tested to see the effects of various lighting strategies. Lighting visualization programs also show reflections, shading, and shadows. Finally, using photographs, the architect can show and manipulate the actual project context, its "entourage," in the digital model. The designer can place the project in its real or in an imagined setting, adding or subtracting other buildings, landscaping, people, furniture, or automobiles.

Thanks to huge CAD memory capacity and ultra-high-speed computer processors, designers can animate digital models and create videos that simulate the experience of walking around, flying through, or flying over a project and its surroundings. You can visit the project on foot, in a wheelchair, on a bicycle, in a car, or in a plane flying overhead, traveling along any path and at any speed. Audio can be added. Zooming functions allow you to move close in or far away as perspectives change. And you can travel digitally not only through or over single buildings but also complexes of buildings, natural and constructed landscapes, neighborhoods, towns, or cities.

Writing

As you can see from the chart, a number of functions in architectural practice entail little or no drawing. However, virtually all functions require some writing, reading, and talking—basic verbal skills critical to practicing architecture. To the surprise of many graduate architects newly employed in architectural offices, much time is spent writing countless e-mails, memoranda, and letters to clients, engineers, product manufacturers, and government agencies. Architects write notes on sketches about their design ideas and specifications to accompany construction drawings. Architects with management responsibility write proposals, contracts, certifications, promotional documents, and reference letters. And firms sometimes prepare and issue lengthy reports.

Specifications can be the bulkiest written output of an architectural practice. To beginning architects, a set of construction specifications can appear intimidating, not only because of their quantity but also because of the esoteric nature of many of the items called for. Much of the jargon and legalese in specifications is probably unnecessary, and certainly much of it is standardized boilerplate language that could be incorporated by reference to widely accepted standards of construction practice. In fact, most sets of specifications are merely rewrites of previously used sets, edited to fit the project at hand. Most firms use and edit standardized, proprietary specifications such as MasterSpec, which greatly facilitates specification preparation.

Specifications designate all the materials, equipment, furnishings, and other products to be incorporated in a building, identifying their type, manufacturer, size, and performance characteristics. For example, specs describe the type of lumber or steel to be used in framing the structure of a building, the type of concrete for foundations, or the type of brick for exterior walls. Architects write specifications that relate to primary building trades and product categories, such as masonry, metals, glass, carpentry, and finishes. Engineers prepare specs related to structural and mechanical systems.

For each project, the architects responsible for writing specifications must delete inapplicable or obsolete specification items from the reference set, modify undeleted items to conform to the new design, and add new specification items not already contained in the reference set that are necessary for the new design. One of the challenges in preparing specifications is knowing how much detail to include because specifying too much or too little can get architects into trouble. Too much can drive costs up needlessly; too little can compromise quality or create ambiguities and disputes. Only experience writing specifications and administering construction can give you the knowledge needed for meeting this challenge.

Architectural liability for professional negligence arises mostly when projects are built but it also can result from misunderstandings during design. Therefore litigation-conscious architects create written or digital "paper trails" documenting a project's history of communication and decision-making. Documentation includes minutes of meetings, telephone notes, e-mails, and memos confirming verbal agreements and approvals and letters of transmittal, among others. Thorough documenters are hard to find because most practicing architects would rather draw and design than write. Thus, reasonably articulate, meticulous, slightly compulsive writers are invaluable.

A thorough paper trail can protect and exculpate the architect when things go wrong. All correspondence, field reports, RFI responses, change orders, and payment certifications must always be written with an eye on the potential for litigation. Obviously it is in the architect's interest to cast favorable light on his or her actions and never to admit making an error, either verbally or in writing. Again, similar to writing specifications, creating a proper paper trail is a matter of knowing what to include and what to exclude.

In many ways the most challenging and critical writing tasks for practicing architects relate not to project documentation but rather to marketing, client contact, and public relations. Principals of firms must spend substantial amounts of time writing prose—for proposals, websites, and portfolios showing their work or for explaining and justifying their design philosophy. Unlike much technical writing, such prose must be pithy but sometimes discursive and always rhetorically fine-tuned. Writing text for proposals is especially important; even the wording of a simple but crucial phrase can either persuade or dissuade a prospective client.

Reading and Researching

Architects read a lot of incoming e-mail, web pages, blogs, hard-copy memos, magazines, and professional journals, similar to everyone else in business. They also read and analyze contracts, research reports, reference books, zoning and building codes, product catalogs, and specifications, often online. And they must read fairly carefully, with total comprehension. Failing to do so can lead to legal, financial, and professional missteps. Moreover, architects read regularly as part of their continuing self-education and sometimes to earn continuing education credits. Most want to know what is happening in the profession, to keep abreast of new projects, new ideas, new trends, new laws and regulations, and new construction products. And to be informed and active citizens of their community, they must pay attention to local news media, not only to follow current events but also to learn about prospective project opportunities in their own community.

Meeting and Talking

Meeting and talking mean engaging in substantive verbal communication of ideas and information. Just as you may be

astounded by the time demands of writing, you also may be
surprised by the number of hours devoted to meeting and talking:
with coworkers, clients, consultants, public agency officials,
committees and boards, manufacturers' representatives, attorneys,
accountants, insurance agents, and bankers. Meetings abound in
architectural practice. There are days when an architect may feel
that architectural practice should be renamed architectural prattle.

The most critical meeting and talking occur when architects are
selling their services, trying to develop business contacts and secure
commissions, and then later when selling their design concepts to
clients or review agencies. This entails persuasion and negotiation.
The ability to convince others of your knowledge, talent, credibility,
and even lovability is indispensable. Indeed, the importance of
public speaking skills for architects cannot be exaggerated because
architects must often stand up and talk convincingly in front of a
group of strangers. Some of the world's most successful architects,
despite diverse speaking styles, are masters of the rostrum. They can
be empathetic and charismatic, articulate and even poetic. With
spoken words and body language, they connect personally with
their audience, discomfort or stage fright notwithstanding.

The art of speaking is also useful for dealing with contractors,
many of them tough negotiators who think nothing of verbally
assaulting reticent, taciturn architects. Architects spend lots of time
in conversation on job sites with construction project managers,
superintendents, and subcontract trade foremen haggling over
prices, the intent and interpretation of drawings and specifications,
scheduling, cost extras and overruns, and, above all, the quality and
craftsmanship of construction work designed by the architect. In
these situations, architects are most effective when they are tactful
yet authoritative, without being pompous or condescending.

Calculating

Calculating refers to the many different types of accounting and mathematical operations that architects perform in practice. Accounting activity in the management of a firm's finances involves keeping track of work completed and worker hours consumed, invoicing clients and collecting fees, paying salaries and other expenses, and maintaining a sufficient supply of working capital to cover the gap between income and expenditures because the latter often outpaces the former. This effort requires diligent record keeping and timely, usually monthly, updating of payables—what the firm owes—and receivables—what is owed the firm.

Another kind of calculating cited in the chart relates to the many quantitative aspects of project design: preliminary estimates of construction costs; construction bids; square footages and dimensions of programmed spaces and areas in buildings; zoning, site, and building code parameters—area, yard and setback dimensions, building sizes and heights, occupancy, and fire egress; quantities, sizes, and costs of components specified; building dimensions; identifying and analyzing points earned for LEED certification; and, in engineering design, types and magnitudes of loads imposed on engineered systems—structural loads, heating and air-conditioning loads, ventilation requirements, water and sewer demand, electrical loads, excavation quantities for cut and fill. Although consulting engineers undertake much of the detailed computational analyses required, the architect must still understand what engineers are doing. In simple construction, such as individual residences, architects often do their own structural design accounting using reference tables and simple formulas.

Architects prepare only very rough construction cost estimates, approximations with varying degrees of reliability. During the design of large, cost-sensitive projects, they and their clients often rely on independent cost estimators. On the one hand, clients expect architects to be knowledgeable about building costs, to be able to predict with some accuracy how much a project will cost to construct, excluding the costs of land, financing, fees, and furnishings. On the other hand, most general contractors know that a project's cost can never be pinpointed accurately until construction documents are completed, and they are usually skeptical about cost estimates done by architects.

Contractors' bids are based on detailed study of construction documents. Estimators compute the exact quantity and cost of labor and materials required for each and every item needed to construct the project as designed. But even before design begins, how can architects and their clients estimate construction costs? They use comparables. If the project being designed can be compared with similar projects for which costs are known, then a somewhat realistic estimate can be generated. To ensure comparability, the architect must consider the geographic location, size, complexity, quality, type, and time of construction of comparable projects. Escalation allowances must be made for inflation if data are not recent. Most comparable cost data are expressed in dollars per square foot of enclosed building floor area, although cost figures may also be stated for other units of size, such as volume (cubic feet), number of beds, or number of parking spaces. Such estimates, no matter how carefully made, are always intelligent guesses. Two different project designs and sites are never wholly comparable and there are always enough special conditions to introduce large margins of error.

Architects' optimism contributes additionally to errors in preliminary estimating because architects are notorious for underestimating the ultimate costs of their designs. This accounts in part for their reluctance to guarantee an absolute construction cost in their agreement with clients. If they did, they often would be obligated to redesign and redraw their projects, perhaps going bankrupt in the process. Prudent architects do their best to predict construction costs conservatively, hoping to look good when bids match or fall below their estimates. At the same time prudent clients should always add a healthy contingency to architects' estimates, no matter how conservative. It has been said that an architect is not trying hard enough if project bids come in under budget.

Client Contact

Client contact is among the most critical activities in architectural practice. When the design team meets periodically with the client to discuss design ideas and review progress, vital decisions about design are made. This is when new ideas as well as conflicts may emerge, when basic formal or technical strategies are adopted, when the realities of budgets and schedules must be confronted. Indeed, face-to-face interaction between architects and clients can disclose the differing agendas of each party as well as offer the opportunity to reconcile those agendas.

Intern architects in large firms frequently complain that they never get to meet or work directly with the firm's clients. They may be too junior in the hierarchy to attend client meetings, perhaps already overcrowded by the presence of a senior partner, a design partner, a project manager, and a job captain. A boss may perceive an employee to be unpresentable because of how the employee speaks or dresses. A few clients prefer to meet with only the nominal head of the firm, notwithstanding the sometimes minimal role played by that principal in carrying out the project. Or there may be intraoffice jealousies, rivalries, and resentments between individuals. One architect may feel threatened or intimidated by another, perhaps because of differences in skills, talents, or personality.

But in almost all small and most medium-size offices, senior and junior architects interact routinely with clients, in part because younger architects may take on a greater share of project design responsibility. This is, in fact, one of the distinct advantages of working for smaller firms. No matter what their size, responsible firms ensure that intern architects have the opportunity to meet with clients, to understand the client's point of view, and to appreciate better the complex forces affecting design.

Government Reviews and Approvals

Another notable subroutine in the day-to-day life of the practicing architect is interacting with government agencies that have jurisdiction over projects. Architects spend considerable time not only researching and interpreting laws and regulations applicable to each project but also persuading local building code and zoning enforcement officials, zoning appeals boards, design review panels, or planning commissions that a proposed design is lawful, conforms to all regulations, and is in the public interest. To accomplish this, architects periodically submit design drawings for review as a design develops, then meet at appropriate times with government agency officials to ascertain compliance. For projects requiring zoning changes, exceptions, or special permits, public hearings are typically required. The architect, client, and often the client's attorney appear at such hearings to explain and justify the project. Thus the government review and approval process can be very time-consuming and costly.

Before schematic design progresses too far, wise architects analyze relevant ordinances to identify key requirements and standards applicable to the project. Yet that is never sufficient to

ensure total compliance, which is why some architects cultivate acquaintanceship with agency officials who can help unravel regulatory mysteries or resolve conflicting interpretations of poorly drafted ordinances. Also many architectural firms retain independent building code and life-safety consultants to help guide design and assist in obtaining approvals. These experts generally know ordinances and regulations backward and forward. Regardless of who presents and explains a project design, not all officials—some feeling overworked and underpaid—are cooperative. Remember that many review officials feel obliged to find something wrong, lest their jobs or purpose be challenged.

Fortunately, there are always officials in every jurisdictional bureaucracy who believe that their mission is to serve the public, including architects. Nevertheless, in all cases, successfully dealing with government agencies demands keen negotiating skills, sensitive diplomacy, flexibility, and firmness.

Relief comes with final approvals and issuance of building permits. Conversely, the architect may learn that despite all attempts to conform to codes while conferring repeatedly with officials, the permit has been denied or delayed because of failure to comply 100 percent with regulations or worse because criteria or official interpretations have changed since last checked. If discrepancies or omissions are minor, the architect may be able to make a quick a trip to the permit office to manually modify the permit drawings on the spot. Otherwise, the architect must further revise the design and hope that such revisions do not adversely affect the project schedule or construction budget.

Consultants and Coordination

Collaboration, not confrontation, is the way architects can and should work with engineering and other consultants. Ideally engineering consultants should join the project design team soon after the architect's work starts. Once schematic design is underway, engineers can begin studying the architect's design concepts and formulate appropriate engineering strategies, advising the architect accordingly. As design development moves forward, preliminary engineering drawings are started. During the construction documents phase, all architectural and engineering drawings and specifications must be prepared and, most critically, coordinated. The coordination process is crucial because the work of each participant affects the work of all others.

Usually the project architect or job captain is responsible for overall coordination, which entails periodic progress meetings, telephone conversations, and e-mail exchanges between architects and engineers. But coordination is greatly facilitated and enhanced by the ability of all members of the design team to share databases and transmit information instantly via the Internet and local area networks. BIM programs enable creation of and access to a digital model of a design embodying every component and system of a project. As the project design evolves, each addition, deletion, or modification of a system component is immediately incorporated and viewable in the model.

Despite digital technology, the coordination challenge is still daunting because no element appears in the model unless a designer adds it. Inside any building there are many places where elements of structure (such as beams or columns), ductwork, pipes, conduits (such as electrical and telephone), and walls all want to occupy roughly the same space at the same time, an obvious impossibility. And many elements are shown in more than one drawing. Design models and drawings are built up in layers. Thus, designers visualize, configure, and identify these elements, layer by layer, relying on BIM programs to insert and show them consistently in each layer of the digital model. If an omission or conflict between elements exists and slips through, it usually will be discovered only when the condition is encountered by the contractor in the field. The contractor may then stop work, alert everyone, request a solution, and mentally pocket the extra funds he is entitled to claim for the extra work caused by the error. In turn, the client may claim payment from the architect or engineer.

Working Digitally

Digital technology has all but eliminated manual drafting and traditional information management techniques in architectural offices. Networked computers, the Internet, local and cloud-based data and program storage, and sophisticated design and data management software allow architects instant access to all their business and project records, including drawings and correspondence; lengthy contact lists for clients, consultants, contractors, public officials, colleagues, and others; frequently used or standardized documents, specifications, details, and drawings; product information, including manufacturing and supply sources; construction cost data (which must be periodically updated); zoning standards and building codes; and general reference data related to the physical and social sciences, geography, cities, historic architecture, and almost anything else that an architect might want to know.

Using digital technology, an architect can generate, study, and refine many more conceptual alternatives for a design than could ever have been contemplated or drawn when design was done manually. There is one risk, however, in designing only digitally. CAD programs and plotters produce schematic design drawings that nevertheless show precise shapes, sharply defined line work, and exact dimensions. Consequently, such drawings can graphically convey the impression that a design is much more developed and

crystallized than it actually is. Clients and others who look at the drawings can be misled into thinking that the design is nearly finalized, when in fact it is still conceptual and inchoate. Therefore architects must make sure that their digitally produced drawings communicate their design in ways that are graphically appropriate.

The computer, although invaluable, is still fundamentally a tool. Unable to think critically or generate creative ideas, it will never replace the brain of the architect. Human beings still must conduct research, visit sites, communicate with clients and colleagues, study and analyze information, coordinate the efforts of others, and, above all, engage in the demanding and exciting act of artful, imaginative design. Computers make it possible for us to design more effectively and more inventively. Yet with all the computer power imaginable, a mediocre architect is still likely to produce a mediocre work of architecture.

Construction Phase Services

Construction phase services and activities contrast sharply with all previous phases. During project construction, architects spend most of their time doing one of four things: (1) visiting the job site periodically to observe work in progress and attend on-site progress meetings with the contractor, owner, subcontractors, engineers, inspectors, and suppliers; (2) reviewing and approving shop drawings submitted by the contractor, subcontractors, and suppliers; (3) clarifying, correcting, or changing—through change orders—parts of the design shown in construction documents, including making final selections of colors or materials not previously specified; (4) preparing construction observation reports and certifications for payment and writing memoranda to the owner, contractor, government agencies, lenders, or file.

During frequently scheduled and sometimes unscheduled trips to the construction site much can happen. You may encounter mud or debris, necessitating ownership of at least one pair of high, waterproof boots. Insurance companies and Occupational Safety and Health Administration safety regulations require wearing a hard hat and Day-Glo vest, which many architects keep at the ready in their car. You can run the risk of exposure to rain, snow, ice, heat, cold, and projecting rusty nails. Disputes and shouting matches can arise before, during, or after job-site meetings. You may have the thankless task of telling the construction superintendent that work in place will have to be torn out and redone and at the contractor's expense. And at times you may experience the feeling of being a persona non grata. But perhaps the most memorable moment is feeling elation, and occasionally disappointment, when your design, previously realized only on paper, is seen in fully constructed form for the first time.

Many architects consider the second activity—reviewing and checking shop drawings—to be among the most boring and tedious of all the architect's construction phase tasks. A shop drawing is a detailed, dimensioned drawing prepared by the fabricator of a particular system or part of a building—such as steel reinforcing or structural members, cabinetry, special equipment installations, railings, curtain wall assemblies—and based on the architect's design drawings. The shop drawing, not the architect's drawing, is used to manufacture the components to be furnished and installed by the general contractor and subcontractor. Shop drawings are sent to the design architect and engineers because the fabricator, subcontractor, supplier, and general contractor all want to ensure that what is to be made complies with the architect's design intent and will fit into the building. If shop drawings do not comply, then the architect and engineers immediately alert the contractor by identifying and explaining the deficiency and requesting resubmittal of corrected drawings. However, even after a shop drawing is approved, ensuring compliance with the design is still the fabricator's responsibility, not the designer's.

In large projects, there can be hundreds of shop drawings with thousands of dimensions and many opportunities for error. You can imagine what it might be like to process and scrutinize every one of these drawings. They are supposed to be submitted well in advance of fabrication and installation but sometimes they are not. Contractors often dump loads of shop drawings in the architect's lap over a short period of time, only to claim later that completion of construction was delayed because the architect and engineers were slow or late in reviewing the shop drawings. Ideally shop drawings should be submitted many weeks ahead of fabrication and installation to allow everyone enough time to review, correct, coordinate, fabricate correctly, and deliver.

All projects necessitate design clarifications and design changes during construction simply because it is impossible, even with digital technology, to produce a perfectly clear, flawless set of construction documents or to foresee all conditions. Contractors frequently send RFIs to architects when they encounter something ambiguous or unclear in drawings. Likewise scores of change orders may be needed. Some are associated with site work and unanticipated below-ground conditions but others result when an owner has a change of mind about some previously settled aspect of the design. Architects always hope that change order frequency, along with design change cost and schedule impact, will be minimal.

Completing construction of a project 100 percent, bringing it to its truly final conclusion, can be a complex end game played out by the key participants. To complicate matters, there are two distinct completion points: substantial completion, when a building can be occupied and used but is not quite finished, and final completion, when absolutely everything is finished. Between substantial and final completion, actions converge. First, the architect thoroughly inspects the building, inside and out, and prepares a punch list for the contractor of still unfinished, missing, or improperly installed items. The contractor and subcontractors, having substantially completed the project, tend to lose interest and even demobilize as they begin to focus their attention on other projects starting up or under way elsewhere. Consequently, they often drag their feet in performing the last 2 or 3 percent of the work itemized on the punch list, items that can be aesthetically crucial to the quality of the building.

Meanwhile the financial end game is playing out. The owner still owes the contractor money, usually including a retainage—monies earned by the general contractor but held back—to ensure completion. The contractor may have pending claims for extras, hoping to collect more than the original contract sum while waiting for monies already due. Each may try to play hardball, the contractor refusing to finish the work, the owner refusing to release any more funds. And there may be other pending disputes. Under standard AIA agreements, the architect—the mediator between owner and contractor—must try to get both parties to reach agreement on what remains to be done, what is owed, and how funds finally will be disbursed. Timing is key because the goal is to move the project from substantial to final completion on schedule. Architects sometimes underestimate the amount of time that all of this can take. And similar to many other aspects of practice, closing out a project requires negotiating skills more than design skills.

Organization within Architectural Firms

An architectural firm may be composed of one, ten, or hundreds of architects. Large firms may also include engineers, landscape architects, interior designers, information technologists, cost estimators, and marketing and public relations specialists. But how are firms structured so that each member of the firm knows where he or she is in the hierarchy or pecking order?

Size of firm is a big factor in determining firm structure. A one-person firm is simple to organize because one person plays all roles. When there are two or more people, however, things become more complex. Most firms are either sole proprietorships, owned entirely by a single individual, or partnerships of two or more partners. The number of partners is unlimited. Firm owners, whether sole proprietors or partners, are entitled to the firm's profits but they also assume responsibility for losses and liabilities. Owners set firm policy, make final decisions, hire and fire personnel, and enjoy other benefits of business ownership.

Many states allow architectural firms to be incorporated but the individual licensed architects who own the firm's stock and direct its affairs are still personally liable for professional negligence arising from the firm's work. Incorporation offers other benefits related to deferral of income for pensions and retirement as well as protection of personal assets from claims related to nonprofessional business liabilities. Otherwise corporations operate much like partnerships. In all forms of organization, the architects who own the firm must provide or obtain the financing necessary to start and sustain operations.

Most firms structure themselves internally in two ways: by rank or by function. Rank-structured firms are headed by one or several senior partners, typically the original founders of the firm. Below them are junior partners, who may play differing functional roles within the firm. Next come senior associates, experienced staff members who help manage operations and may share in the firm's profits but who are not owners of the firm. Then comes the professional staff, usually the most numerous but also the youngest or newest members of the firm. In large offices they populate the studio spaces and do most of the production work. Some of them may be unlicensed interns, only a few years out of school. In smaller firms, such ranking is less noticed, although there are still employers and employees. Finally, there is the administrative staff, indispensable to any business organization of any size. They frequently are the only people in the office who know how much money is in the firm's bank account, how much the firm owes and is owed, who works for the firm and what they earn, and who is scheduled to meet with whom, when, and where.

Functionally structured architectural firms are organized into two broad areas of activity: firm operations and project operations. Firm operations such as business development, marketing and public relations, personnel management, and financial management are supervised by senior partners assisted by appropriate administrative staff members. These partners are primarily responsible for pursuing and obtaining the firm's project commissions and contracts, representing the firm to the outside world, and overseeing the general internal management of the firm.

Project operations are the activities generating the firm's revenue and majority of its expenses. Most firms use a project team approach. The team may vary in size with each phase of a project or one person may play more than one position on the team. A typical team structure consists of the following players:

Project principal-in-charge   This is usually a senior partner who may have been instrumental in making contact with the client and bringing in the commission; acting primarily as a front person, he or she may spend little time producing the work itself.

Project designer or architect　This is a partner or senior associate who takes primary responsibility for conceptual design of the project and is the lead author of the work; he or she may also be the partner in charge.

Job captain or project manager　These are usually an experienced associate, who may also be the primary designer responsible for managing the day-to-day flow of work on the project, including coordination with consultants, maintaining project records and correspondence, and supervising production of digital models and drawings.

Architectural designers　These are staff professionals who do most of the research and labor-intensive, digital production work associated with each phase of design, especially design development and construction documents phases; they meet with consultants and occasionally with clients, contractors, and government officials.

Technical specialists　Large firms often have professional staff members who write project specifications, manage the firm's computer network, programs and data storage, and take responsibility for construction-phase services.

Project teams also may be created through departmentalization within larger offices. Thus there may be a design group, a production (contract documents) group, a specifications group, an interiors group, a landscape group, a cost-estimating group, and a construction administration group. Each group or department may be headed by a partner and senior associates responsible for management of their respective department's activities. This means that a manager could be supervising work on several projects at once. In A/E firms, the engineering departments may also be large; such firms may have more engineers than architects and would be more correctly labeled E/A firms. Departmentalized firms may be very efficient in producing work because of specialization but barriers and competition may arise between departments. Most young architects prefer the team approach because working on a project team in a big firm can be like working in a small firm.

Diversified Services

Much of this book and this chapter focuses on architecture as the design of buildings, describing the design process and how architects participate in that process. But practicing architects and firms increasingly have expanded the services they offer and professional activities they pursue beyond designing buildings. This is not surprising given the multidisciplinary scope of architectural education in North America, the range of skills and interests many architects acquire, and the proliferation of environmental challenges posed by an ever-more complex society and physical landscape.

Therefore it is not unusual to find architects performing services that may seem marginally architectural yet clearly inhabit the realm of physical design: regional master planning, ranging in scale from entire states to counties to cities and towns; master planning and urban design for new communities, educational campuses, and other building complexes such as business parks; urban design for sectors or specific sites within cities, including revising or creating new zoning regulations and design codes; and, in collaboration with engineers and landscape architects, designing visible portions of public sector infrastructure—transportation facilities, roadways, parks, and power plants.

Some architectural firms actually do work on behalf of other architectural firms. One architect, who might have a small firm, can be the designer for a project for another firm and undertake only the schematic design and design development phases of work. A separate firm then prepares the project construction documents. The latter firm may become the "architect of record," certify the drawings, administer the construction contract, and assume most of the professional liability. It is typically a large organization that specializes in such work.

Architects also serve as design consultants advising corporations, community and neighborhood associations, government agencies at all levels, school boards, historic preservation organizations, and cultural and other nonprofit groups. Persistent urban, suburban, and ecological problems will continue providing architects opportunities to confront and address these difficulties along with meeting architectural and construction challenges around the world. In recent decades, US architects have been among the first to step forward to help people, domestically and abroad, who have suffered the effects of natural disasters, war, famine, and grinding poverty. For example, architects designed housing and sometimes helped build temporary shelter in flood-ravaged New Orleans and in Haiti after an earthquake made hundreds of thousands homeless. The devastation along the eastern seaboard caused by Hurricane Sandy in 2012, especially in New Jersey and New York City, motivated architects to contribute to the rebuilding effort.

The Goals of Architectural Firms

To bring this chapter to a conclusion and lead you to the next, briefly consider the various goals firms pursue, either explicitly or implicitly. Explicit firm goals are routinely recited in promotional materials and on websites, always promising great design done within budget, on schedule, efficiently, effectively, and for reasonable cost. Implicit goals are more telling and are evidenced by the kind and quality of work a firm does rather than by what it says it does. With this in mind we can generally categorize goals as follows:

- Pursuing design excellence and aesthetic innovation

- Optimizing services to meet client needs and expectations

- Serving the interests of the community and public, not just the client's

- Burnishing professional reputation and acquiring fame

- Maximizing business volume and firm profits

These goals are not mutually exclusive; a firm can pursue any or all of them. But most firms develop, pursue, and prioritize certain goals that determine their approach to practice and contribute to the firm's brand, image, and reputation. Thus newly graduated architects should be aware of the goals of firms where employment might be sought because such goals are easily embraced by impressionable interns.

One goal is universally shared by virtually all architects in practice: to be hired by a client for a new project. Achieving this goal is the subject of the next chapter.

10 How Architects Get Work

Architects concerned with business development periodically
attend marketing seminars or workshops to learn more about
market research, sniffing out new clients and new projects,
and conducting public relations. Before the 1970s, however,
marketing was rarely addressed or acknowledged explicitly by
the architectural profession as a vital part of practice. In fact,
previous generations of architects believed that overtly marketing
services was unprofessional, a commercial activity associated with
retail trade, the selling of products, and not for those who render
professional services. Actively marketing services conjured up
visions of paid advertising, self-promotion, exaggerated claims,
unfair competitive practices, "specials," and "discounts." Yet
architects have always been naturally competitive, realizing that if
they just sat back, relaxed, and waited for new clients to call, they
might very well starve.

In today's extremely competitive climate, pursuing work has
become so time-consuming and critical an activity in architectural
practice that anyone considering a career in architecture must at
least be aware of marketing goals and methods, not all of which
seem like marketing. We will examine the reasons clients select
architects, how they select them, and what architects do to improve
their chances of being selected.

Getting the First Job

The day you look for your first job in an architectural office is your
first day of marketing: you are selling yourself and the services
you can provide. From your perspective, the architectural firm
is your client, and the best strategy is to make a favorable first
impression. You want the firm to remember you rather than others

interviewed, to like your portfolio of work more than others, to
be more impressed with your personal references, to feel more
comfortable and confident about you in comparison with other
job applicants. You want to look good and you want your "client"
to feel certain that you can and will do the best job possible.

This certainly sounds like a sales pitch. It is! And as often
mentioned in this book, the ability to persuade other people to
"buy" your talent and ideas is no less essential than the ability to
generate and explain your ideas. Effectively selling yourself and
your services requires two complementary conditions: you must
have something to sell, on the one hand, and there must be a need
and a market, on the other.

For that first office job, getting hired can be tough. You
believe you have something to sell—your talent, knowledge, and
skills acquired in school—but you quickly learn that prospective
employers also want experience. You lack the latter. How, you
wonder, can you ever get that first job if only experienced
architects are employable? To gain experience, you must get that
first job. It can seem like a vicious circle, a catch-22 phenomenon,
but eventually most intern architects find that first job. A job
opening and offer occur when a firm realizes it needs new help,
often because of a new contract and project, and believes you are
ready, willing, able, and immediately available. In fact your first job
as an intern is frequently the result of being in the right place at
the right time. Luck and timing are always factors in the marketing
process.

Economic Conditions

Neophyte architects and architectural firms face the same problem
in getting work in addition to normal competition: marketplace
uncertainty and variability. Jobs with firms exist only when firms

have projects to work on and projects depend on many people and forces beyond the control of the architect. National and international economic conditions as well as local economic health greatly affect building activity and consequently the employment of architects. If credit is available and affordable, prices stable, and consumer and business optimism high, society builds. But if money is tight and the economy is stagnant or in recession, building slows down. Understandably architects are bellwethers, sensing shifts in building mood early in the building process through the mood shifts of clients, contractors, lenders, and other real estate and building industry participants. When it is boom or bust for the country, it is generally boom or bust for architects.

Territory

Markets are geographic and territorial. Most individual architects make locational decisions before any other major decisions regarding their careers, and firms must do the same, at least until they achieve regional, national, or international status. Architects must decide where to be—in what state, county, city, and neighborhood—and where to build, which is not limited to only that area immediately surrounding their offices. Selecting a market territory may be influenced by factors such as potential for population and economic growth, preferences for climate and natural environment, urban or exurban amenities, lack of competition, social or business affiliations, and family considerations. Some of these factors have to do with the market itself, whereas others relate to the personal concerns of the architect.

Market territories can be very small or virtually unlimited in size. Most architectural firms concentrate on local markets, rooting themselves in towns, counties, or cities and doing most of their projects within these local jurisdictions, their home turfs. Cities such as Boston; New York; Washington, DC; Miami; Chicago; Los Angeles; or San Francisco are metropolitan areas composed of many local jurisdictions, so architects' practices, though still considered local, may cross multiple political boundaries.

Some architectural firms, as they grow and become better known, expand their territory to include entire states and regions such as the Northeast, the West Coast, the Midwest, or the Sun Belt. Regionally based architects may be known for designing projects whose language of form and material derives from local building traditions that respond to local culture, climate, and ecology—New England, the Southwest, and the far Northwest, for example. A few well-known architectural firms with national and international reputations are able to practice worldwide, doing projects far from where their various offices are located. Their projects may be anywhere in the country or overseas. Somewhat insulated from local market conditions, they may not even compete for local work unless it has national or international significance.

Not all firms with geographically diverse practices are well known or celebrated. A number of large architectural and engineering firms do specialized projects throughout the world, often involving complicated programs and sophisticated technology and requiring many employees to carry out the work over several years. Yet these firms' names are not household words, either within or outside the architectural profession. They provide services mostly to industry, domestic and foreign government agencies, and real estate developers. Much of their work, though large and complex in scope, receives relatively little media attention. But they too are less dependent on local markets.

Types of Markets and Clients

Architects spend a lot of time thinking about the type of market and client they want to pursue. Firms pick their territory but they also must decide on the kinds of projects they want to do within that territory. Generalist architects go after any and all work that comes along and in which they are interested. They may choose to specialize in certain types and sizes of projects if they have a choice, such as single-family residences, multifamily housing, office buildings, health-care facilities, educational buildings, or hotels. They may seek only prestigious, generously budgeted institutional commissions such as museums, libraries, theaters, corporate headquarters, university buildings, or city halls. Or they may stick to the opposite end of the cost-status spectrum, doing only tight-budget, bread-and-butter projects such as shopping centers, low-rent offices and warehouses, factory structures, and moderate-income housing.

Still other firms specialize in historic preservation and in restoring, retrofitting, and adaptively reusing aging architecture. Architectural preservation represents a growing market for architects as US inventory of older, technically or functionally obsolete buildings grows. Indeed, renovating and repurposing old but structurally salvageable buildings, whether or not they are historic, can be a very effective sustainability strategy. It conserves most of the resources—labor, materials, energy, and money— originally invested and permanently embodied in such buildings.

Given the choice, many architects would probably prefer their market territory to be national and international, as well as local, and that their projects be of all types, as long as projects are high budget, visible, and prestigious. Obviously this is hard to achieve. In fact, most architects end up doing what they do for circumstantial reasons. They locate, begin practice, and establish reputations based partly on the kind of work that first comes into the office and gets built. This early work contributes to creating a track record and reputation, the buildup of experience that employers and clients look for. Once on a track with a specific kind of reputation, it can be hard to get off that track but it is not impossible with ample talent, some luck, and much promotional effort.

Selecting Architects for Projects

Why and how do clients select architects? The rest of this chapter answers this question in two ways. First, we will see what clients look for, already hinted at previously. Then we will explore the specific actions architects take to make themselves known, loved, and chosen.

Many years ago, working with architecture students in a required course focused on professional practice, I wrote "An Assessment of Architectural Practice," published by the University of Maryland School of Architecture, Planning and Preservation. We tried to identify reasons that clients choose architects. Our conclusions were based on a limited survey in Maryland conducted by the students, who submitted questionnaires to architects and nonarchitects. Quoting directly from the document are these findings:

> Survey respondents, including architects, were asked to identify the most important considerations in choosing an architect. Following are the frequencies of response:
>
> | | |
> |---|---|
> | Design talent and creativity | 50 |
> | Prior experience in similar work | 33 |
> | Organization and management skills | 29 |
> | Knowledge of practical aspects of building | 15 |
> | Reputation | 6 |

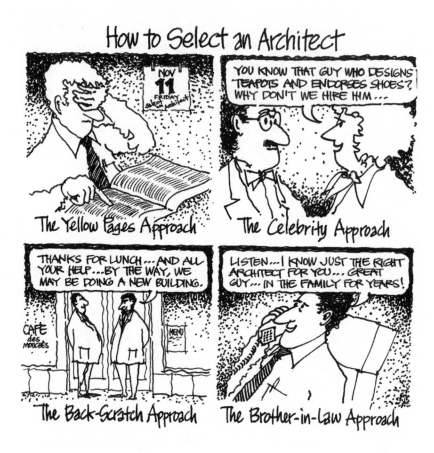

When asked to rank those architectural products that "sell" best, or are most in demand, architects gave highest ranking to "functional design," "competitive fees," and "economy/cost control," and lowest ranking to "building image," "aesthetics," and "innovation/novelty."

Further, having served on several architect selection committees for governmental and institutional projects, I have seen evaluation forms with listed criteria used to assess relative qualifications of competing architects. Such forms attempt to quantify the process. Relative scoring weights are assigned to each criterion. Not surprisingly, sometimes the weighting factors correspond with the described response distribution. Thus we can begin to understand the viewpoint of many clients. With no particular ranking, consider the following criteria for selection:

1. Credentials and professional experience
2. Creativity, inventiveness, style
3. Personal qualities, integrity
4. History of performance and meeting client goals
5. Fees, financial arrangements
6. Rapport with client
7. Convenience in location and accessibility

All these criteria reflect characteristics defining a firm's reputation, what it is known for, and how it is perceived by competing firms and by others in the industry. A client, after selecting and working with a particular architect, may conclude that some aspects of the architect's reputation were unfounded. Nevertheless, in selecting an architect, it is the client's perception of reputation that matters, and those perceptions are shaped by the quality of evidence presented by the architect and by those who know the architect well enough to validate the reputation.

Although most of these criteria are self-explanatory, several merit further elaboration. Consider number two, for example. Some clients are interested in choosing an architect who not only is reputed to be creative and imaginative but who also does work seen to be in fashion or cutting edge. Or they may shop for a specific brand or style, scrutinizing architectural firms' recent projects and verifying their aesthetic track records.

Item four, performance, is critical to many clients. They look for architects who meet deadlines, whose projects are buildable and satisfy budget limitations, whose offices are neat and smoothly managed, and who can provide a long list of satisfied previous clients. This item is closely related to criteria six and seven because for all clients, good rapport with an architect is indispensable. They ask themselves, Can we communicate with each other? Does this architect understand and sympathize with our needs and problems? Are we comfortable working closely together? Do we share the same values and aspirations regarding the project? Will we ever see the senior partner again?

Unfortunately, some clients associate firm size with ability to perform, assuming that only big firms can do big projects. Big firms do not necessarily perform better than small firms, although they clearly have substantial marketing and person-power advantages. Regardless of firm size, it is the project team that counts, and the team available in a small firm may be as large and capable as the team assigned by a large firm. Indeed, one advantage of small firms is that more work is likely to be done by the firm's principals and senior staff, perhaps with more commitment, creativity, and care because such projects are less common and therefore more important for smaller offices.

Matters relating to criterion five can be the stickiest. The architect's ideal client is one who is willing to pay whatever it costs to do the job right but almost all clients are cost conscious to some degree, and for many the cost of architectural services may be a primary factor in selecting an architect. Three disparate forces act on fee negotiations. Force one is what the client believes to be an affordable fee relative to total, anticipated project development costs. Force two is what the architect believes to be an adequate fee given the scope and complexity of anticipated design work. Force three is what the so-called market fee appears to be, that is, what the competition generally would charge. Force one fees are generally below force three fees, whereas force two fees are generally above. Persuading clients to pay fair and adequate fees is not easy in this situation. Occasionally failure to agree on fees can cost architects the job because clients always can find architects who will do the work for less money.

In addition to shopping for fee bargains, some clients may also want to negotiate fee payment terms unfavorable to the architect's cash flow. Thus the total amount of the fee could pose less difficulty than how and when fees are paid. Clients sometimes ask architects to defer receiving payment until some future date or to accept a note (IOU) or ownership interest in the project. This basically makes the architect a banker.

Nevertheless, architects who are skillful negotiators can overcome such difficulties by convincing clients that, in truth, one gets what one pays for. This requires taking time to show the client precisely what must be done to execute the project correctly, completely, and creatively. Time and cost allocations must be shown in detail so that the client understands how and why proposed fees have been calculated. Each step in the design and construction process must be identified and explained. Once the client comprehends the scope of work and the architect's cash flow requirements, and if the client believes that the architect is the right one for the project, then architect and client usually can reach agreement, even knowing that there are other firms that would work for less.

Governmental clients can be the exception because they may be required by statute to choose architects who, after meeting minimum qualifications, offer services for the lowest fees. For this reason some architects do little or no government projects. Those who do sometimes lose money or break even. But such work can pay the rent and keep the staff busy while partners look for more stimulating and lucrative commissions.

But not all public work is frowned on by design firms. Federal, state, and local governments regularly undertake interesting or prestigious projects, such as courthouses and libraries, for which firms eagerly compete, primarily on the basis of professional qualifications and experience, not fees. Occasionally, to select an architect for an especially high-profile project, government agencies sponsor design competitions, inviting several well-qualified firms to submit preliminary design concepts that are ranked by a panel of judges. If all goes well, the competitor whose design is top rated receives the design commission. Sometimes design competitions open to anyone interested, and not to just a few invited designers, are undertaken for such projects.

Occasionally an architect, in an effort to secure a commission, may be tempted to make kickback arrangements, whereby a portion of the architect's fee, after being paid, is returned "under the table" or is "contributed" to an appropriately designated recipient. It is easy to understand why a hungry, ambitious architect might agree to such terms with a client when the proverbial wolf is at the door and a new commission is pending. A more subtle and frequent form of kickback manifests itself when architects offer services to clients for fees that are well below cost, substantially undercutting fees prevailing in the marketplace. This is legal but ethically questionable and ultimately self-destructive. It devalues architects' services in general, increases pressures for further fee cutting among competitors, erodes firms' profits, and compels firms to continue paying relatively low salaries to their employees.

It must now be evident that architects cannot be passive practitioners in today's world. We cannot behave like sellers in a seller's market, when in reality it is usually a buyer's market.

We cannot assume that a combination of aptitude, talent, good credentials, and the right start will lead inevitably to success and an ample supply of work. We must go after work because all of our colleagues do likewise.

It also must be evident that because reputation counts for so much, getting work must mean getting known. Becoming and being known as an architect achieves the same purpose as it does for McDonald's, Google, or Mercedes-Benz: name recognition, product reputation, and branding. Architects are compelled to find ways to promote themselves, advertise their work and their ideas, and let clients and the community know who they are. As we shall see, some architects do this overtly, some in more subtle ways. Some efforts verge on commercial advertising, whereas others lead more indirectly to notoriety, brand recognition, and favorable reputation. However, any one of the activities described here can in some fashion contribute to making an architect known and in turn help to get work. Remember too that not all architects engage in all of these activities. Indeed, some activities are still thought to be unprofessional or even unethical by many architects.

The Direct Approach

The most obvious strategy for getting work is to go after projects directly, using one of several strategies:

- Identify project prospects and leads by reading online and in-print news reports, magazines, journals, and government and business publications, looking for items that advertise or mention future or pending projects.

- Maintain and update the firm's graphically appealing, informative, and easily navigable website showing the firm's most interesting recent work along with firm capabilities, qualifications, and current and past clients.

- Communicate with and cultivate prospective clients; prepare and send promotional materials tailored to appeal to each potential client; express the firm's interest in the client's project; and always mention awards, projects, and special project features relevant to the client's project.

- Disseminate regularly a firm newsletter, in print or electronic form, as well as press releases sent to local newspapers and national journals announcing awards received, significant new projects, new members of the firm, new office locations, and other news; always include images of work.

- If time and finances permit, enter local, regional, national, and international competitions; although the chances of winning may be remote, you can have fun doing them and your competition design can be added to your website, portfolio, and résumé even if you don't win.

- If all else fails, you can advertise (once considered an ethical violation by the AIA). Commercial mass media advertising is legal, but because many architects find it unprofessional and very expensive, few engage in it; however, many firms do act as sponsors for, and contribute money to, public interest or trade organizations, which often acknowledge such gifts publicly in magazines or on TV and radio broadcasts.

The Indirect Approach

The indirect approach to promoting oneself or one's firm is more commonplace. In addition to marketing directly to prospective clients, architects can enhance name recognition and reputation through activities that are less commercial, more subtle, and often as effective as the direct approach. Many architects deem these activities to be more professional than advertising.

- Be socially active. Entertain people, especially those who might be potential clients or might refer clients to you. Membership and participation in appropriate clubs or social organizations may prove fruitful, expanding your network of acquaintances.

- Become civically engaged by joining and participating in community, public interest, business, and professional organizations. Architects can make useful, pro bono contributions and they also can meet important and influential people, further expanding their network of contacts and potential clients.

- Publish finished projects in local, regional, or national media— print and digital—such as newspapers and professional journals. Hometown newspaper articles can be as effective as direct advertising and exposure in professional and trade journals enhances an architect's reputation among colleagues and prospective clients.

- Give lectures and talks to community groups, in schools, and at professional conferences, including those not primarily aimed at architects. Participation in seminars, workshops, and other educational programs further contributes to one's public persona, name recognition, and reputation.

- Submit projects on a regular basis to local, regional, and national design awards competition programs. Typically this requires good photos and drawings presented in a graphically compelling way. Expect recognition to be periodic because work awarded depends largely on the tastes and moods of design awards juries. Publicize such awards whenever possible.

- Write about architecture, either articles or books, if you have time, because writing is very time-consuming. Any subject will do if someone will publish it, although controversial subjects, personal manifestos, and visually compelling material may attract the most attention. Through websites and blogs, the Internet has greatly facilitated dissemination of articles and images, and self-publication of graphically well composed books also has become much easier and more affordable.

• Get others to write about you and your work if you have done something significant or your work has become sufficiently interesting. Being the subject of someone else's writing, even as the object of criticism, can establish you as a celebrity in the eyes of the reading public and among many reading architects and architectural aficionados. This is accomplished most readily when you have friends or acquaintances in the media, particularly journalists who write about architecture.

Self-promotion by architects is easiest when their work is newsworthy or when they become so well established that anything they do or advocate gains an audience. Becoming recognized, respected, and famous is difficult for those who do only competent work and almost impossible for those who do mediocre or uninteresting work. But it may also be difficult if they make no effort explicitly to promote themselves using the tactics outlined. It is not enough just to be good at what you do, to be an expert or a great talent. Something more is needed: you must be willing to tell the world what you do.

Assuming that an architectural firm has established itself and enjoys some kind of positive reputation, it still must face the reality of competition because typically many firms may be perfectly well qualified for a given project at a given time. This means that at some point, firms must use the direct approach to obtain commissions, no matter how successful they have been using the indirect approach. How, then, do clients and architects finally get together?

Generally, architects are selected to do a single project. Unlike doctors, lawyers, or accountants, who usually have continuing relationships with clients over extended time periods, the architect may do only one project for a particular client. If hired again by the same client, it is still on a project-by-project basis. Nevertheless, many successful firms pride themselves on the amount of repeat business they get from satisfied clients who keep coming back for more.

More typically clients hire architects with whom they have not worked before. They find and select them mostly through these avenues:

Personal contact, either social or professional
Referral, based on reputation and experience
A screening process, based on professional qualifications
A screening process, based in part on fees
Client-sponsored design competitions

Indeed, architectural firms get much of their work through referrals and personal contacts. Even then, they must sell themselves because clients often interview several architects before making their final choice. By contrast, government projects, once set in motion, are first announced in newspapers and other periodicals with a request for all interested design firms to submit letters of interest and statements of qualification. Agencies usually appoint screening committees to narrow the list of interested firms to those few they want to interview. After interviewing the short list of firms, they make their choice. Often nongovernmental institutions take a similar approach when selecting an architect.

The Interview
Skill is required to woo and sign a client, and it must be applied especially effectively in that most critical of architect-client

encounters—the interview—of which there can be more than
one to obtain a commission. An interview is like a first date;
initial impressions are vital and enduring. Interviewing is a
performing art. The architect must be charming and persuasive
as well as informative to enthrall and captivate the client. The
romancing is done with words and projected images and videos.
Well-composed, slickly printed portfolios or books, illustrating
with photos and drawings the firm's relevant project experience,
back up the architect's proposal. Proposals also typically describe
the firm's proposed project team, including consultants, the
work schedule, the project management approach, and often the
designer's philosophy and design strategy. This is the proverbial
dog-and-pony show.

Having captured a prospective client's attention, architects still must convince the client that their firm alone possesses the unique qualities the client seeks and that their future working relationship will be ideal. Most important, they must demonstrate their profound understanding of the project and the client, their familiarity with the site and program, their insight into the project's special requirements, and their respect for the budget and schedule. Fees for services are usually the last discussion point during an interview and ideally should be explored in detail only after the architect has been chosen.

Joint Ventures

To compete more effectively, architectural firms sometimes form joint ventures with other architectural firms or with engineering firms. A joint venture is a temporary partnership between two or more firms created for the sole purpose of pursuing and carrying out a specific project; the firms otherwise continue to conduct business as separate entities. Joint venturing can expand geographic coverage and broaden expertise or it can provide a firm access to a market previously inaccessible. Joint ventures are marriages of convenience, transforming small firms into big firms and big firms into bigger firms. Boston firms can become Chicago firms or office-building firms can become hospital firms. Occasionally joint ventures result when clients want a design-oriented firm to team up with a nuts-and-bolts, production-oriented firm. In this instance, the former usually takes responsibility for the schematic and design development phases of architectural services and the latter prepares construction documents and oversees construction.

Architects as Contractors, Construction Managers, and Developers

Some architects keep busy by offering clients construction management or design-build services. In the design-build mode, architects wear two hats: they act as designers and construction managers, performing the functions usually performed by general contractors. Many design-build architects undertake only modestly sized projects, primarily residential and small-scale commercial projects such as office buildings or retail stores. But a number of diversified A/E firms have their own construction management departments and provide such services for larger projects, directly competing with general contractors and firms specializing in construction management.

Merging architectural and contracting functions seems appealing for architects and clients because it reduces the number of organizations a project owner has to deal with and gives the architect full control over construction. But there are financial risks for client and architect if the architect's cost estimates and bids are too low or if the project is undercapitalized and monies run out before completion. A potential conflict of interest exists for the architect; although the client seeks the most value and the best quality (within the budget) from the architect and contractor, the contractor 's objective is usually to build the architect's design at the least possible cost, an incentive to cut corners and compromise quality. If the architect plays both roles, there is no mediator between the owner and the contractor. Ultimately the outcome of design-build relationships depends on the integrity and financial acumen of the architect.

A few architects become real estate developers, designing projects in which they have a significant ownership interest. Being one's own client can be very appealing. The architect-as-developer strategy represents a potentially rewarding but financially risky means for staying busy. Not only can practicing architects earn substantial profits as developers, and potentially more than they can as architects, they also can exercise greater control over the final design within the limits of budgets and marketability because they own the project. Of course, they can lose money, and lots of it, if a project goes sour. Architect developers undertake mostly housing or small commercial projects. Often joined by other investment partners, entrepreneurial architects perform all the functions of the real estate developer—land acquisition, equity and debt financing, construction, advertising, sales, and leasing—in addition to the design functions of the architect.

Projects developed by architects are no more likely to succeed than to fail economically. However, relatively few actively practicing architects have been successful developers and successful architects. Many architect developers have learned the hard way that developing projects is not the same as designing projects. Each requires altogether different expertise, psychic energy, outlook, business skills, and attitudes. Each entails very different risks and requires different kinds of stomach linings. Nevertheless, architects always will be tempted by the perceived liberty and potential profitability of designing projects for which they are also the client.

Design Competitions

Competing for architectural prizes or commissions on the basis of proposed designs has a long history. Many notable monuments and public buildings and a fair number of private ones have been built as the result of design competitions. There are several ways to conduct a design competition but most competitions fall into one of two categories: open or invited. In an open competition, as the name implies, the sponsor generally accepts design submissions from anyone qualified to enter, although qualifications can be restrictive—for example, competitors might be limited by nationality or geographic location. In an invited competition, the sponsor, after first screening the qualifications of architects expressing interest, interviews and selects only a few from whom design proposals are solicited. In both cases, a jury composed of professional designers and client representatives, designated by the competition sponsor, usually reviews the design concepts, ranks them, and selects the winning proposal.

Competitions can be conducted in one or two stages. In the latter instance, there are two rounds of design: a first round to narrow the field and a second round to pick the winner. In open competitions, competing designers receive no compensation for their work. In fact usually they must pay a fee to enter. In two-stage, open competitions, only the finalists who make it past stage one receive a stipend, and even then the often modest fee rarely covers the costs of producing the stage-two design submission, much less the work done for stage one. By contrast, architects invited to participate in a competition among a small number of firms, whether in one or two stages, typically are paid a preschematic design fee by the sponsor. However, these fees also are likely to be nominal, well below the cost and value of the work that the firms must produce.

Some architects believe that design competitions are one of the fairest methods for selecting architects. Other architects hold the opposite view. The former believe that open competitions offer small firms and creative but still undiscovered architects the opportunity to score quickly and emphatically, to make their mark and gain recognition against overwhelming odds, and to win monetary prizes and significant design commissions. They further argue that design competitions bring out the best designers and stimulate the most innovative design thinking, bringing forth design proposals that the average or nonchalant architect, working with a conservative client, might never dream of.

Competition cynics or opponents claim that competitions are inherently unfair because the outcomes often reflect the biases of the jury that selects the winners and fail to address and grapple with the needs or tastes of the client and project users. They claim that competitions favor either well-established architectural firms with ample financial and staff resources, allowing such firms a potential edge in presentation, or, conversely, firms whose work load is slack. Architects who are busy may have difficulty finding time to undertake competitions without compromising the competition effort and their efforts on behalf of their regular, fee-paying clients. Another objection is that many competitions are exploitative and poorly managed, with ambiguous rules and requirements. Architects also have accused some sponsors of being exploitative, taking advantage of architects' willingness to go for the brass ring and using the competition process to obtain design ideas at minimal cost.

A very small percentage of all projects in the United States designed by architects are the result of open or invited design competitions. Frequently, winning designs are never executed because the projects are abandoned, were never real, or proved too expensive or impractical. When a prize and a commission are awarded, the winning architect may still suffer financial loss or be decommissioned, subsequently excused from completing the work for technical, economic, or political reasons. Even worse, his or her design may later be altered and executed by someone else. And in many competitions, vital interaction between architect and client during the formative phases of design is missing.

Ultimately design competitions, as a method for getting work, are a long shot for almost all architects in practice. Competition sponsors and the projects they build clearly benefit from the profusion of ideas and the investment of thousands of hours by

all the losing competition entrants. But competitors, after a costly search for success and recognition, may end up with little more than feelings of frustration, envy, and sour grapes, no matter how much fun was had participating. Yet, to be a winner . . . !

Free Services

One questionable marketing tactic is worth noting: doing work for free. For many years the AIA and the profession in general condemned the practice of furnishing prospective clients with free sketches, designs, or other services without fair compensation. To do so was considered unprofessional and unfair. Yet this occurs frequently. It is the architect's loss leader, the come-on to attract the client's business. But there is nothing illegal about providing free services (unethical, perhaps, but not illegal).

Intense competition among architects, along with more aggressive marketing practices, puts pressure on architects to do a bit of up-front work for free as an inducement to prospective clients. This pressure is hard to resist if you believe that everyone else is doing likewise. I have participated in architect selection committee interviews during which firms, not yet selected and

with no compensation, have presented unsolicited, detailed site and program analyses, plus schematic design concepts, which cost many thousands of dollars to generate. This work is an integral part of basic design services and thus has a measurable economic value that should be paid for. But to gain a competitive edge in pursuing commissions, many firms are willing to gamble and make the investment. Sometimes it pays off, sometimes not.

You surely will face the same pressures during your career. How much free work should be done for a prospective client in the interest of courting that client before you are selected and given a contract? When the contract beckons and the project promises new design opportunities, it is hard to know where to draw the line.

11 Architects' Clients

Most architects are employed by clients who contemplate building something. Some architects think of clients only as sources of work and income but most good architecture is in fact the result of successful design collaboration between a talented architect and an enlightened, motivated client.

A client may be a person, a couple (married or otherwise), or an organization. Partnerships, corporations, nonprofit institutions, and governments can be clients. A lawyer would tell you that an entity needs two things to be a legitimate client: lawful existence as an entity with authority to enter into enforceable contracts; and money or access to money. For architects the latter criterion may pose more problems than the former because there are loads of clients with no funds, many clients with inadequate funds, some clients with barely enough funds, and few clients with unlimited funds.

Architects can have great clients or difficult clients. Great clients are perceived to be receptive to most, if not all, the architect's design ideas, to give the architect wide design latitude, and to spend money in the interest of creating a work of art. They are decisive yet accommodating and they rarely make changes to a design once they have understood and embraced it. Such clients also willingly pay the architect's fees and continually praise the architect's work.

Difficult clients display opposite characteristics. They question not only the architect's ideas but also his or her comprehension of programmatic, financial, and scheduling requirements. They nitpick, complain about costs, and make decisions slowly. Agonizing forever over each design issue, they often insist that the architect generate limitless design studies and alternative schemes before agreeing to one. Even then, such clients think nothing of asking for more changes. And of course such clients may squawk when they receive the architect's bill, wondering how a few sheets of drawings could cost so many thousands of dollars.

Great clients respect the architect as a professional, a creative artist, a problem solver, and a technologist, and they can accept inevitable minor imperfections as part of the price of attaining worthy aesthetic and functional goals. Difficult clients may think of the architect as a necessary but obstructive provider of costly services, insensitive to practical issues, careless, egotistical, and periodically incompetent. Because many clients have only one direct professional encounter with an architect during their lifetime, that unique experience may forever color their perception of what architects are like, making them either skeptical of or believers in the value of architects and architecture.

Household Clients

The most plentiful type of clients are households composed of people who want to improve the quality of their personal living environments, whether an apartment or a house. Household clients—singles, couples, families with children—hire architects because they want to build a new residence or remodel an existing one. In all cases, they seek more or better space, privacy, security, convenience, and comfort, and, in many cases, ego satisfaction. They expect the architect to provide a design that can be built by a contractor within the client's budget, a design yielding a functional, structurally sound, dry, easily maintained environment that is neither too hot nor too cold. But the architect and client typically strive for more: creating a habitable work of art.

A household client occasionally asks the architect not only to design the building but also to furnish and decorate the interior—

selecting furniture, floor coverings, wall and ceiling finishes, decorative trim, colors and fabrics, light fixtures and lamps, window treatments (drapes, shades, blinds), artwork, and maybe even ashtrays. The line between architecture and interior design can blur because domestic interiors are also the province of another profession—interior designers and decorators.

Intervention by the client or by decorators in designing interiors is seen by many architects as unwanted intervention. But all decorators and many clients hold the opposite view, insisting that architecture is concerned mostly with the exterior of buildings and, at best, only the layout and geometric shaping of interior spaces. Inside, the will of the decorator and client, not of the architect, prevails. As a result, many well-conceived works of architecture have been spoiled visually by bad decorating decisions. Conversely good interior design can help cover up bad architecture.

Household clients can be the most demanding of all clients. Their project may be among the most important single undertaking of their adult lives, financially and psychologically, whether a back porch addition, a remodeled kitchen, or a new multimillion-dollar home. Residences are personal and intimate places where ego investment is high. Unique behavior occurs there.

In our homes we sleep, eat, practice hygiene, make love, read, work, recreate, communicate, socialize, or simply survey that tiny part of the world over which we have dominion.

Home represents an investment not only of money but also of self. Thus for the household client, life's most fundamental needs, desires, activities, experiences, and resources are involved. This is why people are willing to commit much of their income and time to their personal dwelling environment. Therefore it is not surprising that household clients can be passionately involved, relentlessly demanding, and intensely emotional when their home is at stake.

Many clients want fur but can afford only fabric. Wanting gourmet quality, they can pay only for takeout. They may expect flawless judgment by the architect, along with speedy service, ability to predict the future, and error-free design and construction. Some clients assume that architects have unlimited control of contractors and unlimited knowledge of building products, not to mention the power to ensure that construction is finished on time and without cost overruns.

For their part, architects often expect household clients to be receptive to their every design whim and proposal, to tolerate delays and errors patiently, and to be willing to increase their construction budget if bids are too high. Architects can fail to warn clients adequately about the limits of the art and science of architecture and construction. The imperfections and unforeseens that may in fact be acceptable to the owners of airports, office buildings, shopping centers, or schools are frequently unacceptable to homeowners.

More than a business relationship exists between architects and household clients. The sensitive designer in effect psychoanalyzes the client, becoming familiar with the client's

personal habits, tastes, behavior, compulsions, and feelings. The
designer may even become enmeshed in the client's domestic
affairs. Creating a new home can be a source of household joy and
unity or it can bring out repressed or unrecognized conflicts and
animosities that otherwise might not surface. Countless architects
have witnessed hostile exchanges between spouses or domestic
partners over some design issue, whereupon the architect is
suddenly thrust into the role of family counselor and peacemaker.
Usually the architect can mediate successfully but sometimes
building a dream house can undo a household relationship.

Architects design houses as much for fun as for profit, although they can make a good living designing homes. Some architects are happy just to break even when working for household clients, some of whom cannot afford to pay the fees required to cover all the architect's time and overhead costs. Most large architectural firms do houses only as a favor to someone. Yet house design continues to receive substantial attention in the media and from many architects, because designing houses for household clients often gives architects the best opportunity for design experimentation and aesthetic innovation. As loss leaders, residential projects also may bring bigger, more profitable work in the future, thanks to appreciative household clients of the past.

Real Estate Developers

Architects would like to believe that their goals are the same as their clients' goals; they frequently are not. In particular, the architect's desire for aesthetic self-expression may be of little or no concern to the client. This is often true in the realm of commercial building, the world of profit-motivated real estate development. Commercial clients' motives are quite different from those of clients' building homes for themselves. The market-oriented client is ultimately interested in one thing above all else: economic success, measured by positive market response and a good return on investment.

The majority of investment in building construction in the United States is commercial development undertaken by private business entities. It includes office buildings, multifamily housing, subdivision housing, hotels, retail shopping facilities, industrial and warehouse buildings, and recreational and entertainment facilities. Many clients developing commercial properties view their projects not as artful works of architecture but rather as investments that produce income, money machines that yield profits. Without the prospect of profit, such projects would never be built. Developers don't oppose good architecture, especially if it adds market value, but architectural value is subordinate to economic value.

A client developing commercial property naturally looks for architects who design attractive buildings that are cost-effective and easy to construct, efficient to operate, and good revenue and profit producers. Here occurs the potential conflict between architect and client. The architect may propose designs that achieve the opposite, costing more to construct and operate without corresponding increase in potential revenue and hence less potential investment profit. If construction and operating costs are too high and revenues too low, the owner will lose money.

Even developers experience self-conflict in dealing with their own self-imposed economic constraints. On the one hand, they must opt for a level of design quality and amenity necessary to capture the targeted market and generate anticipated revenues. On the other hand, they risk offering too little for the price and losing out to competitors who offer more. Accordingly, the architect tries to sell good design to developer clients on the basis of sound business and investment thinking, arguing that better-quality design and increased spending will result in faster and higher rentals or sales. This is a language that commercial clients can understand, although they must be convinced.

To developer clients, the ideal architect thoroughly understands their goals and limitations, along with building economics; always meets budgets and deadlines; readily obtains approvals from building officials and government review agencies; turns out error-free, easy-to-read drawings for easy-to-build buildings; and designs buildings that work well and look good at the same time.

There is no shortage of architectural firms claiming to offer all these things, and certainly some can deliver. Developers learn quickly about architects and the kinds of services they provide. The architect responsive to their aspirations and requirements is the architect they will choose and stick with. As long as a mutually satisfactory relationship exists, that architect will have a loyal client. But let something go wrong and the client will look elsewhere. It should not be surprising that there are architects who are excellent designers but whom many developers would be reluctant to hire.

To many architects, the objectives, values, and attitudes of commercial real estate developers lack vision. Architects argue that too many developers sacrifice human, cultural, or environmental ideals to the so-called bottom line, rejecting attempts by architects to design artfully. Developers, say many architects, fail to provide enough time and money to execute projects properly. They feel that some developers are abusive, demanding acquiescence, get-it-done-yesterday performance, and flawless work, all for insufficient fees. Architects protest that developer clients commonly exploit architects economically, insisting that compensation for services be deferred as a condition for getting the design contract. In effect, extending credit to a client for thousands or hundreds of thousands of dollars is risky and makes architects lenders.

Some developers and many architects believe that art and commerce can be successfully reconciled, although not always easily. It is more difficult to create award-winning architecture in the face of severe economic constraints than when such constraints are relaxed. Although the United States is littered with millions of bottom-line, architecturally banal buildings, there are nevertheless many structures that have succeeded commercially and aesthetically as well. Regrettably there are also many that have been judged aesthetically successful but have failed as investments.

Architects sometimes have sacrificed ideals by turning out mediocre work or by abandoning the commercial sector of the design market to lesser talents. Developers take note of this by pointing to deficiencies they attribute regularly to architects: delays, cost overruns, inefficient or unbuildable designs, unworkable construction details, wasted space in buildings, confusing or incomplete drawings and specifications, incorrect use of materials, and poorly coordinated structural or mechanical systems. Although developers are usually more sophisticated about construction, their expectations concerning professional performance by architects can equal those of household clients.

An astute developer client would probably assert that creating buildings is a business, not an art, and that these tactics are just sound economic practice. If architects can participate in this business and create art at the same time, that is fine, as long as their priorities do not supersede the client's. Some architects are willing to work on these terms; others are not. With each client and project, architects must examine a prospective client's values and compare them with their own. The architect looking primarily for aesthetic patronage will usually not find happiness on the bottom line.

Corporate Clients

Most real estate developers operate as incorporated but small businesses. Corporate clients are different. They often are large, departmentalized institutions with hierarchical decision-making responsibility dispersed from top to bottom. They have multiple management levels, ranging from the CEO down to department heads. Specialization abounds: marketing, finance, production, construction, estimating, purchasing, accounting, project management, property acquisition, and maintenance, to name a few. Each person in the corporation has an interest in what the architect does, which is colored by his or her respective area of responsibility.

When the architect designs for a corporate client, there are really dozens of clients. Marketing managers, concerned with selling or leasing, see the design as a product to be marketed. Construction managers see it as an assemblage of materials and labor. Finance managers and accountants see projects in terms of capital investments, cash-flow projections, statements of profit and loss. Property managers see buildings as machines to be maintained after others have built and marketed them. Then there are those overseeing all: the corporation's chief executive officers and active directors. Their interests tend to be earnings, payable dividends, increased stock value, and corporate image.

Corporate kingdoms may contain multiple territories jealously guarded by their respective territorial overlords, some of whom are subject to delusions of grandeur. Such executives are often assertive and insecure. They want to succeed in corporate life, to aggrandize their authority and status, to perform well if not better than their in-house competitors. Corporate managers want to look good within the company along with doing their job properly for the benefit of the company's customers and stockholders.

Architects have to cope with numerous company executives and company politics when working for corporate clients, deciphering the power structure to figure out who makes the ultimate decisions. Once understood, dealing with corporations can become a game the architect can play and, with luck, master by letting each individual in the corporate hierarchy believe that his or her opinion is indispensable, that his or her needs are paramount, and still seek the trust and consent of the top brass.

Many corporate clients are methodical and unemotional in pursuing their goals, operating in a more orderly, well-documented fashion than other types of clients. They honor contractual arrangements more readily, including payment of architects' invoices, partly because institutional rather than personal funds are involved. And corporations may prefer doing business with other corporations. Therefore architectural firms with corporate qualities often appeal to corporate clients. After all, one corporation engaging in intimate corporate relations with another corporation seems like a natural act. Indeed, it's only human according to the US Supreme Court, which has ruled that corporations are persons.

Entrepreneurs

A frequently encountered commercial real estate client is the individual entrepreneur, the developer whose team is small and who may be building only one or two projects at any given time. He or she may operate using a corporate form of organization or a limited partnership but the mode of operation clearly bears the stamp of one person and one will, unlike most corporate clients.

Entrepreneur clients come closest to being the architect's counterpart. Their egos are at stake, as well as their fortune, if they have one. They are usually willful, decisive, and outgoing, investing much of themselves in their real estate ventures. They exhibit a certain toughness and resilience, plus the ability to make quick decisions based as much on gut instinct as on intellectual analysis. Some have a sense of mission as well as a desire for wealth. To others development is nothing more than a business in which sizable fortunes can be made or lost through financial leverage, the investment of small amounts of the entrepreneur's money, equity funds, and large amounts of borrowed money.

Historically the entrepreneurs of civilization—political, military, artistic, scientific, and religious figures—built monumental architecture and great cities. The spirit, power, and will of such individual figures resulted in work for architects and builders who would have had little to do without the impetus provided by kings, queens, emperors, moguls, popes, generals, and statesmen of the past. The primary goals motivating these historic entrepreneurs were not related to financial investment opportunities or social welfare but their instincts and compulsions were probably similar to those of today's entrepreneurs.

Institutional Clients

The term institutional can mean many things to many people and to different architects. In architectural practice, it usually refers to clients and projects other than those that are primarily investment and profit oriented, although institutional buildings often are used for fund-raising functions. Thus this definition excludes commercial real estate development whose principal purpose is to produce investment income from rents or sales. Further, institutional clients are generally nonprofit organizations, corporate or otherwise, that develop projects for very specific purposes. Typical projects include the following:

Civic buildings such as cultural centers, museums, performing arts facilities

Schools—primary and secondary schools, special schools, university buildings

Religious facilities

Research and health-care facilities—hospitals, nursing homes, clinics, laboratories

Institutional headquarters and administrative facilities

Recreational facilities such as arenas and stadiums

Although a few of these projects may be built for profit-making reasons (such as hospitals and sports stadiums), they are not conventional investment real estate.

Institutional clients operate much like corporate developers in their organizational characteristics, not surprising for institutions that may in fact be legally constituted corporations. The institution itself may comprise a very large constituency, but similar to corporations with countless stockholders, the institution's behavior is really fashioned by a relatively small number of people who are responsible for making policy and managing the institution's daily affairs.

The architect typically works with an institution's staff members and building committee composed of institutional officers and trustees. Others, either from within the institution or from outside, may also serve on the building committee. Outside advisers may be invited to participate because of their expertise, political pull, or social connections. Active or potential institutional financial contributors are obvious favorites for such committee memberships. In addition, project users may be represented on the committee.

Building committees may have substantial decision-making authority or they may serve in a primarily advisory capacity to other decision makers—chief executive and operating officers, vice presidents, departmental directors, and managers. In some cases, architects may have to deal with a building committee supplemented by other ad hoc, specialized subcommittees that focus on only specific programmatic, operational, and design issues. In these circumstances, architects must navigate more carefully because multiple committees can be in conflict with one another. Good communication and documentation become essential, not to mention wise diplomacy.

Institutional clients may be very sophisticated but many have little experience in dealing with real estate development, finance, architectural design, and construction. In this regard, they can resemble household clients, requiring the architect to guide the process more actively. When projects are complex, institutional clients frequently hire development advisers and construction management consultants. They represent the owner's interest in dealing with architects, engineers, general contractors, subcontractors, financial institutions, and government agencies.

They assist in project scheduling, administration, budgeting, cost estimating, accounting, purchasing, and contract negotiation, acting as a go-between and surrogate client. They can greatly facilitate the process of building when relatively naive institutional clients are involved but they can also duplicate tasks usually carried out by competent architects and contractors.

Some institutional projects have stringent budgets, whereas others may be generously funded. Some are financed privately, through fund-raising campaigns and membership dues, and some receive direct public support and governmental allocations for construction. There are many institutional projects, such as cultural facilities or corporate headquarters, for which the public architectural image is important. Here the institutional client must usually provide a budget adequate for such image making by the architect. For high-budget, high-prestige projects—museums, institutional headquarters, and civic buildings—institutional clients tend to select prestigious architectural firms with reputations for creating iconic architecture.

Architects like to do projects for institutional clients because in their view there is much greater opportunity for producing memorable, newsworthy, and photogenic buildings. Moreover, the number of people participating in the development of such projects inevitably increases the architect's contacts and professional exposure. And the experience of doing special projects may well lead to new project commissions of even greater prestige and expressive potential.

Institutional clients are more likely than some other kinds of clients to pay their bills, although not necessarily on time. But architects also complain about complexities of coping with a client who operates like a giant committee, who makes decisions slowly and quasi-democratically, and who can be at odds with him- or herself. Design can take longer because the architect must try to satisfy every stakeholder, every person claiming to represent some part of the institution's interest. This is even more difficult when differing personal agendas, tastes, and ideologies creep into deliberations and decision making. In these circumstances, persuasive charisma and charm, along with persistence and patience, continue to be valuable assets for architects.

Government Clients

Government clients are a subset of institutional clients but government agencies and officials have sufficiently unique characteristics to merit special consideration. Architects interact with three levels of government: local (municipal or county), state, and federal. Each is composed of executive, legislative, and judicial branches. However, most projects are undertaken by specific executive agencies of government charged with specific missions. Therefore, architects need to understand how government agencies behave.

Government agencies at all levels build transportation facilities, public works projects, park and recreation facilities, administrative offices, courthouses, law enforcement facilities, fire stations, public hospitals, and sometimes affordable housing for low- and moderate-income families. Public educational facilities are built by local city or county school boards with funding help from state and federal education agencies. Unique to the federal government are projects for the military, domestic and overseas, and US embassies in foreign countries.

Governments are organized into agencies concerned specifically with these diverse areas. Thus we have departments of public works, transportation, housing and community development, education, economic development, parks and recreation, public safety, justice, health, general (administrative) services, and, at the federal level, commerce, defense, and state. Although funding for construction originates with the legislative budgeting process and is officially carried out under the leadership of the executive, individual agencies actually provide the impetus and management for conceptualizing and implementing projects. And, of course, agencies are themselves corporate-like bodies.

Remember that government's objectives are more complicated than industry's. Private enterprise's ultimate goal is straightforward and simple: profit. The method for achieving the goal is easily summarized: produce and market a product or service. Government, however, must protect and further public health, safety, and welfare. It must promote commerce and trade, tax its citizens, provide security, deliver public services, build and maintain infrastructure, and undertake any other essential tasks that private enterprise cannot or elects not to do. Clearly this is a far more complicated mission to accomplish; although the ends may seem apparent and indisputable, the means are not.

Looking at a government agency as a client, the architect sees a collection of people, laws, and regulations whose purpose is achieving public objectives. Moreover, such objectives usually must be achieved at minimum cost to the taxpayer. Thus capital budgets for most local, state, and federal government buildings rarely enable creation of luxurious, flamboyant, or precedent-setting architecture. Although there are a few notable exceptions, government agencies generally seek attractive, functional, efficient design whenever they undertake construction.

The advantages of working for a governmental client are much like those of other institutional and corporate developer clients. Projects may be large in scope and on occasion of monumental proportions. Large or small, they can have challenging programs and pose provocative design opportunities. Designing government-sponsored projects benefitting the public is intrinsically a source of satisfaction for an architect. Successful completion of one government commission may well lead to another in the same area of specialization. And once a contract for services is signed, architects know that government agencies reliably pay fees earned for services rendered, unless there are disputes.

On the opposite side of the ledger reside some serious disadvantages. They are in effect a mirror image of the advantages. Projects can be banal, mundane, and architecturally unpromising, no matter how talented the architect or well intentioned the government sponsor. Fees can be inadequate, sometimes limited by statute despite the amount of work required of the architect. Negotiating acceptable contracts with government agencies can be excruciating, particularly when officials may argue that other firms could do the project for a lower fee. And if a dispute arises later, many government agencies think nothing of holding the architect's feet to the fire by withholding fee payment, knowing that the architect has little recourse.

Perhaps the worst attribute associated with government clients is bureaucratic mentality. Not all government officials have it. In fact, it is a characteristic not limited to government agencies. Such minds can be found in private corporations, institutions, and architects' offices. But the word bureaucrat has become most closely associated with government. What negatively characterizes bureaucrats? Above all, it is attitude, not competence or expertise, although these too may be in question at times. This attitude manifests itself as a can't-do, no-way approach.

The negative bureaucrat, in contrast to the positive bureaucrat, looks for reasons not to do or approve things. He or she plays as strictly by the book as possible and, when in doubt, says no. Clinging tenaciously to rules and regulations, such persons tend to be dogmatic and inflexible. They abhor uncertainty and avoid making value judgments, the realm in which architects often must dwell. They shun taking risks and responsibility for any actions that are not clearly prescribed for them in writing. Because no code or regulation can ever anticipate every eventuality, negative bureaucrats can be major obstacles in the path of creative architects.

Equally regrettable are bureaucrats who almost instinctively resist innovation, change, or experimentation, despite the potential for fruitful improvement or discovery. Many are motivated by basic job security concerns. They fear criticism and will do almost anything to cover their respective posteriors. Even more discouraging, and infuriating as well are bureaucrats who exhibit suspicion and skepticism concerning the motives of people with whom their agency interacts. Acting ostensibly to protect the public interest and save taxpayers' money, such officials often suspect that private interests are up to something suspicious: cutting corners, charging exorbitant fees, padding expenses, conspiring with other consultants or contractors. Also, similar to some other types of clients, they may demand and expect an unattainable level of perfection.

Agencies themselves, being bureaucracies, can behave this way collectively. Sometimes the architect finds that negativism is the dominant policy, particularly regarding creative architectural design. For example, many school boards and departments of education have adopted regulations and specifications that permit only the most conventional of design solutions for school buildings. The US Army Corps of Engineers is notorious for its strictly "engineering" approach to building design, an approach it demands from the architects it hires. Federal, state, and local housing authorities promulgate design standards and other regulations that can make it difficult for architects to develop innovative housing projects, even to save money or conserve energy.

Architects experience frustration in still other ways when working for governments. Changes in personnel can deter the progress of a project's design because new contracting officials may have quite different views or interpretations of mandates from their predecessors. This can occur most dramatically with changes of administration following elections. Sometimes the project itself may be suspended or terminated. Budgets and building requirements may be altered suddenly, compelling the architect to modify or recommence design.

Once designed, most projects built by government agencies are competitively bid because this theoretically ensures that taxpayers will obtain the best price possible in the construction marketplace. It also means that neither the agency nor the architect knows what the project will actually cost until most of the architectural work is completed. If the budget and interim estimates have been unrealistically low, bids can come as a great shock. In some cases government agencies demand revisions by the architect, without additional compensation, or abandon the architect's plans altogether. At best, this is an embarrassment for the architect and, despite losing money, may make collecting still unpaid fees difficult. Unfortunately this can occur with nongovernmental clients as well.

Many architectural firms never do government projects, whereas others specialize in them. Some firms thrive on collaborating with government agencies but some, after trying once or twice, give up, claiming they only lost money and acquired ulcers. In all cases the type of client you will have depends on the type of architect you become.

Citizens and the Community as Clients

We architects tend to be idealists and reformers, our sights set not only on aesthetic innovation but also on social change. Consequently some of us carry that idealism into the neighborhoods, hometowns, and cities where we live and practice. Many civic-minded architects routinely offer their services—sometimes pro bono, sometimes for nominal fees—to local citizen groups and community associations in an effort to make a difference socially and aesthetically. Community-based design centers, staffed by volunteer architects and architectural students, have been established in many jurisdictions to help needy tenants and home owners improve their dwellings and their neighborhoods. Practicing architects have contributed time and expertise to public schools, homeless shelters, clinics, and other organizations that lack the financial resources to hire and fully pay an architectural firm.

Architects frequently are asked to serve on neighborhood committees, municipal advisory bodies, historic preservation boards, or planning and zoning commissions. They may get paid little or nothing for their efforts but local citizens are invariably grateful for the advice and guidance they receive. There are lots of opportunities in most communities for architects to engage directly in public service, and those who invest the time willingly and effectively are likely to be asked to do more. The challenge is knowing when to say yes and when to say no, given competing time demands. In any case, having the community as a client can be rewarding in two ways. First, it can provide that special

satisfaction that comes from doing good deeds and helping others. Second, and not incidentally, it can increase your public visibility, which may lead you to other kinds of clients, some of whom you will still need.

Many architects realize that public policy directly affects the quality of the built environment as well as US ecology and natural resources. They also realize that government legislation directly affects the practice of architecture and design of buildings. Thus, desiring to be heard and to influence public policy, a number of architects—reportedly more than 1,200 at this writing—have been appointed or elected to public office, becoming municipal, county, state, or federal officials. Perhaps as architects increasingly understand and appreciate the consequences of public decision making, more of them will seek public office as a way to effect positive change for the community as a whole and for the good of architects and architecture.

12 We Who Are Architects

Arriving at this final chapter, you should have a better understanding of the profession of architecture than you did eleven chapters ago. Of course, no book can convey fully the architectural profession's unique value and exceptional achievements, its nuances and peculiarities, its continually shifting values and methods, its daunting challenges and shortcomings. Nor can a book fully portray the remarkable diversity of individuals who call themselves architects. Nevertheless a few additional pages may help round out the book's portrait of architects and the subculture they create and inhabit.

The introduction refers to several popular versions of architects as heroes. These highly romanticized images are misleading and oversimplified. In reality, most architects are decidedly unheroic, although some have idiosyncratic personalities and aspire to be aesthetically heroic. Consider some of their mannerisms and attitudes, their social and behavioral characteristics. As you read, try to envision a particular architect or even the architect you yourself may become.

Architects as Types

Some people seem destined to be architects, possessing natural talents as designers. Others are born into circumstances that facilitate achieving personal and professional goals. Notwithstanding their intellectual and artistic talents, the latter are blessed at birth with social status, useful personal contacts, and perhaps inherited wealth. They have a head start giving them access to a world of potential clients not readily available to others. Comfortable and confident, armed perhaps with innate charm and sophistication, they can choose to practice architecture as an artistic and cultural pursuit rather than as a business. If the elite influence much of what is built, and someone has grown up among the elite, unfettered by subsistence finances, then being an elite architect can be a sure ticket to success.

Another type, the architectural artiste, is defined by manner, not social background or inherent talent and intellect. Through words and gestures, artistes typically express themselves sometimes flamboyantly and often unconventionally. They can be witty, deadly serious, or dramatic, but they are rarely shy and often self-absorbed. They are demonstrative and relish an audience. Much of what artistes do is consciously chosen or fashioned to express their artistic tastes and to put on a show: what they wear, how they live, the authors they read and quote, the diversions they seek.

Common to all professions but sometimes extreme in architecture are the prima donna types. They can be oblivious to and even disdainful toward other people, ideas, and activities unconnected to their own interests, needs, and activities. They often seem arrogant, pompous, vain, and temperamental. Prima donnas also may act the artiste, affecting defiant nonconformity. Some prima donnas, having made their mark, can legitimately claim the limelight. Others are less deserving, their self-estimation, not the estimation of others, placing them on a pedestal. Humility eludes most prima donna architects, who will not hesitate to tell you how accomplished they are.

Architecture always has creative fantasizers who dream up and propose unrealizable projects. The fantasizer is not deterred by matters of practicality, convention, or acceptability. A speculator and risk taker in the realm of ideas, the fantasizer may also take pleasure in being outrageous and iconoclastic, using fantasy as a form of cultural or political criticism and commentary. Stretching the boundaries of style, scale, or technology, design fantasies can be simultaneously satirical, vexatious, symbolic, and enlightening. Often fantasizers concoct fantasy for its own sake, to be whimsical and amusing. Only when pretending to be real or denying reality do their efforts deserve skepticism or dismissal because confusing fantasy with reality can be dangerous.

By contrast, many architects are pragmatic, down-to-earth types. They are practical, get-the-job-done people who prefer reality to fantasy. They may seem anti-intellectual but in fact they may embrace intellectual concepts that also make sense and prove useful. They enjoy building for its own sake and thrive on the nitty-gritty process of design and construction, happily worrying about functionality, costs, and deadlines. Down-to-earth architects, eschewing aesthetic speculation and verbal theorizing, are less concerned about the meaning of beauty than in finding the means to achieve beauty.

Practical architects also may have strong management and organizational skills, reflecting their interest in project implementation. We speak of architects who know how to put buildings together, who are knowledgeable about detailed design, construction materials, technological systems, and construction procedures. But preoccupation with practicality can impede innovative design thinking because frequently the most practical approach is to continue doing what was done before. Thus there is a strong argument for design teams to be composed of those who dream up ideas and those who can execute them.

Architects of any type can be compulsive, even obsessive, about their work. Being somewhat compulsive as an architect is not necessarily bad. Hundreds of tasks in architectural practice require intense, careful, thorough execution. God and the devil are in the details. Thus, being compulsive about pursuing and completing a task 100 percent is an asset in an architectural office where exhaustive, nit-picking, time-intensive work must be diligently and meticulously carried out. Public safety depends on such diligence. Wouldn't you feel more comfortable in a building whose design was scrutinized by a compulsive architect than by an easily distracted, hang-loose architect?

Being obsessive-compulsive is a liability when it becomes extreme and irrational. It leads to intellectual and emotional blindness, eclipsing potentially desirable options and creative possibilities. Excessively compulsive architects alienate colleagues and clients by stubbornly rejecting intelligent, artful compromises. Clinging unrelentingly to beloved geometric forms, styles, materials, or colors, no matter how inappropriate, architects sometimes produce poor architecture driven only by personal obsession with their own bad ideas. Of course, do not confuse irrational obsession with reasoned tenacity and passion. A fine line distinguishes vigorous advocacy from compulsive defensiveness but it is an important distinction.

Architectural offices are full of plodders. Plodders, similar to down-to-earth and reasonably compulsive architects, are necessary in architectural practice. They willingly undertake work that requires steady, laborious, and often tedious effort. They keep on going, plugging away until the job is done. They cope well with drudgery, of which there is a considerable amount at times in architecture. The plodder is persistent but not necessarily obsessive. Faced with an obstacle or change of direction, he or she may adapt readily to changed circumstances. Most plodders generally respect authority and gladly accept instruction or guidance.

The business of architecture naturally engenders business types. Many architects choose to become or evolve into managers and entrepreneurs. Managers like to be in charge, directing people and overseeing operations. They enjoy responsibility and authority. To be effective, they need leadership ability and the ability to make tough decisions in situations of conflict and pressure. Their instincts draw them to organizations and to organizational politics.

In architectural practice, projects and firms require management. In this respect, architecture is like any other business. Firm accounts, finances, personnel, business development, equipment, and physical facilities have to be administered, along with specific, day-to-day project operations. Without strong management, organizational chaos and financial failure are likely. Thus professional managers are among the most critical and highly paid workers, even in architectural practice.

But managers can be a problem as well. Tinkering unnecessarily with administrative structures or meddling inappropriately in firm operations, managers can stifle those working under them. The passive, laissez-faire manager can be just as obstructive by failing to provide adequate leadership and direction. He or she risks letting things slip out of control or slip through altogether. Although the casual manager may superficially maintain amiable relations with underlings, lack of attention and guidance may result in frustrated and demoralized personnel and even mission failure. Good managers may not always be loved but they will be respected, listened to, and usually rewarded, no matter how obnoxiously or pleasantly they may behave from time to time.

Not all managers are entrepreneurs. Entrepreneurs are, above all, risk takers willing to accept the possibility of loss as well as gain. Consciously or subconsciously, they thrive on risk. Entrepreneurs like to create, own, and control businesses or projects. Conscious of the marketplace, they are always alert to new opportunities. Anyone who enjoys generating new ideas and then mustering resources to implement them is an entrepreneur. Entrepreneurs also have to do a lot of networking, which requires many of the social and verbal skills discussed in previous chapters.

The best networkers are extroverts who join and participate in professional, civic, and social organizations, mixing with colleagues and prospective clients. Meeting people, exchanging ideas, gathering information and project leads, and making themselves or their firms more visible and widely known is how architects engage in public relations.

Many architects aspire to be Renaissance persons. The Renaissance in Western Europe, stretching from the fifteenth to the seventeenth centuries, was an age of world exploration, scientific discovery, and secular enlightenment, the age when humanism trumped mysticism and blind deism. It produced some of Western civilization's most creative inventors, artists, architects, philosophers, craftsmen, scientists, engineers, and builders, among them Leonardo da Vinci, Michelangelo, Andrea Palladio, and Isaac Newton. Thus to characterize someone as a Renaissance person, or as a polymath, is recognition of that person's diverse knowledge, talents, skills, and the ability to be a generalist and a specialist.

Such aspirations still make sense for architects. To be an architect requires expertise in a variety of disciplines, coupled with the ability to respond effectively to an environment of increasing complexity, uncertainty, and change. Architects must be able to communicate and work intelligently with carpenters, masons, bankers, or attorneys. Architects must be artists, poets, engineers, sociologists, business administrators, and diplomats. Trying to be a Renaissance person is challenging but many architects come close to it. And although the prolific Renaissance architect of today may not produce cutting-edge or timeless architecture, he or she may very well be the type who has the best crack at it.

Idols and Adulation

Every period, movement, and passing trend in architecture has its architectural heroes and heroines, individuals widely recognized and celebrated within the profession. A few become celebrated public figures. They may be admired not only for their design work but also for their theories and teachings, their critical insights, or their artistic and literary skills. The culture of architecture seems unable to exist without a pantheon-du-jour, a collection of prophets and apostles blessed for the moment by their peers, historians and critics, teachers and students, and especially journalists. Membership in the pantheon changes regularly but there is always a pantheon. And only a few members, such as Frank Lloyd Wright or Le Corbusier, are likely to remain permanent members.

Architectural prophets and apostles stand for more than the Vitruvian ideal of "commodity, firmness, and delight." Rarely does anyone worship architects who are merely competent or even good at what they do. Instead people mostly idolize designers perceived to be exceptional, to be avant-garde. Typically their work is viewed as innovative, iconoclastic, visually and intellectually provocative, perhaps exhibiting in some way the poetic, transcendental potential of architecture. Sometimes practitioner heroes explain and justify the poetic, transcendental nature of their work by writing or telling us about it. Such explanatory discourse can be at best intellectually fascinating and enlightening or, at worst, obscure and unconvincing.

Architecture can be rich in messages. Too often, though, we hear pronouncements of meaning and symbolism that only the heroic architect, acting as messenger along with a select group of sympathetic critics and disciples, can see or interpret. Such interpretations may elude the rest of us no matter how hard we try to make sense of them. Consequently be wary of what you hear and read about idolized heroes. Maintain an open but critical mind. Architecture is full of overworked, tiresome design clichés that are the residue of some heroic designer's once-original ideas. And many unusual, idiosyncratic design ideas, touted by journalists in search of the hottest story, may, in fact, prove to be bad ideas.

The Faces of an Evolving Profession

In my architecture class at MIT in the 1960s, there was only one female; the rest of us were US-born, white males, mostly young and single. Since then demographics have changed dramatically. As many women study architecture as men and I have taught design studios in which women were the majority. Today many US architecture students are of African, Asian, and Hispanic descent. At undergraduate and graduate levels, US architecture schools always are populated by foreign students from Asia, Europe, and Latin America.

Architecture students are not only ethnically and nationally diverse, they also are more diverse in age and socioeconomic background. Increasing numbers study at the graduate level, have degrees and experience in other fields, and are heads of households. No longer is it unusual to see middle-aged men or women studying alongside twenty-year-olds in architecture school.

But some things still have not changed as much or as rapidly as one might hope or expect. White males still dominate the profession. The majority of architectural firm owners and

professors in architecture schools are males. African Americans are
relatively sparse in the architecture profession and on architecture
faculties, as well as in architecture school student bodies, despite
decades of affirmative action on the part of universities.

Women with families face pressures that men do not. During
child-bearing and child-rearing years, devoting full attention and
energies to time-demanding professional activities is especially
difficult for architects who also are mothers. For some women
working in firms, this can result in losing ground to male
counterparts in terms of seniority, experience, and compensation.
Until the 1980s, female architects were still considerably younger
statistically than male architects and therefore less likely to have
attained leadership positions in practice or education. Often
relegated to doing interior design work, women rarely were in
charge of construction administration or seen on job sites wearing
a hard hat and issuing instructions to contractors. However,
women today are increasingly taking their rightful place in all areas
of the profession.

Historically, African Americans in high school and college
have tended to choose careers other than architecture, perhaps
continuing to perceive architecture as a white male profession.
Within African American families and communities, architecture
is still seen as an esoteric profession, one rarely considered by
students who nevertheless might have the requisite talents and
motivation. Even predominantly black colleges have to work hard
persuading students to pursue architecture. Statistically there are
still relatively few African American architect mentors or role
models. Yet in the United States, black architects have a long and
successful history in private practice and government, and African
American graduate architects find jobs as readily as anyone else.

The ethnicity, sex, and national origin of an architect
are irrelevant. Individual ability, knowledge, dedication, and

personality are what matter in architecture. Therefore, no matter who you are, where you come from, or what you look like, if you want to be an architect and have the talent, nothing today stands in your way.

Afterword

Here are a few, brief reminders and parting observations, plus my sincere thanks to you for reading this book.

On Becoming an Architect

- After high school spend at least two years, if not more, pursuing college-level general education before concentrating on architecture in a professional program. Play the field of electives, explore diverse interests, engage in sports, travel a bit, and find yourself prior to three or four years of total architectural immersion. It is difficult to get all this in when you go directly from high school into an intense five-year BArch program.

- In selecting an architecture school, be skeptical of architecture school rankings published annually, in particular the *U.S. News and World Report* college and university survey (typically appearing in March). It purports to identify top architecture schools by sending questionnaires only to deans and one or two senior faculty members of schools granting master's degrees, asking them to rank architecture schools. The response rate is about 50 to 60 percent. The ranking methodology is superficial and seriously flawed. It ignores the views of most architecture faculty members as well as practicing architects and school alumni; it overlooks BArch programs; it assumes current deans and senior faculty members are the most knowledgeable about other schools' curriculum, courses, scholarship, and faculty, a dubious assumption; and, with its focus on reputation, it inevitably pushes image over substance. It should be no surprise that alma maters of deans and senior faculty members repeatedly dominate the list.

- If you are studying architecture but doing poorly or feeling unhappy about it, consider alternatives: taking a year off to work, enrolling in fewer courses, or even changing majors. Architecture is not easy but it should be stimulating, satisfying, and even fun.

- You may want to look for schools offering optional academic tracks for students after completion of introductory architectural studies. These tracks would be alternatives to the traditional track emphasizing and centered on design. Such programs serve well the many architectural students who discover that architectural design is not their strength but who have strengths in other areas: history, urban planning, real estate development, technology, landscape architecture, interior and furniture design, business, and management.

- Architecture schools should aspire to educate fewer but better architectural designers. At the same time they should seek more institutional support for expanding nondesign, nonprofessional components of their programs, offering more courses for undergraduates and others not seeking accredited professional architectural degrees but who are interested in the subject. Nevertheless, the accredited professional program should not be compromised for the sake of nonprofessional, general education.

On Being an Architect

- If and when you marry, consider its impact on your career and your career's impact on your marriage. Marrying and having children at too young an age can be stressful for architects who work long hours for moderate compensation. And there is a lot to be said for marrying someone who is *not* an architect, ideally someone capable of earning a living independently. Even better, marry someone whom you love but who also has money.

- Take your time. There is no rush. You do not have to do it all before you are thirty or even forty. You have much to learn, and architects are students all their lives, capable of learning new things and starting in new directions at any age.

- Know that today's fads and fashions will be stale tomorrow and gone by next week. What seems important now may be inconsequential or forgotten in the future. Architects must embrace more lasting values, just as their buildings must endure for decades or centuries. Even architectural journalists, critics, and teachers are not immune to judging architecture too much by tastes and trends of the moment.

- Resist the temptation to be all things to all people. Practicing architects do best when they are doing architecture. They are different from engineers, contractors, sociologists, financial analysts, or developers. Therefore, as an architectural practitioner,

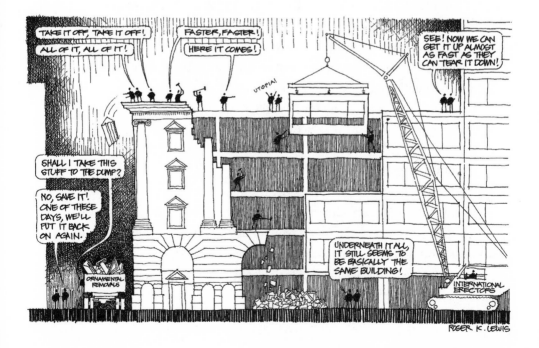

concentrate on improving the circumstances that relate directly to architecture, avoiding periodic forays into other territory just for the sake of economic expedience. Creating good architecture and good cities is a great enough challenge.

• Recall what makes architecture such an appealing profession: the many rewards of designing built form and creating useful, visually rich environments; the fusion of art, technology, and social sciences; the opportunity to exercise community leadership; and the gratitude and recognition bestowed by respectful clients, colleagues, and the public. The impediments, frustrations, financial limitations, and risks with which architects must cope make it an undeniably challenging career. Yet for those with talent, passion, and some amount of good luck, no career compares with architecture.